T0327675

DOMAIN NAMES REWIRED

DOMAIN NAMES ⓇEWIRED

Strategies for Brand Protection in the Next
Generation of the Internet

Jennifer C. Wolfe
and
Anne H. Chasser

www.domainnamesrewired.com

WILEY

John Wiley & Sons, Inc.

Cover image: Leiva-Sposato
Cover Illustrator : © Ian McKinnell / Getty Images

Copyright © 2013 by John Wiley & Sons, Inc. All rights reserved.

Published by John Wiley & Sons, Inc., Hoboken, New Jersey.
Published simultaneously in Canada.

No part of this publication may be reproduced, stored in a retrieval system, or transmitted in any form or by any means, electronic, mechanical, photocopying, recording, scanning, or otherwise, except as permitted under Section 107 or 108 of the 1976 United States Copyright Act, without either the prior written permission of the Publisher, or authorization through payment of the appropriate per-copy fee to the Copyright Clearance Center, Inc., 222 Rosewood Drive, Danvers, MA 01923, (978) 750-8400, fax (978) 646-8600, or on the Web at www.copyright .com. Requests to the Publisher for permission should be addressed to the Permissions Department, John Wiley & Sons, Inc., 111 River Street, Hoboken, NJ 07030, (201) 748-6011, fax (201) 748-6008, or online at http://www.wiley.com/go/permissions.

Limit of Liability/Disclaimer of Warranty: While the publisher and author have used their best efforts in preparing this book, they make no representations or warranties with respect to the accuracy or completeness of the contents of this book and specifically disclaim any implied warranties of merchantability or fitness for a particular purpose. No warranty may be created or extended by sales representatives or written sales materials. The advice and strategies contained herein may not be suitable for your situation. You should consult with a professional where appropriate. Neither the publisher nor author shall be liable for any loss of profit or any other commercial damages, including but not limited to special, incidental, consequential, or other damages.

For general information on our other products and services or for technical support, please contact our Customer Care Department within the United States at (800) 762-2974, outside the United States at (317) 572-3993 or fax (317) 572-4002.

Wiley publishes in a variety of print and electronic formats and by print-on-demand. Some material included with standard print versions of this book may not be included in e-books or in print-on-demand. If this book refers to media such as a CD or DVD that is not included in the version you purchased, you may download this material at http://booksupport.wiley.com. For more information about Wiley products, visit www.wiley.com.

Library of Congress Cataloging-in-Publication Data:

Wolfe, Jennifer C.
    Domain names rewired : strategies for brand protection in the next generation of the internet / Jennifer C. Wolfe and Anne H. Chasser.
        p. cm.
    Includes bibliographical references and index.
    ISBN 978-1-118-31262-9 (cloth);   ISBN 978-1-118-42002-7 (ebk);
    ISBN 978-1-118-42177-2 (ebk);   ISBN 978-1-118-43393-5 (ebk)
        1. Product management.   2. Internet domain names.   3. Internet marketing.
    4. Branding (Marketing)   5. Strategic planning.   I. Chasser, Anne H.   II. Title.
    HF5415.15.W65   2013
    658.8'72—dc23

                                                                            2012022852

10 9 8 7 6 5 4 3 2 1

Contents

Preface

When we set out to write this book, there was still much speculation about ICANN's gTLD program. Some questioned if it would ever go forward and were quite certain that ICANN would never succeed in launching the program. Others wholly questioned the value and staunchly opposed their company's involvement in such a speculative program. Still, others indicated they would respond as required to meet the opportunities in the marketplace. We interviewed thought leaders in corporations, trade organizations, technology, and others from fall 2011 through April 2012 and wrote the book during that time period. ICANN's program did launch in January 2012 and the application period closed in May 2012.

While the book was in production, the Big Reveal Date arrived, and we could finally see who had applied and for what strings. So, we write this Preface to the book to comment upon our research in light of the Big Reveal Date and the nearly 2,000 applications for gTLDs. Most of our predictions on who would apply and how many applicants were right on track. We were noticeably wrong about a few key predictions, however. We thought for sure that Facebook, eBay, and Disney, among others, would apply and they did not. But Google, Amazon, Microsoft, and others did, making bold moves with numerous applications. To begin to understand the implications of who applied, for what, and what it all means, it helps to start with the numbers.

- In total there were 1,930 applications filed.
- Of these, 116 were IDNs (internationalized domain names) comprising Chinese, Japanese, Arabic, and Cyrillic characters.
- There were 1,409 unique strings.
- There are 230 strings in conflict, spread out over 751 applicants. Those conflicted applicants are working deals as we speak to determine what partnerships may form and who will run that gTLD.
- Forty-seven percent of the applications came from North America
- Thirty-five percent from Europe
- Sixteen percent from Asia Pacific
- Less than 2 percent from Latin America and Africa
- Fifty percent of Interbrand's Top 100 global brands applied
- 36 of the Fortune 100 applied
- Fifty-four percent of all applications filed were generic
- Thirty-nine percent of the applications were brands
- Four percent were community applications
- Three percent were geographic applications.
- ICANN earned nearly $350 million in fees

The top contested strings included: .app, .home, .inc, .art, .book., .shop, .blog, .design, .cloud, .hotel, .news, .store, .love, .mail, .web, and .ltd.

Top filers in brands included: Google, Amazon, L'Oréal, Richemont DNS (luxury brands), Dish DBS, Scripps Networks Interactive, Microsoft, Johnson Shareholdings, Chrysler Group, TJ Maxx Companies, and Gap.

While many still question whether consumers will adapt from a .com world, the basic economics will surely drive change. Applicants have $350 million invested in the application fee alone. They will want to monetize their investment and will invest in innovation and invention to evolve consumers from a .com world to a .anything world. So, it's helpful analyze who applied for what in order to understand what trends we may expect.

In our deep dive analysis of the list of applicants, a few key segments emerged in brands: Retail & Consumer Goods; Media, Travel &

Entertainment; Business to Business and Services, and Tech & Pharma. We've included the complete list of applications by applicant in the Appendix, but have provided a breakdown of brands that may be of interest in Figures P.1 through P.4.

Retail & Consumer Goods. Nearly 36 percent of consumer-facing brands that applied are in the retail and consumer goods categories. Within that segment, the lion's share were filed by famous retail brands, followed by automobiles—nearly every major auto brand applied. Luxury brands and fast moving consumer goods closely followed. A few of the big filers included:

Figure P.1   Notable Retail & Consumer Goods Brand Applicants
©2012 Wolfe Domain

Media, Travel, and Entertainment. Approximately 25 percent of the brand applications fell into the media, travel, and entertainment categories. Within that segment, media and travel (hotels, restaurants, airlines) were equally represented, while a much a smaller percentage of games and social networking and sports, movie, and theater applied.

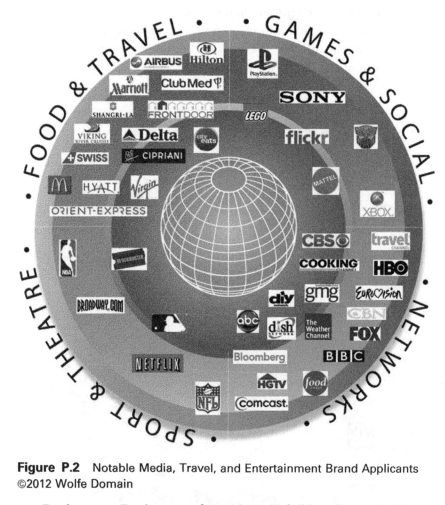

Figure P.2 Notable Media, Travel, and Entertainment Brand Applicants
©2012 Wolfe Domain

Business to Business and Services. Of all brands, nearly 20 percent fell into the business to business, services, and non-profits category. Within this segment, finance and insurance represented the lion's share of those applications, followed by business to business and then non-profits.

Figure P.3   Notable Business to Business, Finance, and Insurance Brand Applicants ©2012 Wolfe Domain

Tech & Pharma. Only 19 percent of the applicants were in the technology and pharmaceuticals category. Within that category, software, equipment, or devices represented the lion's share, with imaging and photography, Internet services, and pharmaceuticals about on par.

In addition to the notable brands that filed, there were more than 900 generic applications (generic terms or words intended to resell second string domains to the public). These will be equally important for companies to consider in developing their strategy. We divided the generics into four categories: company/commerce; sports, media, and entertainment; search and navigation; and lifestyle-related TLDs. We

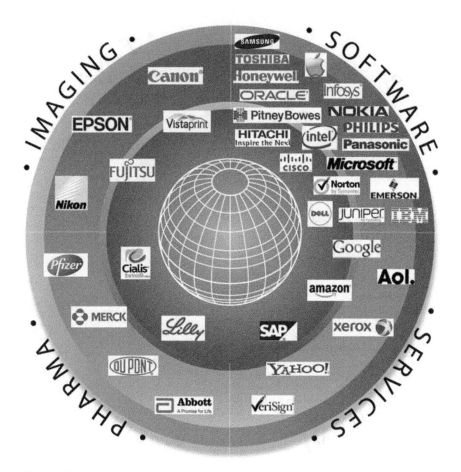

Figure P.4 Notable Technology and Pharmaceutical Brand Applicants
©2012 Wolfe Domain

found the application strings fairly evenly distributed among these categories. (See Figure P.5.) Some of the more interesting generics included:

Agency	Blog	Coffee
Apartments	Book	Compare
App	Buy	Construction
Art	Café	Contractors
Audio	Channel	Cooking
Baby	City	Corp
BlackFriday	Cloud	Coupons

Cruise and	Kids	Rent
Cruises	Kitchen	Repair
Cyou	Land	Restaurant
Design	Life	Review
Dog	Live	Sale
Eat	LOL	Salon
Family	Love	Save
Fashion	Mail	Search
Farm and farmers	Media	Security
Film	Mobile	Shop
Flowers	Mom	Shopping
Forsale	Mortgage	Shopyourway
Free	Movie	Show
Fun	Music	Store
Furniture	News	Studio
Gallery	Now	Style
Game	One	Sucks
Garden	Online	Tech
Gift	Ooo	Theater/re
Gives and giving	Pet	Tickets
Green	Phone	Tube
Group	Pizza	Video
Guide	Play	Vip
Health	Productions	Website
Help	Property	Wiki
Holiday	Radio	Wine
Hotel	Realestate	World
House	Realtor	Yachts
Inc	Realty	You
Insurance	Recipes	Zulu

Now that we have more certainty about how many and what types of generic top-level domains may launch into the Internet, it's a bit easier to begin to see how this could succeed in segmenting the Internet into zip codes of commerce, lifestyle, search, media, and entertainment related categories. Truly, like zip codes segmented to deliver mail

Figure P.5 Notable Generic Applications ©2012 Wolfe Domain

around the country, these gTLDs could segment where your domain name resides within your chosen category on the Internet.

While we still anticipate some if not many of these gTLDs will fail, as is always the case in a paradigm shift, others will succeed and begin the evolution of the Internet. They will build segmented search, communities, and spaces for people interested in the generic categories for which they applied. How long until the shift from .com begins? These gTLDs will likely start to launch in mid-late 2013 through 2014, but we anticipate a two to three year window for consumer adoption.

These numbers and breakdowns are helpful, but we believe a deeper analysis about what companies might do with these domains provides more insightful commentary. We have identified several key strategies that we anticipate the brands and generics are using for their gTLD business. Understanding what they likely plan to do, and why, can provide important information for companies that did or didn't apply. Everyone must be ready to evolve their digital strategy over the next few years and recognize that the Internet will change. This is just the beginning.

The Strategy: Authenticity and Fight against Counterfeiters

There was a big movement by the automobile and luxury goods industries to lock down the distribution channels for their products with TLDs. This trend points toward providing authenticity to Internet users and fighting counterfeiting online. With a TLD, companies like Ford, BMW, Toyota, GM, and Lexus, as well as Tiffany, Hermes, Cartier, Coach, and others can provide second string domains only to their authorized dealerships or sales outlets. Meaning, they only stand behind products sold from their top-level domain. "If it's not a .BMW or .Tiffany, then it's not us—don't buy from it." If they properly educate consumers, this could put a dent in counterfeiters' ability to confuse consumers with typo based .coms and ensure that for these big companies they control their brand by managing their top-level domain. The other big category that will likely benefit from this strategy is the major pharmaceuticals. Essentially, all the big pharma companies applied: BMS, Pfizer, Sanofi, Abbott, Merck, Lilly, and Johnson & Johnson. They can now ensure that only their authorized distributors can sell their products online, ideally providing greater security for unknowing consumers buying drugs online from a counterfeit .com. The finance and insurance industries can also benefit from this strategy to stop those fraudulent imposters from directing consumers via email to a counterfeit .com and provide greater security to their customers. All the major banks and credit companies also applied, including Citigroup, Capital One, Discover, Fidelity, J.P. Morgan, PNC, Prudential, Visa, American Express, Barclays, BBT, as well as insurance companies AIG, Allstate, American Family, Anthem, Farmers, The Hartford, Met Life,

Nationwide Insurance, Northwestern Mutual, Progressive, Travelers, State Farm, and others. Each of these companies can benefit by promising greater security and authenticity, and educating consumers away from fraudulent .coms or other gTLDs.

Who Is Missing from This Strategy?

- Franchises. Interestingly, we didn't see many restaurant chains or other franchise-based organizations. T.G.I. Friday's, Domino's, Burger King, Wendy's, and others didn't apply. McDonald's did, however. The price tag for a gTLD may have been high, but not for these leading brands. They may have missed an opportunity to be a market leader in managing their franchises and consumer connection with their brands by opting out. At a minimum, it would have been an ideal enterprise system for managing franchises and their web presence under an umbrella gTLD.

- Celebrities. Also missing from the list of applicants are celebrities. For many celebrities, their face, name, and likeness are their brand. The ability to control how they distribute the products and services they endorse and to develop their platform for other entertainment opportunities at this more enhanced level may have been missed. For many celebrities, this might be outside of what is manageable, but for those like the Kardashians, Jessica Simpson, Mary Kate and Ashley Olsen, Ashton Kutcher, and others with extensive product lines and businesses around their name, they missed a big one here and should start planning for round two. The only big movie brand that we saw is Hasbro, which applied for Transformers. Q: What might they do with their superhero channel? A: Just about anything.

The Strategy: More Robust Consumer Experience and Data Mining

We also saw a big play by retailers and famous retail brands in the list of applicants. Macy's, Bloomingdales, Gap and its family of brands, TJ Maxx, Polo, Calvin Klein, Home Depot, Pampered Chef, Clinique, Nike, Target, Walmart, Weber, J.C. Penney, and E&J Gallo Winery are among those that applied. A few airlines and hotels moved into this space such as Delta, Swiss Air, Virgin, Hilton, Hyatt, Marriott, Orient Express, and Viking Cruises. Why? They can build a much more robust consumer experience by owning the entire top-level domain. Operating a top-level domain enables these brands to not only build out their retail portal more extensively, but potentially create content and communities tailored to their target audiences. If they build a more customized user experience such that consumers design what they want from their big brands, then these brands have capitalized on consumers telecasting what they want, where they may want to go, when they shop, and what they are looking for online. This bolsters the golden opportunity for brands to gather important research for its purposes and further refine its ability to understand the coveted consumer. In the long term, could this mean these big retailers don't need to hire market researchers? Might they eliminate the need for other distribution channels that cost them money? Or, could they build content and programming to keep their customers glued to their new channel, thereby eliminating other advertising and social media costs? Could the cost to keep a customer happy be reduced through this strategy? All of this and more is possible with innovative thinking and implementation.

Who Is Missing from This Strategy?

- Luxury Retailers. We didn't see applications from Nordstrom, Neiman Marcus, or Saks. Perhaps they don't think their customers would adapt, but they have missed an opportunity to dominate the consumer experience and will be left in a .com world until round two.
- Top Advertisers. Some of the top advertisers in the world opted out on this strategy. Procter & Gamble's family of products, Coca-Cola, Pepsi, Verizon, Time Warner, Sears, Anheuser-Busch, Estée Lauder, Yum! Brands, Mars, Hershey, Kraft Foods, Unilever, Kohl's, and others all passed on the opportunity. While for most of these companies, the reasoning was likely not the price tag, but the internal resources needed to figure out what to do with it, I expect we'll see them carefully monitor what happens in the coming months and years and then they'll be in round two. They also may look for partnership opportunities with those brands that did apply and with generics that fit their brand category.

- Big Social Media. Most shockingly, the biggest social media companies in the world: Facebook, Twitter, Pandora, eBay, Groupon all passed on this opportunity. The price tag surely wasn't the issue for these billion dollar companies. The ability to put smart people on it wasn't either, since they presumably have locked up top technology talent. So, why did they pass? Only they know, but owning and fully controlling their own top-level domain surely could have enhanced their ability to provide consumers a better experience and would have locked down their ability to control their destiny on the Internet. When the Internet is your business, why wouldn't you spend the $185,000 to own your brand? Most of these players have spent millions for a 30-second Super Bowl ad so the potential for a return on investment was certainly there for them to buy at least their core brand as a gTLD.

- Two Big Airlines. United and American Airlines were both missing from the list of applicants, while their major competitors, Delta and Virgin applied. What may happen? Perhaps nothing, but if Delta and Virgin can better serve consumers and provide more customized travel planning experiences, they may win the battle of the skies until round two.

The Strategy: Enhanced Search for Sale

Google, Yahoo!, and Bing all applied. There are approximately 900 generics (101 of which belong to Google), so the idea of search as a business will likely not only continue, but expand, in an exploding Internet. The opportunity to tailor search and even charge for it, whether you are seeking or want to be found, will be enhanced. For consumers, that means it may actually get easier to find what you are looking for with more niched search categories. For businesses, you may be able to tailor your domain and digital strategy to your customers. The search engines may actually start to charge for this premium search and evolve its business model.

It is also likely that the battle for search will expand from the three major players into a sea of generics fighting to own market categories. Brands, too, could compete by offering better search within their brand categories. The implications for search in an ever expanding Internet are long-reaching. With the three big search engines all applying, we anticipate the algorithms will change to incorporate TLDs and could weigh more heavily in favor of finding domains in the more descriptive gTLDs rather than in the saturated .com top-level domain. While Google certainly made the boldest move, could this dilute or enhance its search engine? Are they planning a search segmentation approach? Will Yahoo! and/or Bing emerge ahead in the long run or fall further behind in the search business? Only time will tell, but we know search is going to change and how we all navigate will be led by these three big players.

The Strategy: Corner the Customer with Cloud Computing and Enhanced B2B Services

Most of the global consulting houses and big business to business service providers jumped on the gTLD opportunity: Accenture, CBRE, Deloitte, Dunn & Bradstreet, FedEx, Gallup, KPMG, and PWC all applied. We also saw a significant play by software and devices such as IBM, Microsoft, Apple, Dell, Cisco, Xerox, SAP, AOL, and Norton, who will likely use this as a platform to expand their software capabilities with cloud computing. If the consulting companies and/or the software companies migrate their customers to manage everything in their cloud or gTLD, which is far more robust than the .com approach, will they corner the market on software as a service? Or, will they use their TLD as one big enterprise system to provide security to their customers and box out other .com-based software providers. Once you put your entire business in their hands, how likely are you to move? What extended services could help entrepreneurs and start-up companies have the same power of an enterprise system as the big guys? The strategy will likely pay off for these big players and provide even greater dominance in the global consulting, technology, and services industries.

The Strategy: Catalyst for Disruptive Innovation

Big brands with innovative thinking included: Amazon (76 different TLDs), Google (101), Heinz (ketchup and Heinz), Johnson & Johnson

(Baby and JNJ), LEGO, Transformers, Safeway (grocery, justforu, and two others), SC Johnson (afamilycompany, duck, mrmuscle, right-athome, and other brands), L'Oréal (beauty, hair, makeup, salon, skin, and other brands), Xbox, Sony PlayStation, Microsoft (live, skydrive, docs, and other brands). What does this mean? It means these innovative leaders will likely drive new opportunities and push outside the box, disruptive and innovative thinking to lead the way the Internet is used. It is shocking that more of the "innovative" tech companies didn't apply and use this as a catalyst to drive disruptive thinking about their business models. Of course, for every applicant, the opportunity is ripe to pull creative people together and throw out every assumption you have and rebuild how you do business. Who are the top outside the box thinkers likely to tap into the power of disruptive innovation? Could Heinz build a community of ketchup lovers? Or, Safeway disruptively innovate the way consumers manage and shop for groceries as an overall experience?

The Strategy: Content Distribution— Displacement of Cable

For many major media, sports, and entertainment companies, they understand that traditional television is nearly extinct and cable could be the next go. As the television device and data and fiber optic companies figure out how to evolve flat screens to receive HD on the Internet and deliver it faster to the home, these media innovators are preparing to serve as their own distributor. So, it's not surprising that Comcast and Dish made big plays here—they are anticipating that their distribution model may eviscerate in favor of a new one—the top-level channels of the Internet. It is likely that early adopters will abandon cable subscriptions to their TVs in favor of Internet only within the next few years and wide spread adoption is likely in the coming 5 to 7 years. BBC, Bloomberg, ABC, CBS, Comcast, DVR, HBO, Showtime, Weather Channel, Broadway, MLB, NBA, Netflix, and NFL all applied. They will likely start to build their delivery of content and partnerships with advertisers as they expand these new channels of the Internet. With the big move by Amazon and anticipation that they may partner with some of these content providers, we could see top-level channels providing not just content and information, but the portal for shopping all from the big flat screen hanging on your wall.

Who Is Missing from This Strategy?

- Sports. The big three leagues in the United States applied, but missing were the NHL, PGA, LPGA, ATP, WTA, MLS, and the WNBA.
- Networks & Entertainment. None of the big movie houses applied. We're missing Viacom, which owns MTV, Nickelodeon, Spike, CMT, Dreamworks, Paramount, Comedy Central, VH1, and Go Fish do not apply. Discovery, which owns TLC, Destination America, the Hub, Animal Planet, Warner Brothers, and MGM, didn't apply either. Disney, NBC, ESPN, Lifetime, E Television, and Hulu also opted out. Many others missed the opportunity to build their own channel. Will they buy in round two? Did they strategically opt out? Budget surely couldn't have been the reason for these big powerhouse media companies that rely on distribution to fuel their sales. So, why didn't they apply when others did? The uncertainty and speculation likely drove the decision, but only they know for sure.

The Strategy: Industry Leadership

Many brands may try to corner the market quickly on key consumer needs as industry leaders. We saw this in photography and printing. Flickr, Canon, Nikon, Vista Print, Epson, and Fujitsu all are going after the photography, imaging, and storage of photos top level. Could they ultimately create a different type of social network within their sites by providing a different type of photo sharing? Will they dominate this industry because of their TLD? Will they build apps that tie to a more robust TLD? Of course, in theory, all of the major brands are likely hoping for industry leadership, but this particular category seems ripe for someone to emerge as the leader in digital imagery management.

The Strategy: If you build it they will come—the next community

The 900+ generics in every conceivable category will likely be tapping into this strategy. If they build the community around people who love sports, fashion, hip hop, pets, music, movies—you name it—then they corner the market and build a community of domains that has value to everyone selling to them. How can it work? This is a tough one, even for someone like me who is studying it. But, the opportunity is there, there just needs to be a tolerance for making mistakes in building it, enough money to survive those mistakes, and the perseverance to out-innovate the others.

Top Missing Brands from gTLD List

We know that half of the Interbrand's top global brands list applied for a TLD. That means half didn't. Who didn't apply, why, and what might they do next? While we don't know for sure, we anticipate the reason for these brand giants was not the price tag associated with a TLD, but more about applying resources and building a strategy around it. They opted to take a wait-and-see approach and then determine if it's right for them. If the Internet changes as we anticipate, they will likely partner or align with those that did and plan to apply in the second round. If nothing changes and .com remains the status quo, then they'll report to their stakeholders that they were wise to hold back. But if it changes everything, how will they respond? Will they be able to catch up when every 60 seconds on the Internet there are 694,445 search queries, 168 million emails sent, 70+ new domains registered, and 98,000 tweets, just to name a few? These big brands opted out for now. Will the C-Suite be asking why?

Coca-Cola	Wells Fargo	T-Mobile
Marlboro	Facebook	(Deutsche
AT&T		Telekom)
Verizon		Louis Vuitton

Hewlett-Packard	Red Bull	Nordstrom
MasterCard	Aldi	Neiman Marcus
Gillette	IKEA	ESPN
ExxonMobil	KFC	Motorola
Pampers	Chevron	Kleenex
Shell	United Airlines	Kellogg's
Disney	NHL	Starbuck's
Mercedes	MTV	Tide
Budweiser	NBC	Lowe's
Colgate	Nickelodeon	Walgreens
Subway	T.G.I. Friday's	Bud Light
H&M	Domino's	Costco
eBay	Pandora	Kroger
Pepsi	Groupon	Reebok
U.S. Bank	Twitter	Major film studios
B.P.	Saks	

Brand IDNs

A few brands opted to apply for the internationalized domain name of their brand in Japanese, Chinese, or Arabic. The expansion of the Internet to include characters and languages outside of the traditional Latin languages indicates the increasing trend toward globalization of our economy and the need to think toward future expansion opportunities in these important regions of the world. What follows is a list of the most notable applicants:

Google	L'Oréal	Bridgestone Corp.
Amazon	Samsung	Nokia
Wal-Mart	General Electric	
Volkswagen	VeriSign (.com)	

Top Trends

A few of the top trends we identified that appear to be on the horizon after reviewing the Big Reveal list include:

- Big innovative technology and media companies will lead and drive consumer behavior into a paradigm shift in the way consumers access content, search, and navigate the Internet. They will likely reposition the Internet as a single source of distribution for content in the future.
- A few top levels will emerge as a trusted "go to" source for managing life, business, and interests.
- More companies will have the ability to participate in communities than in the current fragmented .com space. Meaning, because more centralized sources for key themes will emerge, it will actually get easier to be connected to the community you want.
- Search will actually get easier because you can narrow in on the playing field within which you search and more niched search engines will emerge. Finding a .com could become more difficult when the top 3 search engines likely adjust their algorithms to weigh categories of search based upon the nature of the top-level domain (i.e., if you are looking for a dog product, it may search through .pets before it searches through .com or .co).
- Early adopters will capitalize on the loyalty of community followers —members of their organizations or top-level domains—and this access to information will be worth billions to advertisers.
- The latecomers will quickly jump on the bandwagon and find ways to participate, but the roads will already be paved by the early adopters. The hot TLDs may be taken by round two.
- Cable will gradually disappear—mobile devices, tablets, and the ability to find channels on the expanded Internet will replace traditional television and cable. The flat screen on the wall will connect you to thousands of new channels of the Internet, all of which have even more to offer than your current cable box.
- .com will be diluted in favor of a .brand world for authenticity and connection to the brand you seek.

- The companies that make movies and provide entertainment will evolve and need to find ways to respond to specific community groups demanding content to cry, laugh, think, and be connected in a meaningful way to other people. The producers of content will likely integrate social media or community connections with shopping all in one place.
- The idea of technology interfering with direct human interaction could actually evolve and bolster the desire to be part of a community—but now through a global community empowered by a new Internet.
- Global giants will no longer determine what products to create. Instead, consumers will forecast their needs in an online community, and savvy companies and entrepreneurs will respond successfully.
- Many of the generic TLD businesses will fail and new business models will emerge just as in the .com era.
- There will be increased merger and acquisition activity because large companies that did not apply will look for companies that did apply and adopt successful strategies to acquire.
- This will likely spawn innovative activity that may lead to an increase in IPOs of the companies that get it right.
- There will initially be an increased cost to businesses, but those that restructure their approach will realize more economies of scale.
- Brick and mortar retail will need to become a destination source offering entertainment for consumers to continue to come into the actual store and they will need to tie their in-store experience to savings when purchasing other products online. Like Apple, the store is so much more than just a store.
- Thinking about brands has to evolve to incorporate a comprehensive Internet, app, digital, interactive, and IP strategy—none of these can operate independently in a .brand world.

What Does It All Mean?

The Internet is about to dramatically change. More than fifty percent of the world's biggest brands have applied for a top-level domain. And, a few of the big players have applied for many with bold innovative moves. While some brands may have applied out of fear of not applying, they certainly will look for opportunities to innovate and invent around this new opportunity. Many companies may use this as a catalyst for truly disruptive innovation. Regardless of your opinion of the program, with $350 million sunk into application fees alone, change is likely coming as those companies seek a return on their investment. What happens to .com? What other domains might you want to secure when these 900+ generics go live? What brand TLDs should you align or partner with? How do you protect your brand in all of this? We've provided answers to all of these questions in *Domain Names Rewired*, but in a 60 second or less answer: Digital strategy is evolving beyond just placing ads in other social media sites or launching new apps. Brands need to begin to see their digital strategy with domain names in an expanding Internet as the anchor to their plan and then intersect social media and apps into a comprehensive holistic digital brand strategy. Just having a .com is no longer enough in a world of thousands of top-level domains—where does your strategy begin and end? Your anchor—your domain name.

We advise companies to begin a deep dive analysis to understand where your brand, your competitors, and your supply chain fit into the new digital map of brands, generics, geographics, and communities. (See Figure P.7.) Once you understand where your domain name fits as an anchor, you can begin to build your digital strategy around your

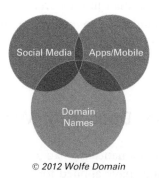

© 2012 Wolfe Domain

Figure P.6 Holistic Digital Strategy ©2012 Wolfe Domain

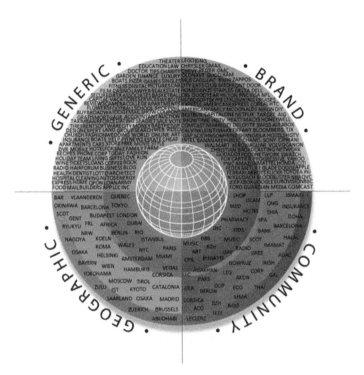

Figure P.7 The Big Bang of the Internet ©2012 Wolfe Domain

anchor(s). Most companies house thousands of .coms. Will you keep them all? Will you buy new ones? Will you apply for a gTLD in round two? Where will you fit into this map of top-level domains? Should you apply for your brand in any or many of the new generics?

It's likely 18 to 24 months before the impact of this initiative is felt by consumers and companies. So, now is the time. Start thinking about it now and learning about what's happening. Begin building a plan so when the time comes, you are one step ahead of your competitors. Whether you applied or not, this book should be a starting point for evolving your digital strategy.

We also encourage you to build a team of people who can bring strategic thinking to this process. It doesn't just belong in the law department or marketing or digital departments—it will take a comprehensive collaborative effort to be successful in this dynamic and changing digital world. (See Figure P.8.)

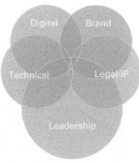

© 2012 Wolfe Domain

Figure P.8 Collaborative Team Approach to Digital Strategy ©2012
Wolfe Domain

We want to thank our many thought leaders for their contributions and
insight. Without them, our predictions would not be possible. We can
clearly see that the future is evolving and while we have tried to identify
trends to help guide businesses in making decisions to be one step ahead, we
know that constant research and knowledge sharing is required. We'll
continue to do our part to gather information and pass it along to you.

For more information go to www.domainnamesrewired.com.

Acknowledgments

Thank you to all of our thought leaders for participating in this project. Your ideas, insights, and perspective were invaluable in understanding what's happening and what we can expect in future trends as the Internet continues to change and evolve.

Josh Bourne
Managing Partner, FairWinds Partners

Sarah B. Deutsch
Vice President and Associate General Counsel, Verizon
  Communication

Claudio Di Gangi
Manager, External Relations, Internet and the Judiciary,
  International Trademark Association

Cynthia L. Gibson
Executive Vice President, Legal Affairs, Scripps Network
  Interactive Inc.

J. Scott Evans
Head of Global Brand, Domains & Copyright, Yahoo!

Nancy H. Lutz
Partner, Kelley Drye & Warren, LLP

Steven W. Miller
Vice President and General Counsel, Intellectual Property,
    Procter & Gamble

Jeffrey J. Neuman,
Vice President, Business Affairs, Enterprise Services, NeuStar, Inc.

Russell Pangborn
Associate General Counsel for Trademarks, Microsoft Corporation

Krista Papac
Chief Strategy Officer, ARI Registry Services

Katherine A. Ruwe
Senior Counsel, Global Litigation and Dispute Resolution,
    Procter & Gamble

Adam Scoville
Trademark and Brand Protection Counsel, RE/MAX, LLC
Ellen Shankman, Principal, Ellen B. Shankman & Associates,
    Rehovot Israel

Yasmin R. Tavakoli
Associate, Kelley Drye & Warren, LLP

Fabricio Vayra
Trademark Attorney, Time Warner Inc.

Nick Wood
Managing Director, Com Laude

DOMAIN NAMES ⓇEWIRED

DOMAIN NAMES: ESCHEWIRED

Chapter One

The New Regime

The debate is over and ICANN is moving full steam ahead to create the next generation of the Internet. What is happening? What will change in how people use the Internet? How will businesses make money from it and what was the reasoning behind it all? How much will it cost companies to protect their brand when the Internet just infinitely grew in size? These are just a few of the questions answered in *Domain Names Rewired*.

In case you hadn't stumbled across the limited and often buried articles in the mainstream media covering this topic, for the first time in the history of the Internet, ICANN (the non-profit organization that runs the Internet and is formally known as the Internet Corporation for Assigned Names and Numbers), has approved the release of up to thousands of new generic top-level domains (gTLD or TLD) such as .yourbrand or .restaurants, to anyone who wants to apply for one. While it is costly to obtain a new top-level domain—at least $250,000 to $500,000 or more in the initial year—this is the new frontier, just like it was when *.coms* became mainstream, full of opportunities to create the future, adopt disruptive innovation and new business models, along with challenges to protect existing business models and brands.

This rapidly changing new regime of the Internet will impact the hundreds of millions of Internet users around the globe, not to mention every business that already has a .com. Largely under the radar of even sophisticated and savvy business executives, when the new Internet launches in 2013, businesses of all sizes will need guidance on how to respond. Those who caught on early and applied for their own top-level domain between January and April of 2012, will be in for the biggest paradigm shift since the Internet began, and potentially capitalize on the next channel of the Internet. Even for companies that didn't invest in the new Internet, they will need to protect their existing .com and brand in an exponentially increasing Internet world and evaluate new opportunities.

In this first chapter, we provide an overview of the business community response to the program, opportunities, new business models, and what is needed to defend your brand in this new regime. Throughout the remainder of the book, we interview global leaders in trade organizations, corporations, technology, and other thought leaders to identify and predict trends.

The rollout of top-level domains includes not just generic top-level domains that are available to any organization and branded top-level domains reserved for legitimate brand-rights holders, but also community groups and geographic locations, with special rules that apply to those top-level domains.

Imagine if you had a heads up in 2004 that social media was about to change everything or knew that the .com bubble would burst in 2000? What might you have done differently? In *Domain Names Rewired*, we hope to give you the tools to take advantage of opportunities and how to prepare for threats to your brand in the next generation of the Internet. But not everyone thinks it's such a great idea. Many are concerned that the cost to brand owners to protect their brand from cybersquatters in a .anything world is too high. They are concerned that there really wasn't a need or desire for this other than to create new opportunities for existing players in the registry operator, registrar, and service-provider industries. We've interviewed thought leaders with differing views and centered our book on providing advice going forward. While the rationale behind the program and process for rollout of the campaign may still be in question, since the debate about whether or not it should go forward is over, we focus on the potential positive outcomes for businesses as a result of this changing landscape, as well as provide tips for defending your brand in a changing Internet world.

An Overview of the Business Community Response to gTLDs

According to a 2010 study conducted by the World Trademark Review (WTR) magazine, 54 percent of global brands responded positively when asked whether their company/client would be applying for a new gTLD; of those brands planning to apply to run a new generic-top-level domain (gTLD), 81 percent planned on making their gTLD their master brand. With these new gTLDs, companies will have an opportunity to cement their brands on the Internet, creating second-tier domains for sections of their organizations on branded gTLDs. In the same WTR survey it was found that 46 percent of in-house counsel said "Yes," "It's Likely," or "Maybe" when asked whether their companies would apply. One respondent in the survey from an international publishing company summed up the opportunity when he was quoted as saying, "We need to be able to provide a safe and reliable web space that will give our customers the trust and confidence to trade with us . . . with our own registry we could control our web estate." In a second study conducted by ABC Namebank in 2008, it stated that there were already some 18,700 companies in the world today that will apply under the new policy. According to these numbers, this will have a global impact and bring a new face to global e-commerce and open doors to what many are calling the new *cyber brands*.

Many corporate marketing professionals see these cyber brands as an opportunity to enhance user experiences by creating a universal signal. These new domains would signal users of a tighter association between online brands, site legitimacy, and even subconsciously signal a company's industry leadership. In addition to site legitimacy, branded gTLDs would reduce unauthorized sales, and issues like counterfeit activities could only transpire outside of a brand's gTLD, making users more confident in their secure purchases and site interaction. Consumers have shown they will be loyal to brands that carry personal meaning. For example, if a user is an avid runner, they will have no fear of clicking on a running.nike site and feel confident it is an authentic product.

Although operating a gTLD means capital investment in initial fees and ongoing operations costs, the opportunity for some companies to maintain control over their brand's online security and community outweighs those costs. If you consider a domain name for many technology companies is its single most valuable asset, is any price too high to have total and complete control over it? Top-level domains and the explosion of the next generation of the Internet in 2013 also presents a unique opportunity for all companies, whether they have applied for a top-level domain or not, to consider opportunities for disruptive innovation; to push the boundaries on how they connect with their consumer, manage supply chains, and distribute their product or service.

According to speculation by our thought leaders, there may be 500 to 1,000 or more new *.brand* TLDs and a similar number of generic TLDs. If companies decide to wait until round two or later, they risk waiting a long time, as potentially thousands of applicants will be evaluated in round one, making the next opportunity to apply for a specific domain less valuable. Our thought leaders estimate the window of opportunity may not open for another five years. Simple logic dictates that it will be at least five years before another round will be up and running. This initial round will not go live until 2013 at the earliest. ICANN has pledged to evaluate the stability of the infrastructure and the process before opening another round. Given the anticipated time for ICANN to approve a new round, modify the guidebook or processes, obtain applications, process applications, and then go live, it couldn't happen much sooner than five years. Five years in the Internet business can make or break most businesses. Accordingly, for companies that can afford it, a wait-and-see approach is not encouraged. Given the significant risk and opportunities available, each company will have to carefully assess that impact and begin developing a strategy. A company's top priority should not just be to ensure they submitted an application that meets ICANN criteria, but that they are developing a solid business case for the domain they chose. With the rise in Internet presence and keyword searches, name identities and how consumers interact with companies digitally is becoming just as important as logos, design, and traditional brand identities, if not more so.

Executing a campaign to interact digitally with consumers can propel a brand to new heights overnight.

The benefits of these new gTLDs, ranging from new branding and marketing opportunities to enhanced security, are substantial, but they also come with costs and potential risk. Most notably, the investment required comes without any guarantee of a paradigm shift to follow. On the flip side, if the gTLDs change the way consumers use the Internet and competitors obtain important top-level domains, companies that wait-and-see may miss an opportunity to dominate in the next channel of the Internet. With or without a gTLD, companies will need to carefully assess the impact, choose an offensive, defensive, or combined strategy and begin developing processes to execute that strategy. This shift in the way information is found by users has the potential to fundamentally change the face of the Internet.

To provide a brief overview of the program, the Board of Directors of ICANN approved a long-debated program to expand the Internet in June 2011. On January 12, 2012, the application period opened for anyone to apply for one of four types of top-level domains (see Figure 1.1):

1. Brand
2. Community (special requirements to qualify)
3. Geographic (cities or regions—special requirements to qualify)
4. Generic terms

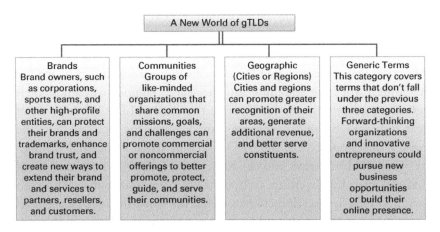

Figure 1.1   The Scope of New Top-Level Domains by Category

The application period closed in April of 2012 for any new applicants. It was expected that there would be anywhere from 500 to 1,000 or more applications, but there were 1,930. ICANN's plan is to review the applications through the remainder of 2012 and start launching the first batch of the new top-level domains in 2013. We completed this book in April 2012 and have added some information following the publication of applicants in June 2012 to Appendix A. We will continue to follow and predict trends as this evolves online. We provide a more detailed analysis of the list of applicants and applications in the Preface.

Potential Benefits for an Organization Applying for gTLDs

Although the application period is closed, to get a grasp on what all of this will mean, it's important to start by understanding the fundamentals and weighing the pros and cons to a business or organization in obtaining a top-level domain. We'll start with the pros for obtaining a top-level domain.

The SEO Impact

Since 2008, when ICANN approved the gTLD plan, registry operators have been evaluating ways to maximize the new TLDs. A major benefit to registering the new gTLDs is the potential impact these domains will have with search engine optimization (SEO). According to public reports by VeriSign, the registry operator of .com, after speaking with the three largest search engines—Google, Yahoo!, and Bing—VeriSign anticipates that if the new gTLDs make it easier for consumers to acquire the content they are searching for, the search engines will adjust their algorithms accordingly to incorporate the new gTLDs. While it is not clear how exactly search engines would adopt the new gTLDs, the registry operators expect the SEO function to be optimized through the new gTLD scheme and, in turn, reduce security concerns about phishing sites by diverting web users to correct websites. Although having to type in long domain names and not knowing specific spellings of company names may lead web users to rely completely on search engines to avoid confusion, the authenticity of the top-level domain will provide greater assurances to consumers that they have found the site they are looking for in their search.

Overall, a short, memorable domain name means fewer impressions are required before customers remember the domain, resulting in improved advertising return on investment (ROI), in addition to improved search ranking for landing pages and second-level domains that are easily associated with the brand by search engines. With the rising number of portable devices being used to access the web, short URLs will become increasingly more valuable since lengthy strings can be impractical for mobile users. Additionally, there are questions about what a strong top-level domain will do to search. If a consumer knows they can go to search.sports and get access to any sporting event they want, they may go directly to the niche site to search for what they need rather than through a big search engine. Search engine optimization depends on the relevance, quality, and popularity of a domain name. While domains may become less important as more and more people access the Internet through new devices and apps, the keywords that they contain will continue to remain relevant.

Because search engines consider keywords within domain names in their search result algorithms, gTLD registrants will be able to register second-level domain names containing carefully chosen words and phrases that reinforce their messaging and positioning. Owners will have the opportunity to control and/or sell second-level domains to third parties, as well as have the ability for significant control over the guidelines of who can register for these domains. For brand owners, selling second-level domains likely doesn't fit the purpose or mission of the TLD, but for generics, this is the primary reason for acquiring a top-level domain.

Second-Level Domains and Navigation of the Internet

One of the benefits of introducing the new gTLDs is improved navigation on the Internet. For example, companies may achieve better navigation through to their websites by having domain extensions closely targeted toward their specific site content. This easier navigation is due to the likelihood that the new gTLDs will be designed to serve consumer needs that the .com domains do not meet particularly well. Some new gTLDs will have the ability to facilitate consumers' Internet navigation and search by more quickly and accurately directing users to websites with the designed content. For example, company-specific gTLDs such as info .yourcompanyname could facilitate the ability for those consumers to obtain general information as well as promote interactions with partners and suppliers with the company.

One additional advantage for owners of a new gTLD should be better and more intuitive navigation for users. Companies will have the ability to break down the new branded domains to focus on more specific audiences (restaurant.vacations, newyorkcity.vacations, bahamatours.vacations, contest.yourbrand, spatreatments.hotelname, yourfavoriteshow.abc, or drama.abc, etc.). Easier access to company content should in turn create potentially better ranking results within search engines. More intuitive navigation could also cut down on advertising expenses to promote a previous unapparent URL. Overall, brands can create an unlimited amount of microsites and landing pages for all of their vertical product lines and sub-brands.

This new system could allow not only for enhanced brand promotion and visibility, but also for secure corporate and client networks (used for purposes such as facilitating the provision of services to clients by creating a dedicated portal site)—which could then prevent fraudulent practices such as offers of counterfeit products through the Internet. In theory, once a new gTLD is awarded, the structure would be in place so that registrants could start registering second-level domain names as soon as the gTLD goes live.

It's important to note that most brand top-level domains won't want to sell second-level domains. ICANN requires that top-level domains that are open or selling off second levels follow a number of fairness rules that brands likely won't want to do. Accordingly, most of the top-level domains selling second levels will be the generics run by registrars, existing registry operators, or entrepreneurs backed with investors hoping to create the next .com, but even brand TLDs will have the opportunity for full control of the second-level domains, offering key strategic advantages in the long term.

> "For better or for worse, ICANN's program for unlimited new gTLDs is set to change the relationship between brands, domain names, and Internet navigation."
> Claudio Di Gangi, Manager, External Relations, Internet and the Judiciary, International Trademark Association

Email

As organizations adopt new gTLDs, email addresses are another aspect of branded technology that could be impacted significantly. In the future, companies could use their new brand gTLD as a simplified email address (name@domain versus name@organization.domain), or, for example, name.nike or name.nbc. If email clients and servers are changed to recognize this format, companies that offer such branded email addresses may be able to potentially strengthen the connection between themselves and their customers, fans, and other supporters and may build interest and attract new Internet interactions. Further, organizations can use this enhanced connection to better understand its customer base without the cost and expense of traditional market research.

In addition, with the ownership of a brand domain, companies also have the option of creating mail exchange (MX) records for second-level domains for resellers, customers, vendors, and so on, (name@vendor.domain), which was not possible in the past. This could also create potential new revenue from the sale of affinity-branded email addresses.

Social Media

Another critical opportunity with the new gTLDs is the opportunity to build a Facebook-like presence. The social-networking giant surprisingly did not apply for its own top level domain. Major brands have used a www.facebook.com/brand URL for campaigns and corporate information targeted towards a younger crowd. Recently, a contributor to *Advertising Age* asserted that company websites may become a thing of the past and provided statistics: Starbucks, in one month, had 1.8 million website visitors versus 21.1 million "likes" on Facebook. It was 270,000 visitors versus 20.5 million likes for Coca-Cola. For Oreo, 290,000 versus 10.1 million.

However impressive those statistics are, they don't tell the whole story. While many corporations have Facebook sites, they are still trying to quantify the value of social media, and they are not abandoning their corporate websites. Facebook "likes" will never be the same as website visitors, in part because you can "like" a company Facebook page without having ever viewed it. While most marketing executives realize the importance of expanding their brand's reach through social media, they also realize that any brand that surrenders itself to simply become a sub-brand of another (Facebook) could be leading to the loss of control of that brand's image, privacy, and even monetization. Having a .brand allows owners to create their own online policy regarding the brand's core web presence and security, as opposed to building a brand presence on Facebook where companies are subject to Facebook's particular policies and security measures. While we can't know the strategic reason behind Facebook's decision not to apply for a gTLD, it does mean there is an opening for an innovative company to build a new social network. While that could surely exist in a .com world, the expansion of the Internet provides the paradigm shift to potentially migrate Facebook friends into more segmented social groups in a more segmented Internet world. Likewise, many of the other social networking companies such as Twitter, Pandora, and Pinterest could all face new competitive threats.

Anti-Counterfeiting

By enhancing brand owners' control over their channels of distribution as the top-level domain owner, the introduction of new top-level domains has the potential to significantly disrupt the abilities of counterfeiters to distribute counterfeit goods and of unlicensed content providers to distribute protected content, which would bolster brand purity. Brand owners applying for new TLDs will be able to approve and monitor all sub-domain registrations made under that TLD. This will give brand owners the control to affiliate themselves with only those entities (partners, licensees, affiliates, resellers, customers, etc.) of their own choice. This will allow them to ensure that there are no unauthorized resellers that are offering counterfeited goods by obtaining domain names identical or substantially similar to their domain names. For example, Apple could create a program whereby only authorized resellers of Apple's goods would be able to obtain a resellername.apple domain name. Such control enhances the brand's value by guaranteeing that consumers will find authentic, legitimate quality goods of the brand and will no longer be tricked into obtaining counterfeit goods, thus decreasing the effectiveness of those counterfeiting channels. From a content provider's perspective, it proves useful for preventing infringement since a content provider has the ability to consolidate its distribution channels such that any online content distributed outside of its TLD would be infringement.

Brands looking to enhance security for their on-line customers will use a top-level domain to signpost authenticity and to guarantee trust.

"Brands looking to enhance security for their online customers will use a top-level domain to signpost authenticity and to guarantee trust. If it does not end in Rolex, it's not Rolex."

Nick Wood, Managing Director, Com Laude

Industry Leadership

The most prominent reason for applying for a top-level domain is to obtain industry leadership and market dominance within a particular industry segment. By purchasing a .brand domain, companies have obtained exclusive leadership of that brand through their 100 percent, ironclad ownership of that name identity. If the public responds as anticipated, a brand or company owning an entire industry category will have complete ability to own the new channel of the Internet within that product category. For example, if an organization owns .style, .news, .movies, or .independentfilms, it can become a single source for all consumers interested in that topic and lead the Internet market space with content, products, and promotions. Because of all of the reasons listed above, an organization can become the market leader in any category in which it owns the top-level domain and box out competitors from owning this new channel.

Some marketing professionals have cited the ability of a TLD owner to build an Internet-based island, controlling all access and content.

Since domain owners will operate the registry that accepts second-level domains, a company can ensure that only companies with whom it has beneficial commercial relationships with, such as partners, co-ventures, customers, and so on, can obtain second-level domains. Marketing professionals have predicted that the domain name system will develop into a directory of leading corporations and that Internet users will become accustomed to associate the top-level branded sites with greater prestige and authority. And, never again will a company have to question in a brainstorming session whether a new product name is available as a .com—they own their own domain and can build whatever contests, promotions, campaigns, or new product lines it wants in its own top-level domain. Companies can then tie their top-level domain to mobile applications or other tools and devices that their target consumer uses to stay connected in a more robust way.

At the time this book was printed, the application period will have closed. While the most telling argument for companies to apply was the ability to control one of its most valuable assets, many will have opted to wait and see because of the cost of the new TLD program and uncertainty. For comparisons, a .com can now be purchased for about $8 a year and a top-level domain will cost about $250,000 to $500,000 to acquire, plus operating costs of about $252,000 per year and business resources toward new business models. It's certainly a drastic difference. But at $8 a year, you

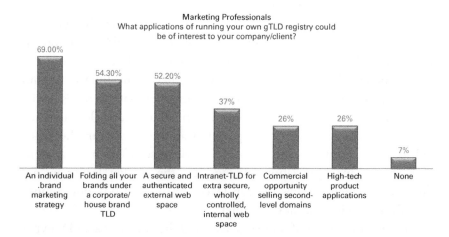

Figure 1.2 Survey of Marketing Professionals' Interest in Top-Level Domains by *World Trademark Review* magazine, December/January 2011

don't own .com—VeriSign does. And VeriSign controls .com. While most top-level domains will partner with VeriSign or another registry operator, at the end of the day, they actually own the domain. For technology companies, that can be an invaluable difference. See Figure 1.2.

While many trademark counsel are fearful of an entirely new domain market, marketing professionals surveyed in the 2010 study by the *World Trademark Review* magazine could see the benefits of owning your own gTLD registry. On the flip side of the pros of applying for a top-level domain are the cons; let's take a look at the risks and cons associated with running a top-level domain.

Potential Risk if Applying for gTLDs

The cost to an organization that chooses to offensively obtain a new generic top-level domain is anticipated to be approximately $250,000 to $500,000 to obtain a site that does not go to an auction (oh yes, if more than one company applies for the same top-level domain, it goes to the highest bidder), and an anticipated $250,000 per year in additional hard costs with the registry operator, plus those additional internal costs to operate the new domain.

Cost and Lost Investment

The biggest risk if an organization chooses to obtain a new generic or branded top-level domain for offensive purposes or just to ensure no one else has it, is that the investment for obtaining and maintaining the TLD does not exceed the return. The most likely scenario is that the general public does not respond favorably to the new top-level domain naming system and that consumer behavior remains unchanged as it relates to domain names. In addition to the application costs, maintaining a TLD will require a commitment of around $125,000 per year for operating the TLD (technical maintenance, escrow costs, etc.), a figure that does not include any internal costs borne by the applicant for its own employees performing internal management of the domain and the marketing efforts it would support. There would also be the additional cost of monitoring and enforcing for all top level and sub-level domains, which would likely amount to around $100,000 per year (although that figure could vary substantially based on the number and nature of the domains obtained).

For mid-market to very large companies, $250,000 to maintain a mission critical capital asset is not exactly breaking the bank. But, for smaller companies it is simply not in the budget.

Failure of Public to Respond Favorably

The additional risk is that if an organization applies for and obtains a new top-level domain and the public does not respond favorably, then the investment of time, money, and resources is lost. It is possible that consumers may continue to search and go to the tried and true .com infrastructure rather than adapt to the new .brand approach. Of course, once an organization obtains the new gTLD, if it determines this consumer response is not as anticipated, it can terminate the new gTLD to cut losses going forward, following some contractual guidelines, but the initial investment is an un-recouped cost.

Consumer Confusion

Additionally, if the public does not respond favorably, consumers may be confused about the new top-level domains and be unclear how to find information and content from an organization's family of brands. Despite ICANN's four-month campaign to raise global awareness leading up to the new gTLD initiative, numerous surveys have shown that the public may not be as enthusiastic about the upcoming changes. The Future Laboratory, on behalf of domain name registrar Gandi.net, found the majority of consumers polled (60 percent) agreed that the liberalization of domain name extensions will change the way they use the Internet, but not for the better. The reasons for negative feedback range from the Internet becoming full of pointless domain names (65 percent), messy and confusing (57 percent), too complex to navigate (46 percent), and out of control (41 percent). Critics of ICANN argue that it is doing too little to promote the program.

Cybersquatting

Owners of trademarks and brands have claimed that a new round of gTLDs might leave them facing an onslaught of cybersquatting and typosquatting, and that their policing and enforcement costs would be substantial. It is possible that the new gTLD program could lead to hundreds, if not thousands of new gTLDs, which is likely to cause brand abuse, such as cybersquatting, to grow exponentially. As a result, the legal costs for brand owners associated with monitoring, registering, and enforcing domain names are likely to rise substantially.

The Business Model—How Can It Work?

To help set the stage for what may transpire as new top-level domains are launched and to start your plan to build and protect your brand, it's important to evaluate and understand the business model for those that did apply. After all, the ability to make money or see a return on investment will drive most top-level domains. And, for branded, closed, top-level domains, since they won't be selling second-level domains, there will have to be a way to monetize their investment.

Today, the online world as we know it is defined by a relatively small number of generic top-level domain names. Currently, there are 21 active gTLD extensions and roughly 270 country-code top-level domain (ccTLD) extensions available for registration. In 2010, there were an estimated 183,000,000 domain names registered to those domains in operation according to Melbourne IT Services and Business Wire. The .com registry had the most domain names of all gTLDs with over 81,000,000 domain names registered as of last year. This newest gTLD expansion to the Internet naming system holds the potential of significant opportunities for branding, cross-media advertising, improving website traffic, and creating new business applications that can help create thousands of new domains in the next year alone and numerous potential revenue streams. See Figure 1.3.

Because the initial investment and ongoing cost is substantial, a clear return on investment analysis is required. What follows is an initial evaluation of potential revenue sources and positive return for an organization for its investment in a gTLD. In many ways, the business model for the new generic top-level domains is not unlike the business model for any Internet site or traditional .com. The unique differentiator, however, is the ability for market dominance and industry leadership by owning an

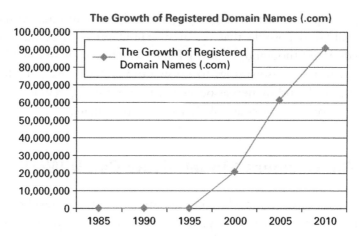

Figure 1.3 Growth of Registered Domain Names by VeriSign and Registrar-Reported Statistics

entire category, and the potential that it changes the way consumers think about and navigate the Internet. While it may be easier to extrapolate why owning .gambling, .sex, .money, or .sports would be valuable, the same model and approach extends to any category, such as food, lifestyle, fashion, music, technology, and so on. It's also critical to keep in mind that for all companies, the opportunity to think in a disruptive way, to toss out old assumptions or business models, and breakthrough to a new, successful model must be discovered in this new and changing Internet.

Content Distribution Channel—What if This Could Displace Cable?

A prime potential business model is the distribution of content and programming, similar to the existing cable network model. If the new generic top-level domains perform as anticipated by ICANN it could become a new channel of distribution—only instead of channels on a cable box, it's top-level domain networks distributing their content directly on the Internet. If this takes hold with consumers looking for programming and content it is possible, in some market segments, that this could replace cable. What if new programming might be on the spring.fashion or election.news channels only and not on the cable networks? If this eliminates the cost of distribution through cable networks or traditional advertising, what long-term impact could this have for an organization's bottom line? This is a slow-building opportunity, but one that should be evaluated as the biggest potential upside of the investment—almost every company is producing some content targeted to its audience. While many argue it's no different than the threat in the .com world, the reality is that by opening up the Internet to so many possibilities, the ability to innovate and push people to a new way of thinking can accelerate the shift that is already underway.

A similar example is the start-up company Hulu, founded in 2007 as a joint venture between a group of several media entities, now between NBC, Fox, Disney-ABC, and Providence Equity Partners. Through its joint-venture structure with content providers, Hulu offers both free and paid content. It functions as an ad-supported site and maintains a subscription-based service, Hulu-Plus, that offers additional programming and user features for $7.99 per month. According to CNET In March 2011, Jason Kilar, CEO, forecasted that the company would hit the $500 million mark for ad and subscription revenue, up from $263 million in 2010 and $108 million in 2009. At that time they counted 627 advertisers and 264 content partners. Hulu is on pace to hit 1 million paid subscribers on Hulu Plus—launched in November 2010—and their advertiser base grew 50 percent, from 194 in the first quarter of 2010 to 289 in the first quarter of this year. According to comScore, Inc., as of May 2011, Hulu accounts for around a third of all U.S. online advertising, generating 1.1 billion impressions of advertisements during the month of April. That means Hulu accounts for around 29 percent of all the 3.8 billion online video ad impressions seen by U.S. Internet users. The report also shows that Hulu is tops for total advertising minutes, at 470, and also for average number of ads per viewer, at 45.

According to CNET, the expected impact that online content providers like Hulu and Netflix will have on consumer behavior, according to 2011 research from Convergence Consulting Group, is that "an estimated 2 million households are expected to have cut the cord and drop paid TV services in favor of broadband video services between 2008 and 2011 . . . Though the pace of cord-cutting is expected to slow this year, it is still happening at a faster rate than in 2008 and 2009." Big cable companies are losing paid TV customers. Comcast reported it lost a net of about 56,000 TV subscribers during the third quarter. The company reported it lost 275,000 basic cable subscriptions during the quarter, but it added 219,000 digital TV subscribers. Also during the third quarter, Time Warner Cable lost 155,000 video subscribers. Overall, 172 million Americans, 81.9 percent of the U.S. Internet audience, watched video online last year and although the .brand domain might not be an overnight success, the potential to build demand surrounding online content is there. TLDs make it easier to build those channels.

Social Media and Ad Revenue

An additional source of potential revenue is in building the social media connection with consumers interested in a variety of business, community-based, and lifestyle issues. If an organization views this as an opportunity to build the next social network of followers in their market category, then it could become the Facebook for people who like that market category and create its own social network. Much like Facebook, an opportunity then exists to gather data and offer promotions, products, and other offerings to its network and community, as well as to research and gather important data of value to advertisers. According to figures released from eMarketer in 2010, Facebook, with about 500 million users, reached about $1.9 billion in ad revenue alone. As for ads, Facebook is serving more than 50 billon display ads per month and is on track to serve 1 trillion display ads per year.

While other social networking sites can't compare with Facebook's numbers, many are still using online advertisements as the majority of their revenue. According to Tim Westergren, founder of the newest personalized online radio service, Pandora, the company made $77 million of revenue based on advertising in just the first nine months of 2010. Similarly, the professional networking site LinkedIn revealed in a filing for an IPO that it made ad revenues of $51.3 million in the first nine months of 2010. Analysts predict that with the IPO filing, future ad revenue could rise to $175 million next year.

Additionally, top-level domain owners in key market categories could build their own Google business model by developing search algorithms in more focused areas. For example, if I want to search only for high fashion or only five-star hotels or only for discounts, sports, or name your category. If I find a top-level domain that I trust and know they will only produce search results that are relevant to me, then that top-level domain owner has a business model like Google, Bing, and Yahoo!.

Subscription Model

An additional model for the new top-level domains is to build subscription-based, second-level domains off of the parent domain with specialized information and content for members only. Sites could charge a subscription, similar to the set up of the *Wall Street Journal*, which made about $60 million in online subscription revenue in 2009. In comparison, the *Wall Street Journal* generated $120 million of online ad revenue in 2009 versus the $150 million of online ad revenue the *New York Times* generated while not charging a subscription fee. The *Wall Street Journal* implemented its subscription fee brilliantly; the WSJ.com site offers some content for free and the whole site is still fully searchable by Google, but if you want to read the entire *Wall Street Journal* online, you need to pay for a subscription, and about 1 million of those users do.

Other popular sites, such as Pandora, Hulu, YouTube, and LinkedIn are all offering upgraded accounts based on the subscription model. In 2010, 25 percent of LinkedIn's revenue came from premium subscriptions, totaling around $61.9 million. Pandora's upgraded subscription service brought in an estimated $12.2 million for just the first nine months of 2010.

Second-Level Domains

In addition, the ownership of second-level domains will be a new frontier in the online world. Owners of the new gTLDs will essentially become registries for that domain, setting its own rules for registration, members, licensees, and even sales to third parties, creating another potential source of revenue. This could bring a possible return on investment as well as create domains of great value, such as resellers .shopping, brand.shopping, or partners.shopping. While this will be the first time companies will have the opportunity to resell online space, the potential revenue could be similar to that of current domain registries selling .com sites. On average, companies charge anywhere from $9.99 to $19.99 per year for domains and with an unlimited amount of second-level domains included with a .brand or .generic, gTLD owners could be looking at a considerable amount of annual revenue from reselling. For example, ICM, owner of .xxx, anticipates earning $200 million a year in sales. It's important to recognize, however, that top-level domain owners were required by ICANN to declare in their application whether they would be open—selling second-level domains or closed—they would control all second levels. Most brands will be closed systems. Closed top-level domains, however, could still be ripe for partnership opportunities, but companies won't be able to simply buy their domain like other open top levels. The majority of the open top-level domains will be run by industry players, such as existing registrars or registry operators, as well as new entrepreneurial companies looking to get into the industry.

Licensing Revenue and Retail Portal—Bolster Anti-Counterfeiting Efforts

Another source of revenue and opportunity is to build market leadership in the top-level domain and then become a retail portal for products and services with other licensed brands and/or direct to consumer products. With global commerce growing approximately 19 percent over the past year and 58 percent of consumers turning to the web to conduct research before making a purchase, the impact domain names can have on a brand's reputation and, ultimately corporate value, is a strong argument for managing domain names as carefully and diligently as other intellectual property. Popular retail portals like BlueFly.com made over $81 million in web-based sales in 2010 alone from more than 698,000 unique visitors. And online shopping in general is on the rise, according to a survey of 2,104 U.S. consumers conducted by Harris Interactive, showing that consumers are spending more time shopping online than ever before, and spending more money, too. The survey found that consumers shop online an average of 3.4 times per month (up from 3.1 times per month in 2009) and that 16 percent of consumers shop online four or five times per month, up from 14 percent last year.

In addition to the growing number of online consumers, by enhancing brand owners' control over their channels of distribution, the introduction of a .brand domain has the potential to significantly disrupt the ability of counterfeiters to distribute counterfeit goods and the ability of unlicensed content providers to distribute protected content. This will allow companies the ability to create retail portals or authorized resellers that ensure security and provide users with a 100 percent guarantee that only authorized resellers are offering your product. For example, the .rosettastone or .tiffanys domain would serve as a constant indication that the products being presented are from the genuine Rosetta Stone brand or Tiffanys brand; not only would this simplify the online retail approach but it also enables the company to maximize the multimedia marketing potential of the brand.

Disruptive Innovation

A final source of revenue and opportunity is to throw out every assumption you have about the Internet business and the brick and mortar business to allow you and your company to imagine a universe with more possibilities. For example, a consumer product company relies primarily on distribution through traditional retailers such as Kroger, Target, Walmart, and other grocery and retail outlets. Although consumers can order those products online from those retailers, in some cases, they can't typically buy direct from the brand owner. But many consumers have become frustrated with pacing the aisles of traditional retail stores looking for favorite brands only to find the retailer has stocked most of the prime shelf space with variations of its own house brand. Often in a hurry and giving up in frustration, consumers buy the house brand rather than the well-known consumer brand. Perhaps this may be a time for those consumer goods companies to rethink their distribution model and, in fact, their entire relationship with the consumer. While most consumer goods companies often cite that consumers don't even know which of their famous brands belong to the parent corporation, the truth is that consumers love their products and are loyal to them—so why not disrupt everything you think, build the relationship at the parent level, and own the entire experience and distribution chain like Amazon? Think about it from the consumer perspective. If I could go to myname.shopping.company and maintain a shopping page with favorites of absolutely everything I love by a big consumer goods company (which I sometimes can't find at the store) and have it shipped to my home right when I need it—I would be captive to their messages and new product offers and my loyalty would only grow. What if I could select all of the products I love and manage purchasing, delivery, and even point of purchase responses in one place? What if I could find the coupons I need all in one place? I would be captive and love them. And, I would likely be interested in other new products they offered because I knew it was high quality and what I wanted. Oh yes, and of course, if they want to advertise to me, they can do it all right there. No more searching—no more forgetting a coupon or having to search for coupons—no more wondering what else they have that I might like. If a consumer goods company follows a similar model, it transforms an aspect of its business model into an Amazon model, and significantly reduces its advertising spend for repeat customers and changes its approach. Now, they don't need to rely on search as much, don't need to run as many ads, and probably significantly reduce a large portion of its cost model. They know what works and what doesn't instantly. Sure, that's completely disruptive and outside the box, but that's exactly what this new expanding Internet can offer.

That's just one example. There are countless others. Were gTLDs needed to think disruptively like this? No, absolutely not; but they can be a catalyst and the ownership of the registry gives the companies that own them more flexibility and ease of managing their web presence with consumers.

There are so many possibilities to rethink everything. Top-level domains were fostered by ICANN to drive innovation. While many brand owners may be applying primarily for defensive purposes or to make sure they don't lose out, they will look to monetize their investment and find new ways of doing things. And, when money gets pumped into innovation or new ways of thinking, there is an incentive to invent and develop around those opportunities.

So we challenge companies, even those who didn't get in on the first round of gTLDs, to think differently and disruptively. Question: How can I tap into the way people are about to use the Internet in a new and different way to transform my business and be entirely relevant and beneficial to the society we serve? The possibilities extend to retail, business to business, technology, everything. You just need the leadership to set the tone to challenge the status quo and a few visionary risk takers to push thinking and champion the idea. There are few opportunities in business that present a unique look at the way in which you do business. This is the perfect opportunity to rethink everything your company knows about its interactive and .com universe.

"The gold rush to get all of the great .coms is occurring again only at a whole new level to get the great .whatever. Most of the applications will be .brand gTLDs. Strategic enterprises are buying them and will, quite predictably, extract value from them. There are many companies that have chosen to sit this one out. When they see the list of their competitors who have likely applied and obtained that important Internet .whatever, their CEOs will be asking who made that decision."

Josh Bourne, Managing Partner, FairWinds Partners

"One of the greatest innovations that will impact the Internet is the expansion to include Internationalized Domain Names (IDNs)—the ability to utilize non-Latin characters. New TLDs in Chinese, Arabic, Cyrillic, Hebrew, and other characters will have enormous consequences, and dramatically transform the Internet."

Ellen Shankman, Principal, Ellen B. Shankman & Associates, Rehovot, Israel

Chapter One Highlights

- The launch of the 500 to 1,500 new top-level domains in 2013 will change the business landscape with opportunities and challenges for business owners and brand owners.
- Top-level domains will include: generics, brands, communities, and geographic regions.

- These new top-level domains will begin to go live in 2013.
- ICANN will likely provide a second opportunity to acquire a top-level domain within a three- to five-year time window.
- There was a long-lasting debate about the pros and cons of whether or not ICANN should allow the Internet to expand at an accelerated pace, but the program is fully underway and this book seeks to provide guidance to brand owners to find new opportunities in a changing Internet landscape.
- There is a substantial cost associated with applying for a top-level domain and there are no guarantees of reward without a major paradigm shift in thinking and strategy by brand owners.
- While there are a number of major risks for those who applied for a gTLD, such as cost, failure of the public to respond to the new system, and customer confusion, there is likely an opportunity for disruptive innovation that will result in new business models for companies to explore new ways of consumer interaction, heightened security, and brand protection.
- The primary benefits in applying for a top-level domain include: positive impact on search, sale of second-level domains or control of second-level domains, changing navigation, social media, and industry leadership.
- For those that applied for a brand top-level domain, there are numerous potential business models to explore including: channels of distribution for content, social media, advertising revenue, licensing and retail portals, reduction in counterfeiting, subscription revenue, and other additional sources of revenue for brand owners.
- The greatest opportunity to come from top-level domains is the opportunity for all companies to rethink their Internet strategy and be challenged to perform disruptive innovation at all levels of the company.
- The launch of thousands of new top-level domains may improve navigation on the Internet with greater focus on consumer needs through a more intuitive navigation system. On the flip side, it could become a source of great confusion for consumers.
- The introduction of new gTLDs can be used to significantly disrupt counterfeiters and the Internet distribution of counterfeit goods.

Chapter Two

The Brand Bubble

I n the late 1990s and early 2000s, the business world went crazy over websites with absolutely no revenue model. Hundreds of millions of dollars were sunk into the .com bubble. Now, those models have evolved into data mining, shopping, and advertising and they are billion-dollar industries. This new regime is likely to be a brand bubble, with a few companies buying Internet-brand real estate in general themes and generics, and big brands putting their stake in the Internet ground to control their brand at a whole new level. What is the brand bubble in the .anything paradigm shift? And, what happens to all those companies who paid hundreds of thousands of dollars or even millions for their .com—what's it worth now? How does it change the brand game? This chapter will continue to probe the big picture issues in the brand landscape and set the stage to begin to create practical solutions and strategies to respond in the next generation of the Internet.

The .com Phenomenon

After years of venture capitalists pouring billions into .coms and often paying millions just to acquire the .com name, only to have the lion's share of those companies completely flame out, is it any wonder that ICANN determined a high barrier of entry was required for the next generation of the Internet? No one may be crying over the lost venture capital money, but everyone has felt the trickle-down impact on the stock market.

For example, according to John Cassidy in his book *Dot.Con*, the biggest venture capital deal of 1999 was $275 million for Webvan, an online grocery store. Two months after starting, it filed for an IPO, which was a new record in the craze of .coms filing for IPOs. It had lost $35 million on sales of just $395,000. Following this IPO, others quickly followed: egreetings.com, mothernature.com, smarterkids.com, ecollege.com, toys.com, pets.com, and kozmo.com. The commonality among all of these companies—they had no revenue—only venture capital backing. The venture capitalists were actually creating wealth out of nothing by speculating and launching IPO campaigns. Journalists soon began to realize that the jig may be up. Pegasus Research International predicted in early 2000, that within 12 months at least 50 Internet companies would have no money left. And on Friday, April 14, 2000, ironically 88 years to the day after the *Titanic* sank, CNBC and CNNfn reported that prices were rising faster than any point in the past five years. Waves of selling began to hit the technology-driven NASDAQ. Afternoon margin calls added pressure and at closing the Dow was down 617.78 points, its biggest ever point drop, and the NASDAQ was down 355.49 points. This was the biggest percentage fall since Black Monday, October 19, 1987. This became known as Black Friday. In just one week, nearly $2 trillion of stock market wealth was eviscerated. This became known as the Internet bubble bursting. Jim Cramer said, "The Gold Rush is over" and the days of entrepreneurs raising money on just an idea came to an end. For companies that created online divisions or tried to spin off Internet businesses, it was time to rethink everything. The .com craze had a string of irrational investing and came to an abrupt end.

A Few of the More Interesting .com Flameouts According to Philip Kaplan's F'd Companies

- Kozmo.com, a delivery service of anything, burned through $250 million before flaming out.
- Furniture.com, after spending $2.5 million for the name, $75 million in venture capital, and a failed IPO, the company died.
- Colo.com was created to build co-location or web hosting; $500 million of venture capital went in and by 2001, with $360 million in debt, they filed for bankruptcy.
- Bizbuyer.com: Investors paid $7.5 million for the domain name business.com and it was out of business months later; $68 million dollars gone and 170 people out of work.
- Eletter.com: $23 million in investors and 100 employees later, they went out of business.
- Buildnet.com: $142 million in funding and 1,000 people ended up in bankruptcy.
- Localbusiness.com: $16 million in funding and 75 employees, it filed for Chapter 11.
- Etown.com: $22 million invested by Best Buy to create a free, online version of *Consumer Reports,* hoping it would drive traffic to their store—it didn't.
- The list of .com startups with millions and millions of dollars and jobs lost goes on and on. The moral of the story—just because you have a good domain name, doesn't mean you'll make money.

We asked the experts how they compared this expansion of the Internet to the dot-com era of the 1990s . . .

"One may liken the .com bubble to urban sprawl. There wasn't much of a structure in place for the commercial growth of the Internet, and many folks registered domain names in an ad hoc manner or based upon what was still available. Now, with new gTLDs, there is a big difference. ICANN, in theory, has established an organized application process that has the potential to privatize certain sectors of the Internet (whether .brand or .industry-based). It's as if an entire zoning project has taken place over the Internet, and this should provide ease of use in a big "dot" extension world. Would you rather live in a city that is zoned or in one that is not zoned? For example, with zoning it's pretty clear where the business district is or where the fashion district is. Overall, new gTLDs should make it easier to find what you need online."

Nancy Lutz and Yasmin Tavakoli of Kelley Drye & Warren, LLP

"Much like in the .com space, the good domains will succeed and the bad ones will fail. It's all about having a good strategy, a good business model and delivering it to consumers."

Steven Miller and Katherine Ruwe, Procter & Gamble

"1994 to 1998 was the wild west of the Internet and birth of .com. It was uncharted territory. The fundamental difference now is that the infrastructure providers are also market participants. The registry and registrar operators are also applying and generating revenue. It creates the potential for a conflict of interest between market participants and those companies that are contracted by ICANN to run the technical aspect of the Internet."

J. Scott Evans, Senior Legal Director, Head of Global Brand, Domains & Copyright at Yahoo! Inc.

Losing money on bad business models wasn't the only problem that emerged during the dot-com era. During the .com years, anyone could apply for a domain name for about $10 a year. The barrier of entry was so low—why wouldn't a bad actor hoard as many domains as possible and then sell them off to the highest bidder? Even after the formation of the Uniform Dispute Resolution Policy by ICANN to protect global trademark rights holders, cybersquatting (obtaining a domain name with no intent to actually use) continues as a pervasive problem (see Chapter

Four). Likewise, typosquatting (misspelling the name of a famous brand to hopefully capture those who type in the desired brand incorrectly) also emerged. In the last 10 to 15 years, the proliferation of .coms and the lack of success for other top-level domains spurred ICANN to create the new generic top-level domain program—allowing the market-driven global economy to create and make successful an expanding Internet. While there have been many complaints about the cost of applying for a top-level domain, the cost, and requirement of a solid business plan and financial standing, means that not just anyone can apply. Only those with legitimate purposes can obtain these top-level domains. And, once they obtain them, they have to follow the rules of the game or they lose their status as the top-level operator. If ICANN had existed or been able to exert this type of control when .com exploded, it might have saved billions and ensured that companies were not exposed to cybersquatters clearly infringing upon their legitimate rights in brand names.

"In the beginning of the dot-com era, businesses were relatively immature as it related to understanding the Internet and how to leverage it. Now, there is a lot less of that factor. Businesses are more savvy and understand the Internet, but they don't necessarily understand the shift to new gTLDs. Sure, we'll see some similarities to the dot-com era where some TLDs will start up and fail, and others will start up and succeed."

Krista Papac, Chief Strategy Officer, ARI Registry Services

"The biggest similarity is like in the dot-com era, where many businesses did not see the need for such a domain or where the benefits were. Perhaps with new gTLDs, like in the .com situation, reasons will emerge. What could be different is an explosion of new business models. Brands or closed systems may migrate to a new way of building and protecting their brands. In open TLDs, certainly some registry operators and registrars will continue to make money through sunrises and sale of domain names."

Russ Pangborn, Associate General Counsel for Trademarks, Microsoft

(continued)

"If it makes it more user friendly, we will see .com-like excitement and innovation. With social media, which didn't exist back in the .com boom, gTLDs could go viral very quickly, particularly if it improves the user experience on the Internet."

Cynthia Gibson, Executive Vice President Legal Affairs, Scripps Networks Interactive Inc.

The History of UDRP

The UDRP (Uniform Domain Name Dispute Resolution Policy) was adopted in late 1999 by ICANN to offer an alternative to litigation in local courts to settle complaints by trademark owners about cybersquatting.

The UDRP created its own definition of "bad faith registration and use" of domain names, and identified some situations that would be considered defenses to a trademark complaint (rights and legitimate interests). UDRP proceedings are binding on all domain name holders in .com, .org, .net, .info, and .biz as well as [ccTLDs] and can result in the cancellation or transfer of the domain registration to the trademark owner. UDRP cases are decided by individual panelists who serve one of four resolution service providers.

Over 7,000 UDRP cases have been heard since the policy was adopted. However, many of the decisions are extraordinarily inconsistent. At present, there is no single entity to which these conflicts can be appealed. Consequently, it is often difficult for a mark owner, domain holder, or counsel for either of them to determine how the policy will be applied in any particular case. For more information about the UDRP itself, see "Using ICANN's UDRP" at http://lweb.law.harvard.edu/udrp/.

It's important to note that the origin of UDRP was very different to how it is today. ICANN asked the World Intellectual Property Organization (WIPO) to produce a report on how Internet domain disputes could be quickly, simply, and cheaply settled to save the Internet from becoming a huge, litigious no-man's land.

WIPO produced a report, with a range of recommendations, and submitted it to ICANN. After significant discussion, it was formed as the UDRP on October 24, 1999. But the policy was solely for trademark owners in dispute with non-trademark owners. UDRP specifically refused to rule on personal names, place names, names of pharmaceutical drugs, and government organizations. Those names should follow their usual course through the legal system in an appropriate jurisdiction. Registrars were required by ICANN to follow UDRP.

Unfortunately, in trying to make the policy as simple and cheap as possible, several important aspects were overlooked or mishandled. This, coupled with over-zealous arbitrators, has turned UDRP into a flawed system. But, ICANN has acted with new mechanisms to resolve disputes in its next generation (see Chapter Four).

The arguments for and against this new top-level domain program stack up—but what's important now is to think about these in context of what happened to the first generation of the Internet. So, let's take a look at the major arguments against the program and evaluate how this compares to the dot-com era. We know there has been strong advocacy by groups such as the Association of National Advertisers and others against the program, with solid rationales for their positions. But, since it is moving forward, we are taking the approach of analyzing it to help business leaders rather than continue to debate the program in this book.

Protecting Trademark Owners

The big cry from advertisers was largely focused on the lack of need to expand the Internet and the Pandora's box of trademark problems that would occur. Dan Jaffe testified before the U.S. Senate on behalf of the Association of National Advertisers and Coalition for Responsible

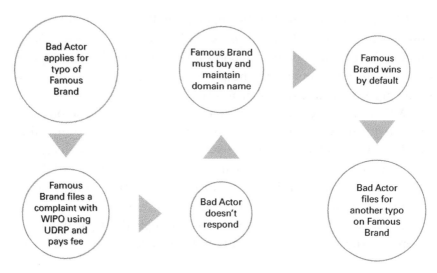

Figure 2.1   Process for Stopping a Cybersquatter

Internet Domain Oversight that the cost and economic harm to businesses would be devastating. We'll cover more specifics about how to protect and defend your brand in this new regime in Chapter Four, but it's worth noting—what would have happened when dot-coms exploded in the late 1990s if the same protection had been in place? Let's take a look at how a cybersquatter may have evaluated his options and whether it would have been worth his time.

When there was no dispute resolution in place, a squatter acquired the domain, then held out for the highest amount of money. Companies would usually settle the matter for less than the cost of litigation. Of course, this was a problem for brand owners—it was blackmail by cybersquattters. Once UDRP was in place, the cybersquatter or typosquatter would acquire a domain infringing on a famous brand. The famous brand would file a complaint using UDRP. The squatter likely would not respond. The famous brand would have to take over the squatting site. The result has been maintaining tens of thousands of domains that most companies don't want. (See Figure 2.1.) And, the squatter just goes out and applies for another domain. While UDRP partially solved the problem, it didn't get to the entire problem.

"Ever since .com was adopted by businesses the game has been unbalanced in favor of infringers. The cost to infringers of applying for an abusive domain name was minimal. They could provide false contact details, put up some pay-per-click adverts and watch the money come in, whilst waiting for an approach from the rights owner. When they got caught, they rarely faced any penalty more severe than handing the domain over. It's like a shoplifter stealing from a store, walking out the revolving door, handing the property over when they get caught, and then walking straight back in again to take something else. The only punishment has been to give back the domains they misappropriated. Now, we are starting to see a system that will have more disincentives. With the URS we should have a faster, less costly tool than the UDRP, which after 11 years really needs to be updated. What's more, brands as gTLD registry operators will have greater lobbying power with ICANN and can push for the existing rights protection mechanisms in the new gTLDs to improve. My vote is for loser pays and enforcement against the registrar if the registrant defaults."

Nick Wood, Managing Director, Com Laude

The result of the too-late and still-developing policies is that the bad actors had years of a free rein and the online counterfeiting industry emerged stronger than ever in cyberspace. Since there was no other penalty to the bad guys, the opportunity to be bad proliferated. Everything from prescription drugs to shoes, handbags, electronics, and language learning software—just about anything could be counterfeited by cybersquatters and sold online because the rules weren't in place to stop it from the beginning and the industry took off. Bad actors looked just like the real brand and misdirected consumers with counterfeit goods using typosquatting sites. Meanwhile, trademark rights holders have been playing catch up around the globe to stop the exploding marketplace of counterfeit goods. And with recession attacking the global economy, more people simply want the cheapest items whether it's the real thing or not.

Simply put, there was no protection for trademark rights holders when the first generation of the Internet took off. In response, a number of mechanisms have been put in place to address this concern and to protect rights holders, consumers, and users of the Internet around the globe. So, it's not really a surprise that brand owners would be concerned about the ability to protect their brand if the Internet evolves to its next level and there are hundreds of additional top-level domains to monitor and protect for the brand. Again, there are more details on all of the safeguards in place and how to use them in Chapter Four, but what's important to recognize is that if these safeguards had been in place in the .com bubble, brand owners might think a little bit differently. And, more importantly, they might be looking at this as an innovative opportunity for market leadership and a better Internet rather than responding in fear, however well grounded that fear may be. ICANN has tried to change the incentives and disincentives for squatters with the Uniform Rapid Suspension system, and while there is still a lot of room for improvement, brand owners have a better process today than they did when .coms began.

> "In the way UDRP worked, the bad actors who were cybersquatting had no incentive to stop cybersquatting. They typically just wouldn't respond to an action and would then go out and do it again. The brand owner would then acquire the cybersquatter's domain and house it with typically thousands of other domains held only as a result of cybersquatters. I am hopeful that with more use of the Anticybersquatting Consumer Protection Act (ACPA) by trademark owners and the future adoption of 'loser pays' policies, we will see a decline in squatting activity."
>
> Josh Bourne, President, The Coalition Against Domain Name Abuse

There's No Need for It

So, let's look at the other big point of contention by those who oppose the expansion of the Internet. We already live in a .com world, they say.

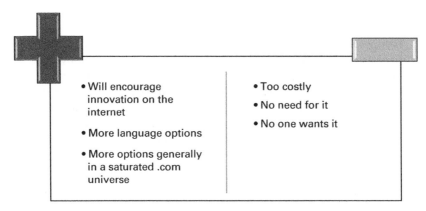

Figure 2.2   Pros and Cons of Top-Level Domains

We don't need any more domain names. The Internet is just fine the way it is. Before addressing the actual claims made about the Internet, think of how shortsighted this sounds in an age of innovation. At a time when global leaders are calling for business and trade organizations to think differently—think outside the box and find new ways to do things better and create more opportunities for all, some leaders are saying, "We don't want to change—why do we need to change?" Not surprisingly, it's the established companies and their representatives advocating for nothing to change. To summarize the testimony given before the senate commerce subcommittee on December 8, 2011, the basic arguments for and against are provided in Figure 2.2.

"Before the ICANN gTLD policy was approved at its board meeting last June, I spent most of my time criticizing it as chaos. After all, there are only so many TLDs that one person can remember. I imagined that, in a world where new addresses are communicated through traditional marketing media, people would have a hard time remembering where they were told to go. I thought that the search engines and registrars would benefit most from this program. If we're all

(continued)

> being told to remember max.pepsi and gifts.jcp more often, because people forget where they are supposed to go, they will go to Google, Bing, or Yahoo!. That said, as I've gone through the process of consulting businesses in answering whether or not to apply—I'd say that more companies are finding new ways of looking at this to ensure the return on investment is there. It does have the potential to lead to new opportunities and innovation."
>
> Josh Bourne, President, The Coalition
> Against Domain Name Abuse

Is "no one wants it or needs it" a good argument? Let's look at a few other product categories and industries that went under after resisting or failing to innovate around change that was coming:

- Phone books and the advertising that supported it.
- Newspapers and the classified ads that supported it.
- Compact discs.
- PDAs.
- America Online—remember when you paid to have your email account and you dialed up to get it?
- Kodak.
- Blockbuster.
- Maps.
- Landline phones.
- Pay phones—ever see one anymore?
- VCRs.
- Fax machines.
- Encyclopedias.
- Floppy disks.

The list can go on and on.

Why would we need to hitch a horse to a wagon when we can ride the horse? Why would we need trains that go so fast—where do we need to get in such a hurry? Why would we need cars? Why would anyone need to have a phone with them all the time and make calls from anywhere? Why have a TV when you get what you need from radio and newspapers? Who would put all their music on a device and walk around with it? Why in the world would you need to connect computers all over the globe? Why would you send an electronic mail or text when you can send a letter? What if Steve Jobs and Steve Wozniak thought Bill Gates had it right and the world didn't need another way of computing? What if they hadn't pushed the personal home computer? Why would we need to think about expanding from .com thinking?

There are plenty of arguments about the problems associated with *how* ICANN is going about this that are all legitimate and should be debated. But to simply cite we don't need it or want to change is does not advance our society or foster what's most critical right now— innovation and opportunity.

In case it's not obvious or we haven't sold you on the importance of constant evolution, change, and innovation to better our world, here are a few other reasons why expanding the Internet may be important.

The .com universe is saturated. Don't believe us? Try to think of a new name for a company or product—the first step is to check what's available in terms of a .com or any URL. Is that fair to entrepreneurs? The big brands and the Association of National Advertisers don't seem to be speaking for every start-up company to come. Entrepreneurs, in particular, would greatly benefit by having more options available and the ability of innovative companies to create new communities in which we can live and manage our Internet lives. And, the current .com structure doesn't provide for use of any language other than Latin-based languages—hardly inclusive of the entire planet of people using the Internet. Further, to develop any expanded use of a well-known .com— such as Facebook or Google, or to run a contest or promotion, the URL becomes complicated: www.facebook.com/nametheprogramhere/more/more or www.chevy.com/contest/enter. To evolve to the next generation of how people want to use the Internet, some changes need to occur and this is the first step towards allowing that innovation to occur in a global marketplace. We didn't need Facebook or .coms before they arrived. That's what innovation is—figuring out something people can't live without before they know that they can't live without it.

It's time to innovate again. Just as entrepreneurs innovated in the dot-com era and new business models and disruptive technologies emerged, now is a time to think innovatively.

The Cost Is Just Too High

The argument that seems to be touted the most is the cost. Some seem to think this is just about ICANN making money. While ICANN will make money from this program, the question of what they do with it is a political issue worth debating since the money should be used to support the Internet community of users around the globe. The real issue on this argument as a marketplace factor, however, is to consider the brand owner's position. First, run a comparison to the amount of money most major brands spend in just one quarter to advertise their brand or what companies spend for a 30-second spot on the Super Bowl. Take a look at the companies who have vocally been against the TLD and how much they spend on their ad budget and traditional media buys. A typical Super Bowl ad runs about $3.5 million for a 30-second spot. A survey of top advertising publications indicate the top advertisers in the world spend between $298 million and $306 million per year in media buys. See Figure 2.3.

So, basically, the companies crying, "It costs too much," are saying the cost of one Super Bowl ad is more advantageous to the brand than taking the time to think innovatively about how the Internet will change and be a market leader in this space. Unlike the .com opportunity that took most businesses by surprise, the next generation of the Internet has been formally announced with a clear time period and an infrastructure to protect brand rights holders. Everyone is playing by the same rules and has plenty of notice to budget and plan for the opportunity to participate. For most big brand owners, the cost is much smaller than what they spend in media that will not exist in a few years. That aside, ICANN has a fairly good reason for creating a high barrier of entry. Think about the benefits to all Internet users. Because ICANN has created a high barrier of entry, the following three big requirements must be met:

1. Ensure financial ability to run the top-level domain. Rather than selling off top-level domains on the cheap, ICANN is requiring that

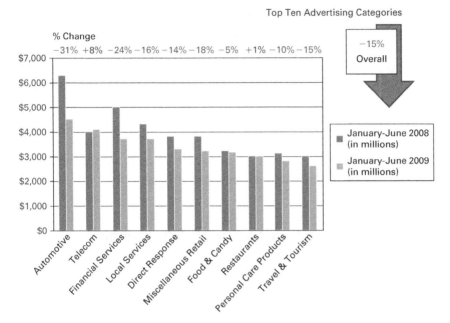

Figure 2.3 Approximate Advertising Spend in Top Ten Advertising Categories

applicants prove that they have the financial capability to run it as a business. So ideally, it's not a business model relying solely on venture capital or IPOs based on concept companies.

2. Ensure there is a business plan. Likewise, ICANN wants to ensure applicants actually have a plan for how they will use the TLD—what's the plan they ask? And, they ask it in a complex enough way that it takes some real thought and analysis to answer the questions.

3. Protection of trademark rights holders. And, finally, ICANN is requiring top-level domain holders to actually protect trademark rights holders and build an infrastructure to create a process and mechanism to resolve disputes.

This differs dramatically from what occurred in the .com bubble. There were no rules then. Any domain could be purchased for a nominal amount of money and cybersquatting, typosquatting, and cyber-counterfeiting emerged. The Internet bubble changed the world forever—social media did, too. Isn't it likely that when millions are again pumped into the Internet that it will also change forever the way people use the Internet?

This is like knowing that the .coms are coming and having a roadmap and a time frame to be prepared. Yet, so many companies have decided to stand strong that this is too expensive, not wanted or needed, and will only confuse consumers. So, while the cost argument sounds like a good one, it's really full of holes for large companies. Large companies can afford it, they often just don't want to invest in new thinking or disruptive innovation so they'd rather wait and see what happens. For small companies however, that's not exactly true.

It's Not Fair to Small Businesses

The final big critique of this next generation of the Internet versus the .com explosion is that it isn't fair to small businesses. While the big players spend more in one month of advertising than the cost of the TLD, the truth is most small businesses can't afford the price tag and wouldn't meet the financial standards required by ICANN. However, that doesn't mean they're boxed out of participating—it just means they won't own the top-level domain. It certainly doesn't seem fair. But again, let's look at what happened in the past. In the .com bubble, initially, it was relatively easy to obtain a .com. The hard part was figuring out how to build a profitable business model around it. Let's take a quick history lesson of what happened to these small or start-up businesses and compare them to the framework and barriers that exist today.

In the dot-com era, early adopters would start up a .com concept business. If they had a good enough idea and a decent team of people, they could usually get some seed money. If they got it to the next level and built any momentum at all, venture capitalists would pump in hundreds of millions and hope that they could get to the IPO. You see, in that time frame, eyeballs and users were the name of the game. And, it captured Wall Street's attention along with the millions of new investors who could now manage their stock portfolios online. Interestingly enough, as though a perfect storm of activity, the news media that covered the markets all day, every day also became part of the landscape. With a flurry of new businesses in IPO mode, news media covering every aspect of it all day, and a surge of millions of new investors putting money into the market, the dot-com era created an economic surge and a period of extended growth.

In John Cassidy's book *Dot.Con,* he details the sequence of events that led to the irrational exuberance of the IPO phenomenon, making start-up founders and their backers worth hundreds of millions overnight, most of the time while still operating at a loss. The rampant irrational exuberance ultimately led to the crash of 2000 (though not quite the crash of 2008). While the market rebounded, this recklessness started a trend that would continue and expand into other facets of business—such as real estate and finance. It started the belief that anyone could be a multi-multi-millionaire overnight if they just had a good enough Internet business idea. Of course, eventually, most of those companies went out of business or were acquired by a bigger company that could sustain the losses until the model was figured out. The bigger company generally just wanted those eyeballs.

Take a look at a few of the prominent acquisitions in Figure 2.4.

But the American dream was alive and well for that time period and continues today with proliferations of incubators and venture capitalists—though they now look for more traditional financial models to

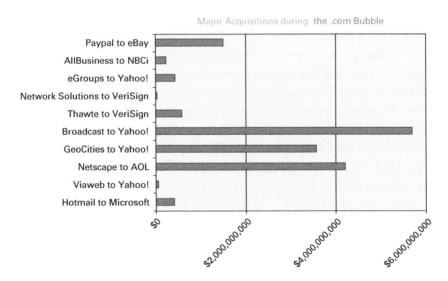

Figure 2.4 Major Acquisitions During the .com Bubble

invest in. So, the question emerges: Was the .com bubble fair to small businesses? To the select few who cashed out after the IPO—yes, absolutely! To those that emerged as technology leaders such as EBay, YouTube, Amazon—yes! To the countless others who lost everything trying to start up a business that failed—maybe not. So, is the price tag of this next generation of the Internet closing out the American Dream? Not really. You see, there are a number of ways an innovative thinker can work within the space that will be created. And, the really innovative thinkers could raise the money with a good enough plan. So, the high barrier of entry is serving one important force in the next generation of the Internet. It is minimizing the chance for irrational exuberance. To get in this game, you have to prove you have a plan and the financial ability to follow through—something even the VCs didn't require in the .com bubble.

In Chapters Six and Seven, we'll detail ideas and strategies to benefit from the next generation of the Internet even if you didn't get in on the first wave to gTLDs.

What's the Value of Your .com Now?

A final important question following the .com bubble—what's your .com domain and brand worth now? The real answer to this question will depend upon how well you execute your business strategy. Your business strategy must evolve to thinking about how this next generation of the Internet will impact your consumers, users, customers, suppliers and stakeholders. This is strategic planning 101. A major shift is about to occur. To think about it requires some heavy lifting and leadership to recognize the importance of it. Your .com could be just as valuable, if not more valuable, if you plan correctly for it. But if you stick your head in the sand and hope nothing will change—your .com won't be worth much anymore. See Figure 2.5.

The value of a domain was determined by 12 main variables:

1. Length—How long is the name?
2. Word count—How many words?
3. Clarity—How well does it describe its content?
4. Memorability—How easy is it to remember?

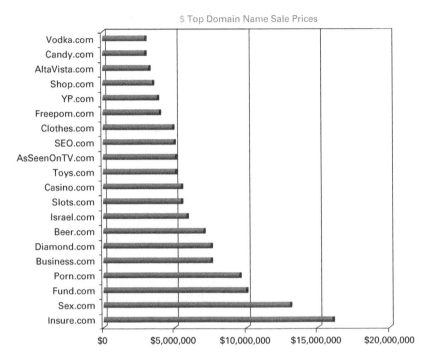

Figure 2.5 Top Domain Name Sale Prices

5. Market size—Large, medium, or small market?
6. Market potential—Is the market lucrative?
7. Market applicability—Does the name apply to the whole market or small portion of it?
8. Hyphens/dashes or numerals? For example, myDomain5.com or music-CD.com (loses value).
9. Any substitute names/synonym alternatives? For example, university.com versus college.com (loses value)
10. Any abbreviations? For example, ppv.com versus payperview.com (loses value).
11. Any variations—singular and plural nouns or verbs? For example, loan.com (singular noun, verb), loans.com (plural).
12. Domain extension/TLD? Is it a .com? (more value than others).

Of all the variables, the three most important factors in assessing domain value are the domain's TLD extension, its market size/potential, and how well it describes its content. But will that change now?

It's All About Execution

.coms got the world excited about the possibility of changing technology. They changed the way we worked and lived in profound ways that no one could have predicted.

Because of the excitement and innovation occurring around .com-concept companies, the stock market exploded into a bubble. Yes, companies were overvalued and the market returned to evaluating companies based upon traditional profit and loss models. But, the allure of innovation and the next big thing remains.

Could .anything also do the same? Could it get us out of this recession? Could it also create new possibilities, innovative thinking, and a little irrational exuberance again? As early adopters figure it out, those big companies that failed to get in the game will surely look to acquisition strategy to fill the gaps. Anytime there is excitement, new ideas, and money being pumped into something, the market tends to rise.

> "What's interesting is that brand owners didn't think we needed .com either. They didn't think people would use a credit card online or use the Internet for gathering information or shopping. Brands are doing the same thing now. History is repeating itself. They will eventually get there with the new top-level domains, just like they did with .com, but for now most of the brands don't think there will be a migration to new gTLDs."
>
> Krista Papac, Chief Strategy Officer, ARI Registry Services

Chapter Two Highlights

- Early .com failures demonstrate lessons learned and our thought leaders share their insights on the similarities and differences between the .com bubble and the potential brand bubble of the new top-level domain program.

- The high barriers of entry required by ICANN to acquire a new top-level domain means that not just anyone can start up a top-level domain company, potentially shifting the dot-com era of irrational exuberance and excitement of idea companies to requiring business models that spur innovation and the investment required for real innovation to occur.
- The players are different, the investors are more knowledgeable about the infrastructure, and there is more competition among registries and registrants that will provide a higher level of services and protect Internet users.
- As in the dot-com era, most businesses don't see the need for the new regime, but there will be an explosion of new business models with new ways of building and protecting brands.
- In a brief look at the history of protecting brands on the Internet through the establishment of the Uniform Domain Names Dispute Resolutions Policy, our thought leaders showcase how we have gone from absolutely no protection to creating some mechanisms to stop cybersquatting and counterfeiting. However, we still have a long way to go to change the disincentives for bad actors to protect not just brand owners but consumers around the world.
- The arguments for this program think that the new regime will encourage innovation, provide more language options, and expand a saturated .com regime; the staunch advocates against the program think that there is no need for the new regime, it is too costly, unfair to small businesses, and there is little interest in a new regime for expansion of the Internet.
- Like in the dot-com era, success in the next generation of the Internet will be all about execution of a new Internet strategy.
- A few predictions begin to emerge:
  - Brands that fail to really consider the changing business model as a result of the expansion of the Internet will fail.
  - Money pumped into invention and innovation will follow the brands that invested in top-level domains with a clear strategy for return on investment.
  - New entrepreneurial models will emerge in a .anything generic universe.

- Brands that understand how to connect with their consumer and give them what they want when they want it will be the most successful.
- .com will be diluted in a .brand universe.
- Thinking about brands has to evolve to incorporate a comprehensive Internet, application, digital, interactive, and intellectual property strategy—none of these can operate independently in a .brand world.
- Companies will need to get focused on a few core brands or find themselves in the brand bubble that burst.
- Merger and acquisition activity will increase for those companies that failed to apply for a top-level domain and must look for potential partners.
- While there is a bigger universe to protect, trademark owners have more tools available today than they did in the .com explosion. They need to think more strategically about their approach using a return-on-investment methodology rather than just a defensive cost structure in the annual budget.
- Small businesses may be boxed out by the price of .anything, but still have opportunities to innovate within the generics, communities, and geographic top-level domains.
- New versions of entrepreneurs will emerge when ICANN opens this up for the second time.

Chapter Three

Building Your Brand and Social Media

D igital and social media have become a top line revenue generator for media companies. Facebook is one of the largest advertising companies in the world, outpacing traditional media. Google is doing the same. Consumer product companies are focused more than ever on digital advertising and creating a sense of community out in cyberspace to build brand loyalty and create market dominance. How are these leaders planning to adapt to a changing Internet and build communities with their consumers when instead of the .com directing traffic its .anything? Who has declared that they will apply and what might they do with it?

The Emergence of Social Media and Online Communities

In 2004, a paradigm shift in how the Internet would be used began at Harvard. Sticking to a simple idea that Facebook needed to be cool and a place people wanted to connect with their friends, the founders built the site and the people came. No, they didn't have a revenue model and they didn't want advertisers. They would figure it out. Not surprisingly, Silicon Valley got it and pumped the necessary funds in to turn it into a multibillion-dollar company. In 2000, after the .com bubble burst, who would have thought that hundreds of millions of people around the globe would be connected through just one website and put up pictures and share every thought of their day? Likewise, Twitter emerged with a similar concept—just in short sound bytes emulating the way we all live our lives now. YouTube captured the desire for all of us to be creators, not just purveyors, of content. The amateur professional began to emerge. Pandora jumped in and recognized that we can all create customized radio stations just by telling its algorithm what kind of music we like. And, Amazon, acquiring Zappos and other major shopping portals, has become the place for many people to shop—not just for books, but just about everything. Consumers have their profile saved in one place and can even pay annually for two-day shipping on just about everything. How much easier could it be? Universities are creating online distance learning programs where you can connect with people from around the world to share ideas, knowledge, and information in a way never available before. Millions of people talk with loved ones more frequently on Skype from around the globe than they ever would have by phone. Groupon changed the way we thought about the coupon. Pinterest evolved the simple collage concept and evolved it into a burgeoning new hobby and business for the companies and brands that long for their consumers to follow them and pin them into every aspect of their lives. And, of course, who could forget Second Life. If you're unhappy with the lot you've been handed in real life—simply go into Second Life and create whatever you want. Some are even reportedly becoming millionaires in the world of Second Life, where people create new identities, new homes, build new products and services, and sell them in Second Life currency, backed of course by real life currency—credit cards.

Experience with Social Media Marketing

In a study by Social Media Examiner, when they asked participants to rate their experience using social media marketing, about half have less than one year of social media marketing experience. More B2B companies have been using social media longer (52.6 percent reported one year or more) than their B2B counterparts (46.2 percent indicated one year or longer). In 2010, only 31 percent of marketers were using social media for one or more years. Now that number has grown to 50 percent.

A few of their findings:

- 72 percent of marketers who have been using social media for more than three years report it had helped them close business.
- At least 73 percent of marketers plan on increasing their use of YouTube/video, blogs, Facebook, and Twitter.
- A significant 77 percent of marketers plan on increasing their YouTube and/or video marketing. Businesses with 1,000 or more employees indicated this is a key growth area, with 82 percent responding affirmatively.
- At least 64 percent of marketers plan on increasing their use of search engine optimization and email marketing.
- As of October 2010, 49 percent of businesses are investing in social media.

How Tech and Social Media Companies Cashed Out in 2011

An excerpt from Mashable Business, December 26, 2011. http://mashable.com/2011/12/26/social-media-ipos-acquisitions-2011/

Social media's first test of investor enthusiasm came in May, when LinkedIn went public. Judging by the initial success, LinkedIn passed the test with flying colors. Shares doubled on May 19, the day the company went public, and though they have fallen off a bit since, were still way above opening price at press time.

LinkedIn's roughly $6.4 billion valuation is mostly based on hope of future growth. The company turned a small profit ($4.5 million) in its second quarter, but then lost $1.6 million in its third quarter. However, the network grew its revenues by 126 percent that quarter and it keeps bulging with new subscribers (the current figure is 130 million). With three revenue streams—advertising, recruiting, and premium subscriptions—Linked is one of the safest social media investments, but at this stage, is bent on growth over stable profits.

LinkedIn's rather pacific IPO was followed by another low-key IPO for Pandora Media in June, but in July the debt ceiling standoff and the European monetary crisis spooked the market. That caused another of the year's most anticipated IPOs, Groupon's, to be delayed until November.

Though Groupon had a strong showing the day it went public, within a few weeks, the stock had fallen so far that it just about wiped out any gains achieved that first day.

And Zynga, which had also pushed back its IPO after the summer's market crash, eventually moved ahead with its plans to go public late in the year. However, it also suffered a dip in stock price.

Given the limited amount of companies going public and their ho-hum stock performances, the comparison between social media IPOs and the dot-com bubble is pretty weak. The latter era actually lasted from 1995, when Netscape went public, until the 2000 Super Bowl, which was notoriously flooded with dot-com ads for companies that would cease to exist within a year or two.

In comparison, the trickle of social media IPOs will likely end whenever Facebook goes public (reports say that will happen next April). You call this a bubble? Somewhere, the Pets.com sock puppet is laughing.

Since the writing of the Mashable article, we have learned that Facebook is in for its share of problems as a public company and the transparency required in understanding its revenue and profitability model. According to Bloomberg News on July 28, 2012, Facebook had lost about $34 billion in market value since its May initial public offering. We also now know that Facebook did not apply for a brand top-level domain, nor did it apply for any of the many generics. Will this help or hurt the social media giant?

What's Next?

Social media built the infrastructure for us to live our lives online and through apps on our mobile devices. It allows us to find others like us and build communities to form relationships, share knowledge and ideas, and live and work all online. Devices such as mobile phones and tablets mean we can take that online experience with us anywhere. We can get directions, make reservations, move money around—we can do everything online. In fact, we are so accustomed to everything being customized to what we want, that we get annoyed when we have to watch regular television on cable and listen to the ads that have little to do with our life. The answer—simply control your digital recordings from home. Or, better yet, just get all your content from Hulu or other online sources. It's not hard to extrapolate where this is all headed. Traditional television—meaning without cable—is extinct. Cable is next unless they emerge into this next generation of the Internet. In the future, we'll likely have one or two places that we aggregate everything we do. The movies, music, and shows we want to watch. The places we want to shop. Where and how we transact the business of our life, how we learn and where we learn, and, most importantly, whom we trust.

This is where the next generation of the Internet comes in. Those who think strategically about it realize that if they can create a safe place for their audience to come to buy their product, share information, and live their lives—they will be a market leader. For the average person, the

Internet is saturated. They may have picked a handful of sites and apps they trust, but the next generation is to really take it to the next level. In all likelihood, cable will soon be obsolete and everyone will get their content, information, and live most of their life on the Internet using tablets or flat screens hanging on a wall and connected to the Internet. Telecommunications companies know this and are positioning themselves for this transition using fiber optics and more advanced, faster technologies. Brick and mortar stores will have to integrate the overhead and cost structure into loyalty online and offer something unique, such as an in-store entertainment-oriented experience coupled with the online experience to keep people coming in to the brick and mortar store. Service businesses will have to integrate delivery into something more seamless and community-oriented, and offer thinking that's different from everyone else.

Our thought leaders weighed in on their thoughts about social media and the new top-level domains.

> "For all companies, the paradigm shift will come in determining where to put your brands and where to reach your consumers. This is where the marketers and agencies will really need to develop a strategy. With an expanded base of possibilities, finding the right solution and place to market your brand will require more planning and forethought than ever before. Each brand will need to be laser focused to succeed."
>
> Steven Miller and Katherine Ruwe, Procter & Gamble

> "Social media won't necessarily change. It's still all about creating something of value. What could have an impact is that, depending upon how you run it, a top-level domain social media system offers some great sense of security."
>
> J. Scott Evans, Senior Legal Director, Head of Global Brand, Domains & Copyright at Yahoo! Inc.

> "Social media may change and adapt because there will be more control at the top level of security and DNS services if there is jenwolfe.yourtld. It's a level of control, a branding opportunity and

why new registries do this? For .com to implement new security extensions or protocols, or create other technological advances, would require more work than to expand these capabilities as a top-level domain. To implement anything new in such a large name space is a huge ordeal. In addition, there are so many things that need to be considered, where as if you have your own name space, you can gather information as the owner of the top-level domain, which you can't do at the second level, such as gathering additional levels of end-user statistics and behavior."

> Jeffrey J. Neuman, Vice President, Business Affairs,
> Enterprise Services, Neustar, Inc.

"People will be confused at first. Just as they were when the Internet first started, but brands that do this right can actually move away from Facebook and other social media and build their own communities. It's tremendously powerful for a brand to be able to say to consumers, if it doesn't end in .ibm or .apple, it isn't us."

> Krista Papac, Chief Strategy Officer, ARI Registry Services

"Something is going to come along in social media. A mere decade ago we didn't have Facebook or Twitter. Changes occur in such a short period of time and we have no idea what will be next. Facebook and Twitter are very well entrenched, but that doesn't mean there isn't room for more."

> Russ Pangborn, Associate General Counsel for Trademarks,
> Microsoft

"It's possible that if someone comes on the social media scene and does it well in the gTLD space and differently, then it could open up new opportunities."

> Cynthia Gibson, Executive Vice President Legal Affairs, Scripps
> Networks Interactive Inc.

"Businesses have continually underestimated the socialization of the Internet. Internet users adapt very quickly. Users pick up on something innovative and then it is exploited. Many Internet users spend much of their lives within social media. Within Facebook, we're not comlaude.com we're just Com Laude; within Twitter we are not comlaude.com but just #comlaude, so domain names have largely lost their relevance. This will be the

(*continued*)

key difference of the new gTLDs from .com—the speed with which people adapt."

Nick Wood, Managing Director, Com Laude

"Ultimately it's all about 'trust.' If consumers/users learn to trust a .brand TLD, they will go there. If they trust that search engines provide better results, they will rely on those. The most important factor for whether or not these take off is one of 'trust.'"

Ellen Shankman, Principal, Ellen B. Shankman & Associates, Rehovot, Israel

It Could Change Everything

Let's speculate for a moment on what some of the big social media players and technology companies could do and how it could change everything. Given the hundreds of millions of users of Google, Bing, Yahoo!, and Facebook around the globe, they will likely push the education front and convert people to the next generation of the Internet. So, let's start with them. An important caveat: this is pure speculation by the authors to illustrate what we could expect. Even in instances where we have interviewed someone from one of these companies, no information or strategy was provided and nothing speculated in this section was derived from that interview.

Facebook

Facebook did not apply for its own brand TLD nor any generic or category gTLDs. We speculate, however, that they would have had many options, but the simplest would have been to create the yourname.facebook. This would allow each person to create their own unique page before the dot rather than after, presumably allowing the company even greater control over each and every user's page as a registry operator and allowing for greater flexibility in how users build within their network. Facebook could also partner with retailers to build contests and promotions and provide advertisers more flexibility within their own account such as: Gap.facebook. This could create enhanced capabilities for advertisers and increased revenue for the social media giant. Most consumer products are already promoting their Facebook page in their media buys so if Facebook can simply take it to the next level and become the platform for advertising to the world's population, they may become the biggest media monopoly since the Hearst empire. Consider the same concept for musicians, movies, really anything that needs to go viral could be launched within Facebook. Is the gTLD needed to do this? No. Facebook already does this and more today. Owning the top-level domain just takes it to the next level and serves as a catalyst for the talented engineers at Facebook to think in a new way. Facebook could evolve into content creation or limitless new opportunities.

Google (YouTube)

Likewise, Google could change its search engine so you simply type in toplondonrestaurants.google and see what comes up. They, too, can create layers upon layers of common searches, trends, and industry segments for searching within Google. For example, they may have a page dedicated to golf.google. On that landing page, I can find anything I want about golf or I can search only within the golf category and find places to spend money related to golf. Google could build communities of people who love golf and provide all of this information and promotional opportunities to anyone selling golf related products and services. It could be further segmented as well. For example: Chicago.golf.google—now I can find courses and products and services just in Chicago. The ability to further segment and make searching within narrow categories becomes more intuitive than it is today. And, at the same time, Google becomes the centralized place to gather important market data.

Another option for Google is to become a centralized portal for content. By owning YouTube and acquiring other sources of content, it could go to the next level by simply becoming an aggregator of content and attempt to replace cable as a centralized portal for categorized content. For example, they could create a kids.google channel that is dedicated to programming for kids. They could offer beneficial services to parents by narrowing in on age-appropriate, subscription-based content on one channel of .google. Or they could have independentfilms.google and be the place to go to watch indie films. The list goes on and on. They have the loyalty and the infrastructure and if they dominate search—why wouldn't they?

Microsoft

Microsoft too, has many options like Google. They can use their Bing platform to compete in the same way with new business models. Although that may be off strategy for the software giant, it is certainly a wide open field for them if they use .bing in the same way or tie their entertainment division of .xbox into a channel for games. But, they also have a more traditional strategy. They have already invested heavily in creating a cloud-computing environment to sell their software as a service much more economically than ever before with bundled one-computer licenses. They have the opportunity to help businesses create their entire Internet/Intranet infrastructure using the .microsoft base. What if I could cost effectively run my entire IT infrastructure for my business using yourcompany.microsoft? As an Internet portal, if it saves me money and is easier, why wouldn't I?

Canon

Canon was an early declared applicant. Their likely use will include allowing consumers and photographers to build their own home page. For example: yourname.canon. On my personal home page, I can upload photos from my phone or digital camera and manage all of my photos. I can build photo books for myself or others as gifts, buy unique items using my photos, and generally manage the photos that make up my life. If they are the early adopter and I find this to be the safe and secure place to store my photos (unlike Facebook where I can get tagged or it is automatically connected to everyone in my friend network), then this becomes a more safe, secure, go-to location for my photos. And, Canon can likely sell me other related products, services, and build communities of amateur photographers. They could even build packages of vacations and trips that center on photography. The list of opportunities to innovatively build services that connect with people who love photography is limitless.

Deloitte

This accounting and consulting worldwide giant was smart to quickly jump on the TLD bandwagon. With their trademark locked up, they don't have to worry about an auction and can use their new .deloitte to build not only an intranet for managing employees, but an extranet for clients. If Fortune 500 companies could have companyname.deloitte as their unique portal to manage all projects Deloitte is doing for them, they may have an edge over others still trying to hammer out bugs in current extranet infrastructure. Likewise, each employee or independent contractor of Deloitte could have their own page where schedules, travel, and projects could be managed. If I work for Deloitte and I can have a yourname.deloitte page, how much easier is it? I can quickly get online to determine my schedule, travel arrangements, instructions, as well as maintain constant updates of my progress on my work so my boss knows what's going on. It takes knowledge management and process infrastructure to a whole new level in an environment where Deloitte owns the registry with complete control over it.

Time Warner

As a global leader in media and entertainment with businesses in television networks, film, and publishing, Time Warner stands a lot to gain by taking its brand into the next generation of the Internet. They could easily dominate the migration to the Internet as a source for content. It's not hard to see how this could play out: hbo.timewarner, or movies.hbo, or mypage.hbo with all the programs I like on a paid subscription basis. But then the question becomes, if I can go direct to movies.hbo—why do I need the middleman—what happens to the cable operators? There are certainly pricing and business strategies to be worked out to answer that question—but that's exactly the kind of new innovative and strategic thinking that will be required.

Amazon

We now know that Amazon made a bold move applying for many generics with an intention to run those as closed systems, for their benefit or the benefit of their affiliates. For the fulfillment and distribution powerhouse, this provides incredible opportunities to dominate the shopping experience and partner with brands and retails of all types of products that need to be delivered direct to the consumer. If they migrate into content production, they could ultimately be in the advertising agency business by creating content tailored to sell products, much like the soap operas of years ago, but have a one click option to buy whatever you like. If you see someone wearing something you like, you can buy it. See a great piece of furniture or a design that you like, you can buy the entire package. It's not hard to see where they may go with this and the ability with one account and free shipping to capture the hearts of consumers.

Generics, Such as Movies, Music, Independent Films, and Wines

In addition to the brand top-level domains, imagine what could happen with the generics. For example, if I can have myname.movies—I customize exactly what I want related to movies. Or, what if I could manage all of my shopping or music at myname.music or myname.shopping? Likewise, industry segments could emerge within these generics. Or, the generics may allow brand owners to buy up space within their new top-level domain. For example, .movies could sell exclusive second-level domains to the entertainment industry. We already know that .xxx has made tens of millions selling various second-level domains in the adult entertainment industry. But, what about the other generics? It's likely to see key partnerships emerge among industry leaders. In all likelihood, unless a lot of money and effort goes in to the execution of a generic, it will fail like .travel or .tv. But, if a big player puts its money and execution plan behind it, the generics could be incredibly successful. And, for those large companies that did not apply for a top-level domain, acquiring a generic may be the way to bridge the gap.

Communities, Such as Banking, Finance, Groceries, Locally Grown, and Coupons

Finally, communities will also form and can likely create secure environments. For example a community of .bank could emerge and all of the banks could obtain a second-level domain, such as jpmorgan.bank, and then I know I am on the one and only secure site. .bank might have more rigorous standards to protect the security of online transactions, so I feel safer working with banks using .bank rather than .com. Likewise, locally grown could emerge as a community of local farm growers. They could build a way to authentically find locally grown food and build economies of scale in online marketing through the use of this community. The traditional coupon industry, plagued by Groupon and Living Social, could also emerge to create a one-stop shop for discounts.

For any top-level domain, the name alone will not mean success. .travel and .tv largely failed because they failed to execute and build a critical mass away from .com. The big difference in the age of social media and online communities is that if Google, Amazon, and Microsoft take people into the next generation, the floodgates will open on what is possible. Then, each TLD better have a good plan and be able to execute on it—that's what will mean the difference between success and failure.

"A great example that we have been working on is the community-based application for .pharmacy. In this community, we intend to solve a huge global problem: 'How do I find the most cost effective, safe prescription drugs for me and my family?' As a community dedicated to ensuring only legitimate information about diseases, health, and the drugs that have been developed to solve problems, .pharmacy will serve a great need around the globe and help the counterfeiting of prescription drugs. This is a perfect example of how a community-based, top-level domain can really serve the needs of the world's Internet users."

Josh Bourne, Managing Partner, FairWinds Partners

Major Findings from the 2011 Social Media Marketing Industry Report from Social Media Examiner

- Marketers place high value on social media: a significant 90 percent of marketers indicate that social media is important for their business.
- Social media marketing takes a lot of time: the majority of marketers (58 percent) are using social media for 6 hours or more each week, and more than a third (34 percent) invest 11 or more hours weekly.
- Marketers seek to learn more about Facebook and blogging: 70 percent of marketers want to learn more about Facebook and 69 percent want to learn more about blogging.
- The top benefits of social media marketing: the number one advantage of social media marketing (by a long shot) is generating more business exposure, as indicated by 88 percent of marketers. Increased traffic (72 percent) and improved search rankings (62 percent) were also major advantages.
- The top social media tools: Facebook, Twitter, LinkedIn, and blogs were the top four social media tools used by marketers, in that order. Facebook has eclipsed Twitter to take the top spot since our 2010 study.
- Social media outsourcing underutilized: Only 28 percent of businesses are outsourcing some portion of their social media marketing.

Chapter Three Highlights

- The emergence and proliferation of social media, online communities, and how consumer product companies are focusing more than ever on digital advertising and creating a sense of community to build brand loyalty, will continue and explode when many consumer brands operate their own top-level domain.

- In a few short years, social media has changed the way companies interact with customers, ranging from the powerhouse Facebook to Twitter, YouTube, Groupon, Pinterest, Pandora, and more; all focused on meeting the desire of people to feel connected to meaningful and relevant content and experiences in an ever-connected world.
- Today, more businesses promote their site on Facebook and Twitter than their own website. Owning a top-level domain could change that.
- Our thought leaders share their ideas about how social media may change and adapt under the expanded Internet and proffer that if the technology and social media giants shift to a top-level domain way of operating, the rest of the world will follow, and this will likely spur innovation out of necessity.
- We speculate, and only speculate, on possibilities and ask the question, "What if the new gTLDs change everything?"
- More predictions emerge:
  - There will be exponentially more options to build and protect your brand by building communities in an expanding Internet environment.
  - There will be opportunities to partner or collaborate to build communities that mean something—especially if you didn't apply for a top-level domain. Discover who did and might be a good partner for you.
  - You must carefully survey the environment of generic and community-based top-level domains to understand where you fit in.
  - You must carefully survey competitors to understand how you become the market leader instead of them.
  - You don't have to abandon .com, but you will need to map where it fits in the Internet regime with competitors and within your market category.
  - You do need to understand your markets and stakeholders. You may have more than just one or two and they may all be looking

for something different. Remember, build the community first. Facebook taught this lesson, an important new business lesson for long-term success in the next generation of the Internet.

- Traditional television—meaning without cable—is extinct. Cable is next unless they emerge into this next generation of the Internet.
- A few sources we trust will emerge as aggregators of content. Consumers will select a handful of sites and apps they trust to manage their entire life and world online.
- Brick and mortar stores will have to integrate their overhead and cost structure into loyalty online and offer something unique, such as an in-store entertainment-oriented experience coupled with the online experience.
- Service businesses will have to integrate delivery into something more seamless and community-oriented and offer thinking that's different from everyone else.

Chapter Four

Defending Your Brand

There's no doubt that when this launches and there are hundreds of new top-level domains, the burden of monitoring and protecting your valuable brand from getting into the hands of the wrong person will exponentially increase. The business world has already been shell-shocked with the number of .com domains they maintain just to make sure no one misdirects customers to their site (including misspellings and the proverbial yourbrandsucks.com). If they could apply for yourbrandsucks .anything on hundreds of new sites, then the once primarily administrative task will change into a daunting initiative that is absolutely necessary to protect the reputation of your brand and your company.

However, it's not quite the same as in the dot-com era. Before moving on to strategies to defend your brand in the next generation of the Internet, let's take a quick look at what emerged in the dot-com era. Some of the biggest problems encountered by brand owners, quite unexpectedly, were:

- Direct cybersquatting—For about $10 a year the early adopters quickly moved in and bought up valuable brands. Because there were no dispute resolution policies initially, brand owners fought the hard battle of forcing government and the Internet community to build the mechanisms. But, the genie was out of the bottle—a new industry had emerged.

- Typosquatting and cyber-counterfeiting. As cybersquatting earned its name, so too, did typosquatting and cyber-counterfeiting. Meaning, a slight typo in the domain name redirects the unknowing consumer to a counterfeit site designed to sell a cheaper, counterfeit product.

- Yourbrandsucks.com and the like—the haters. Likewise, another brand of .coms emerged much to the dismay of brand owners—the haters—those who wished to include something negative about your brand in the domain name itself. Creating not just a legal, but also a public relations problem, most companies, likewise, were unsure of how to respond to the haters.

After years of invoking the Internet community to create uniform dispute resolution procedures and the U.S. government to enact laws to prevent and punish the wrong doers, there is finally a framework for protecting legitimate brand owners, such as the Anti-Cybersquatting Consumer Protection Act, the developing global Anticounterfeiting Trade Agreement, as well as ICANN's Uniform Dispute Resolution Policy. The result for big brand owners is acquiring scores of domains with various spellings and variations just to block out others from having it. This requires maintenance and an administrative process and budget. It also requires ongoing search and policing to stop brand infringement in a world of hundreds of millions of websites. The biggest challenge for most has been managing the administrative requirements while balancing the legal requirements with the public relations ramifications. For example, Harry Potter, owned by Warner Brothers, faced countless sites of people who didn't hate, but loved Harry Potter. The problem was—they were misusing the brand. The company had to and continues to have to carefully evaluate the public relations outcry that would come from shutting down those loyal followers who simply want to worship their beloved Harry and company. Accordingly, collaboration among public relations personnel, lawyers, and technical managers to carefully address this issue is required and will increase in the new gTLD landscape.

In light of the challenges encountered in domain name protection over the past 10 years, most companies have adopted their strategies for policing and protecting their brand in the current domain space. Is it any wonder those whose job it is to do so didn't want to make it that much more difficult by expanding the Internet?

But the next generation is coming and a slightly new approach to defending your brand will be required. So rather than see this as a burden, look for the opportunities for broader and greater global protection by forcing companies to think bigger and broader than they have in the past. This is something that is long overdue for most companies. This means that you need to incorporate global trademark protection and a deeper understanding of how global brands are built and protected to have something valuable in the next generation of the Internet.

The New Domain Name Landscape

Before moving on to building your defensive strategy, it is helpful to overview the programs ICANN has created in this new top-level domain to assist in defending your brand.

UDRP

The Uniform Dispute Resolution Policy was introduced by ICANN in late 1999 in response to an outcry from the business community trying desperately to protect brand names from cyber- and typosquatters. The purpose of the program was to provide faster, less expensive, and binding resolutions to all domain name disputes that recognized trademark rights holders while also allowing from some legitimate use. While this approach was much better and faster than litigation, brand owners complained that it ultimately caused them to house thousands of domains they didn't want just to keep others from having it as the ultimate outcome of the proceedings. And, while it was less expensive than litigation, if outside counsel was involved, each dispute could easily cost $10,000 or more despite fees of only a few thousand dollars paid to the organizations approved by ICANN to oversee the dispute resolution process, including WIPO (the World Intellectual Property Organization), National Arbitration Forum, Asian Domain Name Dispute Resolution Centre, and others.

URS

The Uniform Rapid Suspension system will be implemented as part of the new gTLD program by ICANN. It is anticipated that URS will have a filing fee of $500, and a proceeding is expected to last between three and five weeks. A successful URS will result in suspension of the domain for the remaining duration of the registration, and placement of a notification of the dispute on the website. The URS is limited to, and should be used for, clear cases of trademark infringement. While it's difficult to predict, a number of experts estimate that up to 50 percent of the claims that are now filed as UDRP claims will be filed as URS proceedings. The URS is not, however, without controversy. Many brand owners have expressed concern that, even with the lower URS filing fee, the cost of pursing cybersquatters across a wide range of gTLDs will be exorbitant. Unlike under the UDRP, the domain owner may file a response up to 30 days after a decision has been rendered, and a registrant can seek *de novo* review of a URS decision. In addition, a complainant that prevails under the URS will not acquire the infringing domain name. Instead, the domain will be suspended until the end of the current registration period, and will become available for reregistration on a first-come, first-served basis, unless the complainant pays for a one-year extension to the initial suspension period. Moreover, brand owners will still need to seek UDRP protection to address cases that are not clear infringement and those where they would like immediate control and ownership of the disputed domain name. As you will see from our thought leaders, this is a step in the right direction, but much more is needed to truly change the incentives or disincentives for wrongdoers and greater protection for legitimate brand owners. For disputes where there is a clear controversy over the rightful owner, the UDRP will likely continue to be the proper venue for resolution.

Objections to Top-Level Domains

From the time the list of applicants for top-level domains was posted in June 2012 until early 2013, if you have the standing, you can file an objection to any top-level domain application that you believe legitimately infringes upon your rights. Application objections will be heard by three independent dispute resolution providers selected by ICANN. While the primary point of objection will be for violating trademark rights, companies can also object on the basis of potential confusion with an existing TLD application; if there is a public interest at issue with an application; and/or if it violates the community standards required for a community based application. For brand owners, the key issue will be proving that there is a likelihood of confusion with their brand that is probable, not just possible, to actually confuse consumers. Numerous other factors will be considered in terms of the applicant and objecting party. The fee will typically be between $2,000 for a single panel and up to $12,000 for a panel of three experts plus any outside counsel costs that may be incurred in the objection process.

Trademark Clearinghouse and Sunrise Periods

One way that ICANN is working to protect brand property rights, is by the establishment of a Trademark Clearinghouse.

The Trademark Clearinghouse will be a global/central repository for trademark information to be authenticated, stored, and disseminated, pertaining to the rights of trademark holders around the globe. It has been designed to increase protections and reduce costs for trademark holders and start-up registries alike.

The Trademark Clearinghouse will accept and authenticate rights information, and will support both trademark claims and sunrise services, required in all new top-level domains launched in this program. It is expected to play an important role in the launch of the new TLD program and to ensure the ongoing protection of trademark rights. Through an RFP process, ICANN selected Deloitte as the Trademark Clearinghouse in Europe. The Clearinghouse will be required to provide two primary functions:

1. Authentication and validation of the trademarks in the Clearinghouse.
2. Serve as a database to provide information to the new gTLD registries to support pre-launch sunrise or trademark claims services.

There are three main benefits that the Trademark Clearinghouse will bring to brand owners and registries. These are:

1. The Trademark Clearinghouse will not only allow trademark owners to publicly declare all of the trademarks they own, but once a trademark has been submitted and validated into the central repository, the trademark owner will be given preferential treatment

in terms of registering relevant domains during sunrise periods. For example, Nike will probably not apply for the .sport new gTLD in order to obtain nike.sport. However, when the .sport registry releases .sport domains during the sunrise, landrush, and general availability phases, Nike will be one of the first organizations allowed to apply for nike.sport.

2. The Trademark Clearinghouse will not only be a source of information that brand owners can log into to see who owns trademarks, it will also provide a notification service to trademark owners who have submitted their trademark information into the database. For example, if an organization did not apply for a new gTLD containing their trademark, they will receive a notification email from the Trademark Clearinghouse to tell them if someone else tries to register domains containing their name under a new gTLD. Using the same example, Nike may decide not to apply for Nike.games. However if someone else tries to apply for Nike.games, Nike will be notified and must then respond.

   This notification service is also important for potential registrants, too. For example, if someone tries to register Nike.games, they will receive an alert from the Trademark Clearinghouse warning them of the potential infringement against the Nike brand as well as the prospect of going through the Uniform Rapid Suspension System (see the following).

3. The third reason this is so important is that the Trademark Clearinghouse for brand owners is the introduction of the Uniform Rapid Suspension System (URS), as briefed above. The URS is intended to provide an expedited procedure for addressing clear cases of infringement against trademarks. The URS is designed to provide a faster (and less expensive) means to stop the operation of an abusive site, while the UDRP provides for transfer of a contested domain name to the rights holder. Rights holders seeking to pursue cases of infringement could use either or both procedures.

   Because the Trademark Clearinghouse acts as an information and notification service, it will provide a level of protection against trademark infringements, but it will not fully protect against individuals registering domains containing trademarked names. The Trademark Clearinghouse (and its new URS process) will provide trademark owners and registrants with the necessary information to either dispute a potential new gTLD, apply for it during sunrise phases before the domain becomes available to everyone, or think twice about applying for a domain because it is owned by someone else and could result in the URS process.

To help trademark owners manage their brands in an expanding Internet, ICANN has integrated two provisions to assist trademark owners seeking to protect their brands in the gTLD second-level domain registration process: the Trademark Claims Service (TCS) and the sunrise provisions. Under the TCS, for a defined period of time (at least the first 60 days of a gTLD launch), the Trademark Clearinghouse will provide notice to registrants whose prospective second-level domain matches a mark in the Clearinghouse. The owners of the corresponding trademarks will also be notified of the match. While the TCS is not a perfect system, when coupled with the mandatory sunrise provisions, the likelihood of widespread infringing on the registrations of second-level domains will be diminished. Under the sunrise provisions, for at least 30 days before the public launch period for a new gTLD, a trademark holder that is registered in the Clearinghouse may preregister domain names that include its mark.

Anti-Counterfeiting

While ICANN has not developed a specific program to stop counterfeiting, there is a way to educate the public and call attention to counterfeiters. For companies that have secured their own top-level domain, they can promote to their consumers that the only way for the authentic brand experience is through the top-level domain and to redirect their .com and other sites to the one authentic.yourbrand. Additionally, if you don't have a top-level domain, it's time to look at any community top-level sites in your industry category and determine how you obtain a domain name in that community, assuming that the community is going to protect the community by screening second-level domain holders for authenticity. Additionally, participating in sunrise periods and the Trademark Clearinghouse, will help to ensure that a counterfeiter doesn't secure a cybersquatting site. According to a report by the Coalition Against Domain Name Abuse, under current law, cybersquatters face statutory damages between $1,000 and $100,000 per domain name; however, courts rarely award damages greater than $1,000. Cybersquatting has evolved into a worldwide operation that exposes consumers to fraud, identity theft, and harmful counterfeit products. Much of this is a result of cybersquatters obtaining names through third-party providers (registrars or agents) without any penalty.

"Hopefully the cost of the gTLD application will eliminate bad actors from the top level. It's important to understand the players in the industry. For example, some bad-actor registrars have made a lot of money by playing the system, securing second-level domain names and then seeing what works (i.e., they keep the ones that make them money and dump the ones that don't, at no or minimal cost to them). An expanded gTLD space is attractive to these registrars, making them competitors as much as they are vendors to .brand top-level domain applicants and anyone doing business on the Internet. Although most are very reputable, there are some that are not looking out for consumers and are just looking for ways to make money—often infringing on brand-owners' rights to do so. These registrars or their former employees are likely applying for gTLDs and we, as a brand-owner community, need to monitor these applications and continue to demand that brand-owner rights be protected."

Fabricio Vayra, Trademark Attorney, Time Warner Inc.

Counterfeiting Statistics

- Rogue websites selling counterfeit physical goods attract more than 87 million visits per year. (MarkMonitor, *Traffic Report: Online Piracy and Counterfeiting*, January 2011.)

- Rogue websites generate more than 53 billion visits per year. (MarkMonitor, *Traffic Report: Online Piracy and Counterfeiting*, January 2011.)
- MarkMonitor estimates that global sales of counterfeit goods via the Internet from illegitimate retailers will reach $135 billion. (MarkMonitor, *Seven Best Practices for Fighting Counterfeit Sales Online*, September 2010.)
- G20 governments and consumers lose $125 billion annually, including losses in tax revenue, from counterfeiting and piracy. (Frontier Economics, *Estimating the Global Economic and Social Impacts of Counterfeiting and Piracy*, February 2011.)
- Digital piracy costs the global economy $75 billion annually. (Frontier Economics, *Estimating the Global Economic and Social Impacts of Counterfeiting and Piracy*, February 2011.)
- http://theglobalipcenter.com/pressreleases/us-chamber-highlights-report-indicating-rampant-traffic-online-counterfeiting-and-pira.

Our thought leaders weighed in on the programs:

"Companies will want to take advantage of the Trademark Clearinghouse. It could potentially serve as an efficient way to direct any legal proceeding to authenticate your trademark rights around the world. Ideally it will help not just in sunrise or trademark claims processes, but in UDRP or URS proceedings, as well. Companies will also need to evaluate sunrise periods and determine which ones make sense for their business. They don't necessarily need to apply for everything."

Adam Scoville, Trademark and Brand Protection Counsel, RE/MAX

"Depending upon the pricing of the Trademark Clearinghouse and how it functions in actual operation, it could be of

(continued)

tremendous value to companies. For example, if the cost is reasonable enough that I can register all of my brands in the system, use this as a source to streamline sunrise registrations, and receive notifications of online brand abuse, then it could be very valuable. If, however, the cost is too high to register all of my brands, or the brand abuse notifications are short-lived, I'd be inclined to find less value in the system."

Fabricio Vayra, Trademark Attorney,
Time Warner Inc.

"The Trademark Clearinghouse will be extremely important for brand owners to participate in and to get their marks in the database so that notices can go out as part of the trademark claims process. Once trademark owners realize the number of domains that will be available, they need to be selective about which sunrise program in which to participate. Extremely famous brands might need to participate across the board, but most brands need to be very selective and focus only on the communities where they will be most impacted. Each top-level domain will resolve similar or identical brands in its own way. They will lay this out in their application with ICANN. Some may auction off identical brands, some may offer a first-come, first-serve. Trademark owners with competing rights need to be prepared and make good strategic decisions about what really matters and what will really cause confusion or dilute your brand. It's hard to watch someone else get your brand in another TLD, but in the end you really have to decide is it worth it—do we really need to worry about it—is it really going to confuse consumers? There's room in this universe for all of us. That's why the TM office registers only in certain classifications—not exclusive across everything. We live in a world of co-existence and need to make choices on what to pursue."

Jeffrey J. Neuman, Vice President, Business Affairs,
Enterprise Services, Neustar, Inc.

"The cost to companies to protect their brands is likely to increase significantly. Because Procter & Gamble has so many brands, this is a big issue. Companies will likely need to significantly increase resources to monitor their brands across up to 1,000 new top-level domains. When the new gTLD applications become public, it will be important to monitor what is happening on a regular basis. It is equally important to take advantage of the required rights protection mechanisms including sunrise provisions and the trademark clearinghouse."

Steven Miller and Katherine Ruwe, Procter & Gamble

"Brand owners, through associations like INTA (International Trademark Association), have served as a leading voice in the evolution of the name space, successfully advocating for new measures to protect organizations and consumers from online crimes and illegal forms of hacktivism."

Claudio Di Gangi, Manager External Relations, Internet and the Judiciary, International Trademark Association

"Unfortunately I think we will also see brand owners who coexist in the real world battling against each other. In the mad world of ICANN two or more owners of identical or confusingly similar registered trademarks will find themselves in a contention set—for example, UBS and UPS, NHL and DHL, Visa and Viva, IBM and BMI, ABC and CBC. In the real world, these organizations coexist. Currently they are invited by ICANN to discuss resolving contention in the application process between themselves, meaning that only one of them can proceed. If they cannot reach a resolution they go into an auction with the highest bidder winning. The loser faces Permanent String Preclusion—meaning they are locked out of the highest level of the domain name system forever. This is an unacceptable situation that will inevitably lead to litigation. The fear of this is driving defensive registration at the top level in the first round."

Nick Wood, Managing Director, Com Laude

"Brand owners should not participate in every sunrise. If you are in pharma, do you need to participate in a .jewelry sunrise?—probably not. You must be strategic about where

(continued)

there is actual confusion. .xxx was unique. Most brand owners have had to deal with the porn industry and, for instance, children's brands have to be careful. So, even if you didn't have any intention whatsoever of being a part of the adult content industry, you had to protect your brands from any consumers associations with .xxx. Xbox, by way of example, was a concern for us because the association with the letter "X" is shared by the adult content industry and the Xbox brand has been targeted for infringement by the porn industry in the past. The URS needs to be faster and cheaper then as it is currently anticipated. That said, ICANN is still working to determine a service provider. If URS is in the $300 to $500 range and you can secure a takedown in a week and you don't have to transfer it to your portfolio because it will simply be blocked for a period of time, then yes, URS will be incredibly valuable. If, however, this is not the case, if it costs more money or doesn't result in the blocking of the domain name, then UDRP may still be the way to go."

Russ Pangborn, Associate General Counsel
for Trademarks, Microsoft

"Most brand owners are concerned about cybersquatting, phishing, fraud, and other abuses arising from the new gTLD. For the near future, there are inadequate protections in place to ensure consumers find the genuine websites for trademarked products and services on the Internet. Many registries will intentionally locate themselves overseas and out of reach of U. S. cybersquatting laws and the costs that will be incurred by companies just to protect their brand could be significant. The wholesale introduction of mass numbers of new gTLDS will result in chaos at the expense of businesses and consumers. We believe, in the new world of expanded domain names, cybersquatters may be more discriminating in the names they choose to steal, but will do so across a much wider scope of new generic tlds. The new generic top-level domains, especially, could easily become havens for spam, phishing and spyware, and bad actors."

Sarah Deutsch, Vice President and Associate
General Counsel, Verizon Communications

"The UDRP has been one of ICANN's greatest successes. The URS was intended to fill in the holes left by the UDRP for 'slam-dunk' cases, to make it faster, cheaper, and easier, and to address multiple domain names in one action. Whether it will prove an effective option utilized by companies, after being watered down from the original IRT (Implementation Recommendation Team) proposal, remains to be seen."

Ellen Shankman, Principal, Ellen B. Shankman & Associates, Rehovot Israel

The Slippery Slope

Once you start to build your plan for protecting your brand, the next looming question is, What if a competitor secures a critical generic as a closed system, such as .shopping, .media, .news, .sports, .programming, or some other variation of an organization's brands and/or industry categories and plans to box me out? Or, what if a competitor applies for a second-level domain in a generic with plans to box me out? And, what do I need to do to protect myself in general? Let's start with understanding the negative consequences and then move on to strategies.

Competitive Analysis

A detailed audit of an organization's global brands and competitors is essential to complete this defensive analysis, but what follows is a brief overview of potential negative consequences.

Consumer Confusion

If a competitor obtains the generic market categories of an organization, it is highly probable that consumers will mistakenly go to that generic top-level domain site. This will cause consumer confusion and could potentially convert an organization's consumers into a competitor's consumers. Lost Internet traffic means lost ad revenue and a substantial increase the likelihood of a diminished consumer base.

Brand Dilution

Likewise, if a competitor obtains a critical market category of an organization, the brand value of the company's brands will diminish significantly. If a consumer is looking for an iPad tablet on Apple, but instead finds mytablet on.technology and the quality is not the same, it is probable that the value of an iPad will be diluted if consumers mistakenly believe there is a connection. Furthermore, many studies have shown that brand dilution associated with one brand within a family of brands is very likely to not only harm the target brand but also the related brands. In 2007, The Coalition Against Domain Name Abuse estimated that so-called cybersquatting costs companies worldwide more than $1 billion annually in diverted customer sales and enforcement expenses. The list of coalition companies includes Coca-Cola, Dell, Yahoo!, AIG, Eli Lilly, HSBC, Hilton, Wyndham Worldwide, Verizon, and Marriott. Depending on the brand owner's industry, the total impact of cybersquatting on a single brand could be tens of millions of U.S. dollars when factoring in the value of lost leads and sales, costs of brand dilution, consumer confusion, poor customer experiences, and millions of lost unique visitor impressions each week. Excluding less-tangible costs, such as lost goodwill and poor customer impressions, the impact of cybersquatting on trademark holders is in excess of $1 million per brand, per year. Some well-known brand owners will face losses many times this figure.

Lost Market Share

If a competitor owns the top-level domain in a similar market segment and the top-level domain has the anticipated consumer response, it is likely that an organization may lose market share in terms of viewers and/or consumers. Similar to the fragmentation of cable, America's Big Three networks started losing viewers after the advent of cable in the 1970s and since then the networks have seen their viewership slowly erode. It's a matter of basic math—with limited choices, it is easier for a product to become a best seller. With more choices that reflect diverse tastes, it's a lot harder. According to 1990 Nielsen figures, ABC, NBC, and CBS were averaging 71 percent of the total viewing audience in prime time, but with the growing number of cable channels in the early 1990s, the Big Three networks started rapidly losing viewers. By the 1991 season the Big Three networks were down a combined 24 percent, while basic cable channels increased their combined viewership by about 2 million homes. Similarly, with the onslaught of numerous new domains, there is the potential for fragmentation of the Internet that an unlimited number of new gTLDs could cause.

Monitoring

If competitors obtain critical top-level domains to an organization's overall market strategy, constant monitoring and market research will be required to ensure that second-level domains sold on those sites do not infringe upon or dilute an organization's family of brands.

"Because of the myriad of unknowns with new gTLDS, we will likely see a number of legal actions or dispute resolution proceedings with novel issues that will take time for judges or panels to decide. While some issues may shake down fairly quickly, waiting for precedential decisions on key aspects that regulators may not have considered might test the patience of stakeholders as we anticipate where new gTLDs will lead."

Nancy Lutz and Yasmin Tavakoli of Kelley Drye & Warren, LLP

The Best Defense Is a Good Offense

There are a number of steps necessary to build your defensive strategy. But, of course remember that sometimes the best defensive strategy is to start thinking in an offensive way: How do you capture your market share and not just protect but cultivate and build your brand? All too often, companies only look at how to stop infringers, rather than looking at how to boost their own brand value and presence.

- Audit your brands and clean house. You absolutely must start with an audit of all of your brands and sub-brands. This is the perfect time to do some housecleaning. What brands are you using? What will you continue to use? What gives you the greatest market share? Can those brands be protected globally or just in the United States? Does your long-term strategy require any rebranding? These are all important questions that require an audit and analysis of your current brand portfolio. Rather than immediately begin with, "How do we protect everything in our portfolio?" ask yourself: "What should we be investing in for the future?" When paradigm shifts occur, taking stock of what you have and placing value predictions on the future is essential.
- Audit your domain portfolio. Likewise to auditing your brand, it's time to also audit your existing portfolio of domain names. Companies large and small often maintain far more domains than needed just to box others out or just in case they later have a strategy that will use it. While you can certainly continue to do so, this is a good time to really evaluate your overall domain name strategy in light of the changing Internet. Because it will become so much more saturated, you actually may need to maintain fewer sites than before. And, are you investing properly in educating your consumers about how to find your authentic brand on the Internet?
- Objecting to top-level domains. You will have until December 1, 2012, to object to current applications for top-level domains. All brand owners should survey the list of applicants to determine if other applicants are infringing upon your brand, particularly if you have superior trademark rights or if you have other concerns about a top-level domain and then oppose their top-level domain within the time period. If you have global trademark rights, you may be able stop others from using your brand as a top-level domain. It's important to remember, however, that this is a global system. So, just because you have a trademark in the United States in one particular classification does not mean you are the only one

with trademark rights. In a complex environment, it's quite likely more than just one other business in the world has a similar trademark right, not to mention the scores of similar names in different product categories such as: Delta faucets and Delta airlines—they both have the same trademark rights in the context of the top-level domain.

- Expand your trademark protection. Evaluate if your current trademark portfolio will provide the protection you need under the ever-changing dispute resolution rules. Where might you expand your business in the future? If the expanding Internet increasingly expands your business globally, you may need more protection than you have today. If you find that you don't have the global protection you may need for your brands to survive scrutiny under the new dispute resolution rules, begin the application process to protect your brands around the globe. The global economy is moving all businesses in this direction, so evaluate options to cost effectively protect your core brand and sub-brands around the globe. Prioritize what is most important to protect and what will produce the return on investment.

- Survey the applicant list twice. You will want to carefully survey the applicant list twice to determine not only potential infringement on your brand so you can object or oppose to those applications, but also to identify the generics and communities in which you may want to apply during the sunrise period. When reviewing the list of applicants, it's a good idea to also start to flag what generics or community top-level domains may fit your long-term strategy.

- Register with the Trademark Clearinghouse. You will also want to register your portfolio of trademarks with the Trademark Clearinghouse. While there is still some debate about the cost benefit analysis of doing so, in all likelihood, the cost to register your marks for most businesses will be such that it simply makes sense to register. This gives you one worldwide source to point to that you have these registered trademarks and can then provide a basis for you to participate in sunrise periods and be notified of potential infringing marks.

> "I recommend that as soon as the applications list is posted that brand owners carefully scan the list. They need to think about it broadly—not just about brands. You need to know the rules and use the rules. For example, you need to consider using the comment period because even if you don't want to object, you might want to post a comment for ICANN's evaluators to review in the relevant period."
>
> Fabricio Vayra, Trademark Attorney, Time Warner Inc.

- Monitor open sites. Once top-level domain sites go live in 2013, develop a monitoring process for keywords, phrases, or brands. There are a number of companies offering this service as a watch service that can cost effectively provide you important information not just for protecting your brand on the Internet, but also having as a heads-up to what competitors are doing. Also, recognize that monitoring services can also double as market research to know what your competitors are doing. All too often, only the lawyers review the search reports scanning for potential infringement. This is an important function, but you can also pass this information to business leaders to apprise them of what could be happening with competitors, how consumers who love or hate your brand are responding, and even to know who is trying to copy you can be critical to your business strategy.
- Evaluate your internal processes for brand and domain management. Can you create greater economies of scale in the way you develop strategy both offensively and defensively? Should you centralize this function into a business unit that measures itself not as a cost center, but in terms of profits, losses, and traditional financial models? Can you create incentives to cross over disciplines and work outside of silos to maximize your impact? To function in this new world, technology, marketing, legal, and executive functions must work together. All too often, this function is left just to IT or legal but it really should be a cross-functional team that evaluates the changing Internet landscape. When everything could be at stake in the future of your business, why would you leave it to just one department?

Remember that the best defense is also good offense—use this as an opportunity to evaluate your high-level brand protection strategy: What are you protecting? Why? How do you maximize resources? Limit the number of sub-brands without clear strategies that include brand protection. And, always balance public relations and perceptions with your brand-protection strategies. A good legal decision intended to minimize risk can often be a very wrong public relations decision or fail to maximize opportunities. Brand protection is more about brand building, and if you don't clearly know what you are building, then what are you protecting?

Our thought leaders added more predictions and advice for protecting your brand.

"One potential benefit of operating a .brand gTLD would be for those who constantly deal with online counterfeiters. For example, if only authorized distributors are permitted to use the .brand extension (e.g., distributor. brand), anyone selling the goods outside of the .brand gTLD space may be readily identifiable as an unauthorized user. Trademark owners could run a search or algorithm to locate websites that do not end with the .brand extension but sell the branded goods, giving them an immediate snapshot of potential infringers to investigate."
Nancy Lutz and Yasmin Tavakoli of Kelley Drye & Warren, LLP

"For companies with many brands, this is the perfect opportunity to build a strong, cohesive, and consolidated domain name management strategy. The new URS procedure definitely provides for economies of scale in bringing numerous infringements into one proceeding against numerous infringer aliases. Unfortunately, for many large companies, the function of opposing domain names has been scattered across departments; ranging from trademark/legal, to IT, and sometimes even by specific brand categories. For companies with scattered enforcement structures, this may amount to duplication and lost economies of scale. Looking at how to go forward in this

(continued)

environment, this is the perfect time to use the URS rules, costs, and proceedings to build economies of scale."

Fabricio Vayra, Trademark Attorney, Time Warner Inc.

"The biggest issue will be protecting your brand. Yahoo! owns over 28,000 domains and only about 150 or so are used. The majority has been obtained through litigation or the UDRP. Now, add 1,000 more top-level domains to monitor—the impact is staggering. The Trademark Clearinghouse is just a database. And, while sunrise could be helpful, it only covers identical brands. Typosquatting is just as big of a problem as direct cybersquatting, so sunrise isn't really helping us there. Brand owners should also realize that while sunrise can be helpful, that they are really just funding the operations of that top-level domain. .xxx earned $17.6 million dollars in 6 weeks during the sunrise period. A true rights protection program will be a tapestry of solutions."

J. Scott Evans, Senior Legal Director, Head of Global Brand, Domains & Copyright at Yahoo! Inc.

"I have never been of the philosophy that you must have every single extension. A few select brands may legitimate have that concern. But, the majority of the brands that are out there don't need to worry that if they don't protect in.yournewtld or that they will be found to not be adequately protecting their rights. That's been a paranoia of the trademark community that's never been held true. I've seen a lot of domain name registrations that have annoyed me, but we don't need to fight to get the name back because in the end I didn't believe there would be any real consumer confusion or dilution of our brand. Of course you should look to see if there is any counterfeiting, then you need to stop that site, but the majority of typo- or related squatting sites are parked and they are just looking for you to buy it from them. For budgetary reasons, you don't have to go after everything."

Jeffrey J. Neuman, Vice President, Business Affairs, Enterprise Services, Neustar, Inc.

"At the top level, brand owners have a couple of questions to ask themselves: What type of brand do you have? Is there a risk of a third party pursuing the same string? If so, do you need to object through the formal IP objections process? On the other hand, If you don't pursue your.brand and someone else pursues the same string, your brand could face permanent string confusion. If this gTLD expansion acts as an inflection point on the Internet and you did not participate, what will be the impact to your company?"

Russ Pangborn, Associate General Counsel for Trademarks, Microsoft

"gTLDS ups the ante in digital and brand protection—you'll have to be more vigilant as you look at your brand. I think it's helpful that the cost of entry was high, so that you're not going to have Joe Smith squat on your name for $20, but it also means that if someone else got your brand in this process, it will be hard to get it back. The risk of losing your brand here is much higher. The stakes are much higher here of losing control of your brand if you don't apply."

Cynthia Gibson, Executive Vice President Legal Affairs, Scripps Networks Interactive Inc.

"To be successful, brand owners need the trifecta—marketing, IT, and legal—of brand strategy and protection and they must also have an executive sponsor. If leadership doesn't help them cross silos and work together, they will have a lot of problems."

Krista Papac, Chief Strategy Officer, ARI Registry Services

"Yes, there will be more top-level domains. No, you don't have to protect your name in every single new top-level domain. First, it doesn't make economic sense. And, second, Lancome.shoe is not a real risk so why register it? .com is an appendage we are all accustomed to using because it is what we were given. There weren't any logical options at the time, so we used the catchall—.com. Now it's time to marry together risk tolerance and meaningful extensions that are directly tied to your products and services rather than just buying up everything. Most brand owners today have domain name portfolios that contain defensive registrations. Brands can reduce the costs of

(continued)

maintaining their defensive registrations if they rethink their strategy in the new, expanded top-level domain space."

Krista Papac, Chief Strategy Officer, ARI Registry Services

"At the second level, traditional trademark protections face a potentially high volume of enforcement that is required. Brand owners need to take a real hard look to do this strategically. Budgets are shrinking, not growing, so if there are hundreds to thousands of sunrise periods the fees associated with participating in all or even many will be impactful. It's tricky. You have to carefully determine what could have a negative impact on your brand or if there's a top-level domain that could negatively impact your customers finding you, then you need to participate in sunrise. The brand protection mechanisms should hopefully be beneficial. Brand owners are facing a very busy time ahead. Most are defensively holding thousands and thousands of domains—it gets expensive. Microsoft has in excess of 50,000 domains and only a small fraction are actually used. Most of it is online enforcement. You can play whack-a-mole and just keep trying to take sites down, but eventually it gets easier to just knock them down and then hold it."

Russ Pangborn, Associate General Counsel
for Trademarks, Microsoft

"A tapestry of rights protection mechanisms is needed to protect brands in this new space—the ability to pre-register or challenge domain names up-front, and to take down domain names at the back end."

Ellen Shankman, Principal Ellen B. Shankman & Associates,
Rehovot, Israel

Chapter Four Highlights

- As the Internet expands exponentially, the cost to protect your brand does not necessarily have to follow. Careful strategy is required to analyze the cost/benefit analysis of the new tools available to you.
- There are numerous strategies for defending your brand under the new regime. Protection programs in the existing and future domain space

include the Uniform Dispute Resolution Policy, Uniform Rapid Suspension System, Trademark Clearinghouse, and sunrise periods.

- You will have until December 1, 2012, to file an opposition to any top-level domain you believe infringes on your brand.
- Our thought leaders weigh in on how to save costs and increase effective protection of brands by centralizing the function of brand domain management within your company and maximizing economies of scale that can come from the Trademark Clearinghouse and URS system.
- There is still a lot of room for improvement in dispute resolution proceedings, including greater penalties to bad actors and greater long-term abilities for rightful brand owners to lock up their brands across the Internet from bad actors and protect consumers from counterfeit goods.
- In addition to brand protection analysis using ICANN tools, brand owners must also assess the negative consequences of other top-level domain owners on their brand including any unintended consumer confusion, brand dilution, and lost market share.
- Brand owners may consider monitoring potentially infringing activity as not just a legal defense strategy, but also a competitive and industry analysis tool that leads to greater innovation.
- There may be a lot of chaos in the initial stages of the new top-level domain launch. Our thought leaders offer proven techniques and suggestions for using the new ICANN systems and finding opportunities to thin out domain portfolios as a result.
- A few predictions emerge:
  - Brand owners may ultimately have more lobbying power in ICANN when they represent the lion's share of registry operators. This could have long-term positive implications for brand owners to influence policy decisions to stop cybersquatting and counterfeiting.
  - Companies can actually improve their overall Internet strategy by taking the challenge and fear about brand protection and turning it into an opportunity to audit, evaluate, and improve the way you build and cultivate brand identity on the Internet.
  - Rather than increase costs, companies can maximize greater economies of scale by using brand protection mechanisms as offensive strategies to build their brand in an expanding Internet universe.

- In the short term, there will be confusion and likely most companies will increase their spend on brand protection until they can re-engineer the process to efficiently evaluate the return on investment associated with brand protection activities.
- The importance of creating a brand that can be protected in a global community of trademark rights holders will become more important than ever. It's no longer just checking to see if it's available or clearance, it's a whole new level of thinking about what you are building, cultivating, protecting, and why.

Chapter Five

Behind the Scenes

The big question for so many businesses is: How will this impact search engine optimization? Anyone involved in media, consumer products, or the sale of just about anything knows that understanding how people get to your website, or find and access your apps for mobile devices, is critical to success.

While this is by no means an in-depth, technical assessment of the many tools available for search engine optimization, it can serve as a high-level overview to understand what may come next. Because the Internet is about to change dramatically, it is probable that consumers will initially be confused and rely on search more heavily. So, let's start with understanding how search engines work and how it is changing the way people use the Internet. Think for a moment about yourself and how you use the Internet. Do you typically type in a domain name or do you go to a search engine? You may have a few favorite domains, but if you're not sure where to find what you want, you use a search engine. So when you type in your search, what happens?

How Internet Search Engines Work

There are hundreds of millions of web pages available, waiting to present information on an expanding variety of topics. When you want to find something on the Internet, you likely go to Google, Bing, or Yahoo! to start your query. Search engines have four functions: crawling, building an index, calculating relevancy and ranking, and serving results. Many factors influence where a site appears in web search results:

- Number of other sites linking to it
- Content of the pages
- Updates made to indices
- Testing of product versions
- Discovery of additional sites
- Changes to search algorithms

Internet search engines are special sites on the web that are designed to help people find information stored on other sites. There are differences in the ways various search engines work, but they all perform three basic tasks:

1. They search the Internet—or select pieces of the Internet—based on important words.
2. They keep an index of the words they find, and where they find them.
3. They allow users to look for words or combinations of words found in that index.

Early search engines held an index of a few hundred thousand pages and documents, and received one or two thousand inquiries each day. Today, a top search engine will index hundreds of millions of pages, and respond to tens of millions of queries per day. See Figure 5.1.

Web Crawling

Before search became the most critical part of Internet and digital marketing, there were search engines in place to help people find information on the Internet prior to the 1990s. Programs with names like Gopher and

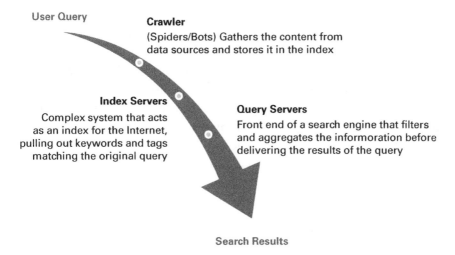

User Query

Crawler
(Spiders/Bots) Gathers the content from
data sources and stores it in the index

Index Servers
Complex system that acts
as an index for the Internet,
pulling out keywords and tags
matching the original query

Query Servers
Front end of a search engine that filters
and aggregates the informoration before
delivering the results of the query

Search Results

Figure 5.1 How Search Engines Work

Archie kept indexes of files stored on servers connected to the Internet, and dramatically reduced the amount of time required to find programs and documents. In the late 1980s, getting serious value from the Internet meant knowing how to use Gopher, Archie, Veronica, and the rest. But, that was before mainstream use of the Internet.

Before a search engine can tell you where a file or document is, it must be found. To find information on the hundreds of millions of web pages that exist, a search engine employs special software robots, called spiders, to build lists of the words found on websites. When a spider is building its lists, the process is called web crawling. In order to build and maintain a useful list of words, a search engine's spiders have to look at a lot of pages.

The usual starting points for spiders are lists of heavily used servers and very popular pages. The spider will begin with a popular site, indexing the words on its pages and following every link found within the site. In this way, the spider system quickly begins to travel, spreading out across the most widely used portions of the web.

Google began as an academic search engine. In the paper that describes how the system was built, Sergey Brin and Lawrence Page give an example of how quickly their spiders can work. They built their initial system to use multiple spiders, usually three at one time. Each spider could keep about 300 connections to web pages open at a time. At its peak performance, using four spiders, their system could crawl over 100 pages per second, generating around 600 kilobytes of data each second.

Keeping everything running quickly meant building a system to feed necessary information to the spiders. The early Google system had a server dedicated to providing URLs to the spiders. Rather than depending on an Internet service provider for the domain name server (DNS) that translates a server's name into an address, Google had its own DNS, in order to keep delays to a minimum.

When the Google spider looked at a page, it took note of two things:

1. The words within the page.
2. Where the words were found.

Words occurring in the title, subtitles, meta tags, and other positions of relative importance were noted for special consideration during a subsequent user search. The Google spider was built to index every significant word on a page, leaving out the articles "a," "an," and "the." Other spiders take different approaches.

These different approaches usually attempt to make the spider operate faster and allow users to search more efficiently, or both. For example, some spiders will keep track of the words in the title, sub-headings, and links, along with the 100 most frequently used words on the page and each word in the first 20 lines of text.

According to SEOmoz's *Beginner's Guide to SEO*, Bing engineers recommend the following to get better rankings in their search engine:

- In the visible page text, include words users might choose as search query terms to find the information on your site.
- Limit all pages to a reasonable size. One topic per page.
- Make sure that each page is accessible by at least one static text link.
- Don't put the text that you want indexed in side images.

Likewise, Google recommends the following:

- Make pages primarily for users, not for search engines. Don't deceive your users or present different content to search engines than you display to users, which is referred to as cloaking.

- Make a site with a clear hierarchy and text links. Every page should be reachable from at least one static text link.
- Create a useful, information rich site and write pages that clearly and accurately describe your content.
- Keep the links on a given page to a reasonable number—fewer than 100.

Meta Tags

Meta tags allow the owner of a page to specify key words and concepts under which the page will be indexed. This can be helpful when the words on the page might have double or triple meanings—the meta tags can guide the search engine in choosing which of the several possible meanings for these words is correct. There is, however, a danger in overreliance on meta tags, because a careless or unscrupulous page owner might add meta tags that fit very popular topics but have nothing to do with the actual contents of the page. To protect against this, spiders will correlate meta tags with page content, rejecting the meta tags that don't match the words on the page.

Building the Index

Once the spiders have completed the task of finding information on web pages, the search engine must store the information in a way that makes it useful. There are two key components involved in making the gathered data accessible to users:

1. The information stored with the data.
2. The method by which the information is indexed.

Each search engine has a different formula for assigning weight to the words in its index. This is one of the reasons that a search for the same word on different search engines will produce different lists, with the pages presented in different orders.

An index has a single purpose: It allows information to be found as quickly as possible. You'll find, for example, that the S section of the dictionary is much thicker than the X section. This inequity means that finding a word beginning with a very popular letter could take much longer than

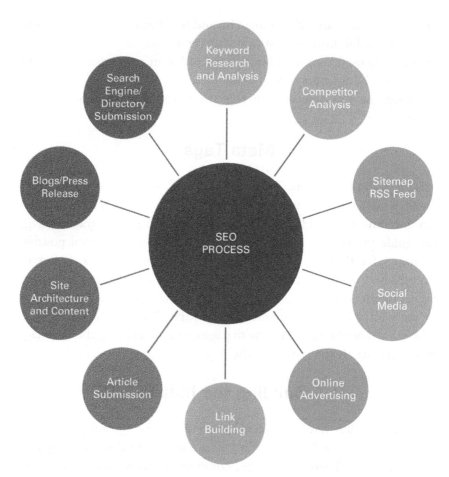

Figure 5.2   Search Engine Optimization Process

finding a word that begins with a less popular one. The combination of efficient indexing and effective storage makes it possible to get results quickly, even when the user creates a complicated search. See Figure 5.2.

The Next Generation of Search

In all likelihood search will change because people will use the Internet differently. If you can search within certain trusted top-level domains, will you still go out to the broad Internet search that produces thousands of results or will you go to a more refined search that produces results more on target? Will you sacrifice privacy to search on sites that deliver what you want but share that with marketers? How would you search if these options were available?

- tophotelsnewyorkcity.google—thousands of results
- tophotels.newyorkcity—fewer results
- fivestarhotels.newyorkcity—even more narrow
- greatdeals.newyorkcity
- search.bing
- search.golf
- search.shopping

Could this eliminate the need for big search engines that search everything in favor of more refined areas of the Internet, like ZIP codes or zoning? Rather than looking through everything, you go to trusted sources. This provides interesting new revenue models for those top-level domains that capture industry segments and interests. They could own search in their category and search is worth a lot. .travel failed. But.vacations could succeed if it is one place to search for the information I want about planning, managing, and tracking my trips, particularly if they built a place for me to search, purchase, and manage all aspects of my trips.

Will Google, Yahoo!, and Bing adapt their business models? No one knows for sure. Will new search engines emerge? It is not yet clear if or how the major search engines will adapt their algorithms. In all likelihood, given their mandate to deliver consumers what they are looking for, they will, but exactly when, how, and whether it is free to all companies is another story. Since all three have applied for their own series of top level domains, it is anticipated that the search engines could evolve and weigh the top-level domain more heavily in terms of categorizing the nature of the search. For example, if you have only a .com, that space may be more diluted than if you have a brand.golf and the user is searching for something in golf—the store in .golf may be found before your store in .com is found. There's no guarantee this will happen, but it is a possible outcome.

It's quite likely that to show up in search in an expanding Internet, companies may have to pay a premium to search engines, further bolstering the revenue models of these directors of the Internet. And, consumers may have to pay a subscription to access really good search engines focused on giving them what they want. If the Internet is expanding, what would you pay to find what you want faster? Search engines certainly have a big challenge, but equally a lot to gain in the expanding Internet space.

Our thought leaders provided their perspective.

"Search engines will rise in importance initially because people will be confused. The algorithms will adjust to the new domains. Then, there will be a greater specialization in terms of search. People will want to search within smaller segmented online marketplaces."

J. Scott Evans, Senior Legal Director, Head of Global Brands, Domains & Copyright at Yahoo! Inc.

"It will be interesting to see how new gTLDs affect search and the ability of consumers to navigate the Internet. Search engines will certainly adjust to incorporate the new domains, but only time will tell if the expansion will bring clarity to the search process for consumers."

Claudio Di Gangi, Manager External Relations, Internet and the Judiciary, International Trademark Association

"The big unknown question is how Google will address this issue and what they do with their algorithms. Traditional searches are becoming less and less useful because of ranking and sponsorship opportunities. It's becoming difficult for users to get meaningful information using traditional searches. It's like trying to find a needle in a haystack. If there is more robust content, whether by category or brand, it may bring better order and organization to the Internet. People will move to what's easy—very quickly."

Cynthia Gibson, Executive Vice President Legal Affairs, Scripps Networks Interactive Inc.

"Keyword searching will become increasingly important. When consumers are looking for one of our brands, they will likely go to a search engine to find us."

Steven Miller and Katherine Ruwe, Procter & Gamble

"The really generic spaces—.web, .generic—will draw more attention to the big search engines because it will be more important to find what you are looking for in a bigger space. With highly differentiated spaces and brands, however, search engines will have to pay more attention to top-level domains. Search engines are all about leading users to the most efficient spaces that consumers want. Search engines that are more specialized or more easily adaptable may have an edge in the future."

Jeffrey J. Neuman, Vice President, Business Affairs, Enterprise Services, Neustar, Inc.

"It's hard to know what's going to happen with search. Ultimately, it probably won't be that different than how search engines tread a .com domain. Most of what you will do in your search engine strategy will evolve from what you already do in .com, just in an expanded universe."

Adam Scoville, Trademark and Brand Protection Counsel, RE/MAX

"There is a lot of opportunity for brands—making the customer experience more memorable and themselves easier to find. If brands execute correctly, consumers may not need to use search as much to find information about the brand or its products and services. Brands can engage with their customers in a way they never could before. It's similar to the cool factor Apple has established with its customers. Companies have complete control to pick whatever brand name they want in terms of new products and services and will always have the name available under their own top-level domain. This will create a shift to new ways of navigating and searching the Internet."

Krista Papac, Chief Strategy Officer, ARI Registry Services

(continued)

"This is such a massive expansion of the domain name space at an accelerated pace so it's hard to know exactly what will happen. Initially, most people won't change their habits, but once there are 200 to 500 to 1,000 new extensions, people may need to depend more on search engines to help them navigate this new space. I think you will also see more specialized top-level domains where consumers will naturally navigate to a category or a particular brand as Internet habits change. The other hot area will be the regional top-level domains that are trying to create jobs and focus on local entities—.london, .miami—a local region will be the driver behind it. There are opportunities there."

Russ Pangborn, Associate General Counsel for Trademarks, Microsoft

"People will be ever more dependent upon search engines. It may be more difficult to know what's real and what's a fraud online."

Sarah Deutsch, Vice President and Associate General Counsel, Verizon Communications

"Search engines don't currently pay much attention to the extension in their algorithm. Much more important factors lead to scoring in organic search. However, search engines may have to account for the extension in order to deliver their primary mandate—relevant search results. If something like .cartier ensures genuine products, it may be ranked higher to provide relevant search results."

Josh Bourne, Managing Partners, FairWinds Partners

"One of the interesting things the gTLD process offers brands is the opportunity to appear in the browser exactly as they do on the billboard or a shopping bag. Most companies spend years and millions of dollars developing their brand. They don't like having to add .com or a country code extension to the brand. In some parts of the world .com is seen as being the American extension; in other parts ccTLDs are seen as political, inextricably associated with the party in power. It is a confusing hierarchy of extensions that consumers do not understand. If consumers can see that brands are in the browser and can find them without going through a search engine then that is an interesting development and probably a good thing. Do I really want to count on Google offering free search forever? Putting your brand in the browser where your consumer can find it with total trust is a really interesting concept."

Nick Wood, Managing Director, Com Laude

Chapter Five Highlights

- The implications of the new top-level domain program on search are far reaching. Most companies rely on search to drive consumers to their website. Apps are largely taking over search. So, what happens with search—no one knows for sure.
- Existing search algorithms like Google, Bing, and Yahoo! operate by crawling millions of available pages and evaluating certain key criteria, such as the number of other sites linking, content, frequency of updating, and relevance to the scope of the search.
- Current search indexing does not weight heavily to top-level domain, but in theory, this would have to change when we go from 21 generic top-level domains to more than a thousand.
- Our thought leaders offered a few predictions:
  - New search mechanisms that are more focused could emerge, such as top-level domains dedicated to searching specific categories of search.
  - Big search engines could splinter their search to provide for more customized user-based experiences.
  - Big search engines may begin to charge in a different way to use their search engine. Consumers could pay a premium for better search and companies may pay even more for enhanced results.

- Ultimately, search could be used less once people understand how to navigate the new Internet. Then, they may have a few go-to sites and spend most of their time there.
- Brands have an incredible opportunity to redirect how people find them and reevaluate their entire search strategy. Now is the time.

Chapter Six

Forecasting the Future

This is definitely a time when forecasting the future of your brand is really about creating and protecting the future for your brand. Entrepreneurs and savvy global giants will profit from and dominate the new Internet. But, will future opportunities be available to do the same? How can you create your own future in the new top-level domain Internet world?

We've already discussed how the .com bubble and social media changed everything without notice. It doesn't take a PhD in history to know that any type of expansion of the most powerful communication tool ever to be used by humans will change the way we live and work. It simply can't and won't stay the same. And, when you consider that some of the world's leading technology companies will likely apply for top-level domains and will seek out opportunities to monetize it—meaning shift consumer use of the Internet—then it becomes clear we need to start to think about this differently. Once you accept those fundamental truths, we can look to other paradigm shifts or big changes for guidance. Our thought leaders, too, have helped us to piece together likely scenarios of what will happen.

A History Lesson

Let's take a look at a few paradigm shifts that could serve as guidance to us.

ZIP Codes Arose Out of Necessity and Then Created an Industry

In 1930, the U.S. Postal Service still moved the bulk of its domestic mail by rail through the major railroad hubs of the nation. More than 10,000 mail-carrying trains crisscrossed the country, moving around the clock into virtually every village and metropolitan area. By 1963, fewer trains, making fewer stops, carried the mail. In these same years, 1930 to 1963, the United States underwent many changes. It suffered through a prolonged and paralyzing depression, fought its second World War of the twentieth century, and moved from an agricultural economy to a highly industrial global leader in business.

The social correspondence of the earlier century evolved in an accelerating pace to business mail. By 1963, business mail constituted 80 percent of the total volume. The single greatest catalyst for the exponentially increased volume of business mail was the computer, which brought centralization of accounts and a growing mass of utility bills and payments, bank deposits and receipts, advertisements, magazines, insurance premiums, credit card transactions, department store and mortgage billings, payments, dividends, and Social Security checks traveling through the mail.

In June 1962, an Advisory Board of the Post Office department made several primary recommendations. Most importantly, and similar to the expansion of the Internet, the department was to give priority to the development of a coding system.

Over the years a number of potential coding programs had been examined and abandoned. Finally, in 1963, the department selected a system advanced by department officials, and, on April 30, 1963,

Postmaster General John A. Gronouski announced that the ZIP code would begin on July 1, 1963.

By July 1963, a five-digit code had been assigned to every address throughout the country. The first digit designated a broad geographical area of the United States, ranging from zero for the Northeast to nine for the far West. Two digits follow this and more closely pinpoint population concentrations and sectional centers accessible to common transportation networks. The final two digits designate small post offices or postal zones in larger zoned cities.

ZIP Code began on July 1, 1963, as scheduled. Use of the new code was not mandatory at first for anyone, but, in 1967, the Post Office required mailers of second- and third-class bulk mail to presort by ZIP Code. What followed in the years to come was an expansion of the use of mail and the ability to target specific households in specific areas meeting certain demographics to marketers, allowing for greater specialization. An industry was born, including direct mail providers, advertisers, printers, paper companies, market research companies, and the like. All because of ZIP codes. Could gTLDs be the ZIP codes of the Internet—providing us guiding sources to find what we want more easily or deliver content to use based upon segmentations much greater than just where we live?

Railroads, Like gTLDs, Met with Opposition

The development of railroads was one of the most important phenomena of the Industrial Revolution. With their formation, construction, and operation, they brought profound social, economic, and political change to a country only 50 years old. Over the next 50 years, America saw bridges, depots, and other structures that displayed the glory of rail locomotives crossing the country.

Baltimore, the third largest city in the nation in 1827, had not yet invested in a canal. But Baltimore was 200 miles closer to the frontier of the West than New York and soon recognized that the development of a railway could make the city more competitive with New York and the Erie Canal for transporting people and goods to the West. The result was the Baltimore and Ohio Railroad, the first railroad chartered in the United States. Others soon followed. Although the first railroads were successful, attempts to finance new ones originally failed as turnpike operators, canal companies, stagecoach companies, and those who drove wagons mounted opposition. Tavern owners and innkeepers whose businesses were threatened also mounted opposition. But the economic benefits of the railroad soon won over the skeptics. Shares were sold to fund the construction of the B&O Railroad. In only 12 days, the company raised over $4,000,000. Perhaps the greatest physical success of nineteenth-century America was the creation of the transcontinental railroad. Two railroads, the Central Pacific starting in San Francisco, and a new railroad, the Union Pacific, starting in Omaha, Nebraska, would build the rail-line. The two railroads met at Promontory, Utah, on May 10, 1869, and drove a last, golden spike into the completed railway, changing forever the way people would live their lives. It's not surprising that in hindsight we understand the importance of the railroad system. Change is usually met with resistance, particularly by those who stand to lose business or standing. And, they often cry out that consumers don't want it or need it and it's just too costly for everyone to even consider.

These arguments have been put forth in the gTLD debate, but also in the debate against the railroad system. This is why there has been such resistance to the gTLD program. Most people couldn't understand why it was necessary or why it would benefit consumers. But, businesses will find a way. Brands are concerned about the cost to protect them, but this transition may be what is needed to reform the cybersquatting industry. The change is coming, like railroads, and it could change everything in the next generation of the Internet.

Software as an Industry?

In 1981, when Bill Gates sold his computer operating system to IBM, he specifically carved out the software from the deal. IBM didn't think software was a stand-alone product so they agreed. Years later, Microsoft is one of the largest companies in the world and fuels the technical infrastructure of global businesses. It was referred to as the Deal of the Century and put Microsoft on the map. A single transaction created the software industry. But, it's more than just the transaction. It's that the establishment of the time didn't believe that software was a product or an industry. In hindsight it seems shortsighted, but even the great and powerful IBM missed this one.

So, it's not surprising that very smart people are opposing the top-level domains. It's hard to take risks and see changes coming. It's hard to believe or get behind something that might not work, particularly for established players. That's why it takes entrepreneurial thinkers, people like Bill Gates, who are willing to think outside the box about the possibilities to advance technology, society, and business.

"An important history lesson to consider as the Internet evolves is to look at the auto industry. In 1945, World War II came to an end. The German and Japanese economies were decimated. The United States helped them rebuild their infrastructure and industry. American industry and particularly the Big Three American car companies experienced an unprecedented time of growth and prosperity. By the 1970s, though, the gas crisis hit and Volkswagen and Toyota, with smaller, more fuel-efficient cars, were winning in the battle of the marketplace. Detroit failed to see the need to innovate and didn't want to think that anything would change. By 2008, they were asking the U.S. government to bail them out."

J. Scott Evans, Senior Legal Director, Head of Global Brand, Domains & Copyright at Yahoo! Inc.

It's much easier to think that nothing will change and do nothing. That's why so many very large companies, with the financial wherewithal to purchase a top-level domain, failed to do so. It's hard to innovate—it takes a lot of work. But, it's not too late for companies large and small.

"The biggest issue for consumers and the next generation of Internet users is that ICANN follows through on providing proper mechanisms for consumer protection and security. This ultimately means brand protection.

(*continued*)

If ICANN does its best to ensure that consumers are not confused and does not foster, facilitate, or permit squatting, then this could be good for consumers. Consumers could find that certain gTLDs such as .bank may actually provide greater security and protection than bank sites in .com. This could be true in a number of categories. Most of us in the brand community are pleased that ICANN has put in place the Uniform Rapid Suspension (URS) and the Trademark Clearinghouse mechanisms, but also believe that ICANN could have done more to protect brand owners and that they should continue to be accountable to brand owners as part of their duty to consumers and the Internet ecosystem as a whole. ICANN will have a delicate balancing act as the Internet expands to ensure that brand owners are protected, businesses can function, the technical infrastructure is stable, and that consumers are protected, all while providing free access to information and speech."

Fabricio Vayra, Trademark Attorney, Time Warner Inc.

"Broadcast television and the distribution of all entertainment will change. Just as the music industry had to change, so will television and films. An important lesson, though, from the music industry: the legitimate distribution models succeed. The illegitimate ones fail."

J. Scott Evans, Senior Legal Director, Head of Global Brand, Domains & Copyright at Yahoo! Inc.

"It's hard to determine exactly what will happen. The biggest issue for most brand owners is the question of whether this was really necessary. Will the societal benefit of expanding the Internet really justify the cost? Maybe for users in some specific instances it will, but for brand owners, only a select few will really figure it out. So while the future is hard to see, there is a real question for a lot of brand owners as to whether this was really necessary. For those companies that just acquired their top-level domains to make sure no one else acquired them, the looming question will be whether they do anything differently or innovatively from what they were doing on .com. "

Adam Scoville, Trademark and Brand Protection Counsel, RE/MAX

"There certainly will be opportunities for generating revenue, but how much is anyone's guess. By way of example, .mobi has received a lot of attention since its launch in 2006 because of its current success in registering approximately 1 million domain names. Assuming .mobi domain names cost $8 per year to renew, .mobi would have grossed $8 million in revenue just from yearly renewal fees. On the other hand, a company operating a closed registry would not have the same revenue stream, but perhaps they would say, 'We moved up in position and beat our competitors by building a stronger connection with consumers through our branded gTLD.'"

Nancy Lutz and Yasmin Tavakoli of Kelley Drye & Warren, LLP

"It's really difficult to predict what will happen because we've never had this many. Usually there have been one or maybe two top-level domains launched at a time but never 500 to 1,000. Most of those were considered failures. The ones that have succeeded are not simply running a top-level domain registry, but by using their infrastructure to actually run the back end for third parties (like many of the new gTLD applicants in this round). Most companies are being very secretive about their plans. Why would they announce their business strategy? This makes it hard to predict, but it is going to change. This will have a powerful impact on developing countries and countries that function in languages other than Latin-based languages. This will open up the Internet in a whole new way for them."

J. Scott Evans, Senior Legal Director, Head of Global Brand, Domains & Copyright at Yahoo! Inc.

"The new TLDs will spur innovative thinking. It already has. Prior to .biz and the other TLDs being launched in 2001, VeriSign was running their registries using on an antiquated protocol. But in 2001, with the new gTLDs, a new standard came out when the pool of registry operators expanded. I truly believe that without the new registries in 2001 introducing competition into the marketplace, some of the innovations such as dynamic updates, DNS security extensions, thick Whois, and other innovative uses of the DNS would have never come to fruition. Since we have

(*continued*)

these registries in place there have been drastic improvements on the registrar and registry market. Most registries in the future will not be able to just have the .com model associated with selling names—they will need to have other services that they offer. This will provide high levels of service and protect users."

Jeff Neuman, VP, Business Affairs, Enterprise
Services, Neustar, Inc.

"If it turns out that this makes it easier to find information, the people who have gTLDs will have a big advantage to protect and promote their brand."

Cynthia Gibson, Executive Vice President Legal Affairs,
Scripps Networks Interactive Inc.

"Brands sold primarily online could benefit from a top-level domain by providing authenticity and overcoming counterfeiting. They'll need to educate consumers, though, to go to their top-level domain versus any other website on the Internet. For consumer goods sold through retail, this may not have as big of an impact."

Steven Miller and Katherine Ruwe, Procter & Gamble

"When assessing the impact of unlimited new gTLDs on the public interest, the main determination will be whether their potential benefits, such as possible improvements in online communication, exceed the external costs of expansion, such as consumer confusion and the misappropriation of intellectual property."

Claudio Di Gangi, Manager, External Relations, Internet and the
Judiciary, International Trademark Association

"I think you'll see increased M&A activity because some companies didn't buy and want in. You'll also see some players acquire generics because there is a mistaken belief that running a registry is like printing money. But there is a lot of responsibility in running a registry. It's part of the fabric of the Internet and a lot goes into running such critical infrastructure. A lot of people think this business is something that is easy to do and anyone can start it. There will be some failures out there and other registries will be there to pick them up "

Jeffrey J. Neuman, Vice President, Business Affairs,
Enterprise Services, Neustar, Inc.

"There will be a resegmentation of the domain name space. We will see innovations we never dreamed of and people will use domain names and navigate the Internet differently than they today. It's up to you—the top-level domain owners—will you give them a better experience? That is what will drive usage."

Krista Papac, Chief Strategy Officer, ARI Registry Services

"This will create a new digital nomenclature. Internet media is critical to businesses to bolster their brands. There are likely to be 1,000 to 2,000 applications in this round and most of those will be branded applications filed by strategic enterprises. The remainder will be .generics—an entrepreneur or current industry player who wants to sell domains to the public. There will be many geographic TLDs who want to sell domain names to the public as well. The brand registries will be almost entirely closed. So, for example, .att—if AT&T applied for and got it—will be a closed system. A myth that exists is that consumer behavior will have to change. I don't believe that to be true. These brands are already spending billions in advertising and will continue to do so. As soon as they all start redirecting consumers to .brand, they will get it and adjust their behavior."

Josh Bourne, Managing Partner, FairWinds Partners

"It's easy to 'panic' when seeing the list of the anticipated more than 2,000 TLDs. It's important to remember that not all new TLDs are going to prove viable. Companies may care to let some of the dust settle in determining their registration and enforcement of second-level domains."

Ellen Shankman, Principal, Ellen B. Shankman & Associates, Rehovot, Israe

Interactive Initiatives and their Outcomes

For other guidance on what to expect, let's look at a few more recent innovative interactive initiatives and their outcomes.

CNN—iReport Website

The Story   In 2006, CNN first created its iReport initiative. The initiative was designed to have individuals from all over the world aggregate and share anything they deemed newsworthy in the form of video, images, text, and audio. It began after user-coverage of Hurricane Katrina, the Asian tsunami, and the London bombings was seen as more compelling and timely than what traditional news outlets were able to create and compose.

The site was launched as a subpage of CNN in August 2006, but after its popular inception, CNN later acquired the domains iReport .com and I-Report.com for $750,000 and on February 13, 2008, a beta site was launched, with a complete launch following a month later.

Risk versus Reward   The biggest risk with CNN's iReport campaign was whether they would be able to trust user-generated content (UGC). What they found was that UGC could be successful with the combination of unique human viewpoints, professional journalism, and the ability to filter and curate the material. CNN has more than 753,000 iReporters registered all over the world and has received an iReport from every country in the world, with an average of 15,391 iReports each month, but they only vet between 5 to 10 percent of the iReports that are received. They have created a best-of-both-worlds scenario, where they have access to an abundance of real-time breaking news with the ability to filter and edit it.

Outcome   The outcome is that CNN's iReport site has an average of 2.1 million unique users each month, after less than five years of being launched. In 2007, the *New York Times* even described the word I-Reporter as one of 2007's buzzwords. Since then, CNN International has gone on to create an international, weekly half-hour TV show showcasing the most newsworthy and entertaining iReports on the site.

Overstock.com — o.co Rebranding

In 2010, Overstock.com spent $350,000 in a purchase deal to buy o.co from the Colombia-based domain registry *.co*. Currently o.co is being redirected to overstock.com, but they have already incorporated the change into their new logo of "o.co . . . also known as overstock.com." See http://adage.com/article/news/overstock-rebranded-o/227995/ for more information.

The Story

Risk versus Reward The genesis of the .co domain is through Colombia, and while country codes usually take a hit in Google rankings, .co is part of a unique set of ccTLDs (.tv, .me, .co) which are treated like gTLDs or generic domains like .com, .net, or .org. While .co is about to hit its one millionth registered domain in little under a year of service, and is about to set up a stable pricing plan for one letter and two letter domains, it is still extremely unknown to the public and, compared to .com's hundred-million-plus domains, is relatively unproven.

Outcome While it's still early to gage the success of Overstock.com's rebranding, polled users agree that the site is easier to access, view in mobile devices, and remember. In addition, the new domain minimizes confusion and hassle when translating the word Overstock into other languages, so the company can rebrand internationally with not only a universal domain but with a logo that is recognizable all over the world. In an interview with Overstock's CEO Patrick Byrne, he says that the percentage of people using o.co versus the traditional URL is going up substantially every day and that ".co is more consistent with how we're trying to brand ourselves now, as a savings engine. It's the simplest way to explain what we do."

Facebook Connect

The Story

In 2007, Facebook launched a new feature called Beacon; with its purpose being to allow advertisers to publish activities on a user's news feed as well as allow users to share third-party links with other Facebook users. The service was controversial and became the target of a class action lawsuit in September 2009. The lawsuit alleged that Facebook and its Beacon affiliates violated a series of laws, including the Electronic Communications Privacy Act, the Video Privacy Protection Act, the California Consumer Legal Remedies Act, and the California Computer Crime Law. Because of the suit, Beacon was eventually shut down. The controversy was based on privacy issues; users didn't want to see information or advertisements they hadn't requested, as well as they didn't want their activity published on third-party sites without their consent. While the Internet is open and built for collaboration, individuals are still concerned about their security and that's where Facebook went wrong. So in 2009, they tried again with a new service called Facebook Connect and this time got it right.

Risk versus Reward   After the demise of Beacon, it was a risk for Facebook to attempt another third-party integration service. In their settlement, not only did they have to discontinue the Beacon service but also create an independent foundation devoted to promoting online privacy, safety, and security, with money coming from a $9.5 million settlement fund. But Facebook was determined to create an integration service because they knew it was a risk that would pay off if they did it right, allowing users the ability to fully collaborate on the web.

The first thing they did was to adjust the name to stay consistent with their brand and for a sense of legitimacy. The new service simply offered third-party sites the opportunity for all Facebook users to connect external content with their Facebook accounts. The service promoted security by having users sign-in with their Facebook username and passwords before allowing any information to be shared between sites. Facebook Connect made it easier for users to take their online identity all over the web and share their interests while still promoting security.

Outcome   By September 2009, Facebook launched Facebook Connect on mobile sites and applications just as it did on the web, joining over 10,000 websites and applications that had already integrated the service.

By the end of the year, sites that used Facebook Connect as an alternate to account registration saw a 30 to 200 percent increase in registrations on their sites; a 15 to 100 percent increase in reviews and other user-generated content; and for each story published on Facebook, they saw roughly three clicks back to the site. Nearly half the stories in the Facebook News Feed get clicked on. This creates opportunities for the site to encourage more user actions—knowing that each one may result in three new visits to their site. With other models like search, there's nothing you can do to increase user traffic besides optimizing for keywords.

Interestingly, none of the companies referenced above with forward thinking digital strategies applied for a gTLD. Perhaps they've had enough risk in the digital world for now, but it is interesting to see them take such risks in some areas and not in others with regard to an evolving digital landscape.

Chapter Six Highlights

- Understanding what might happen as the Internet changes requires looking at historical paradigm shifts. History has taught us that most changes of big proportion come with opposition. Most people don't like change. But change is required for innovation to occur.
- When ZIP codes were introduced, they were intended to segment the United States and make mail delivery easier and faster. It helped create a direct mail industry and change the way companies market their products and services to consumers. It was the birth of market segmentation based upon geographic location.
- The canal companies, turnpike operators, stagecoach companies, and wagon drivers, as well as the tavern owners and innkeepers who served them, initially opposed railroads. No one thought they were needed at the time.
- Bill Gates sold his computer system to IBM in 1981 and carved out software from the deal. IBM didn't think software was a stand-alone industry, just like some don't think we will ever evolve from .com.
- The United States auto industry was on top of the world and a leader in making cars after World War II because they were the only game in town. Believing nothing needed to change, however, they found themselves out-innovated when the German and Japanese industries were rebuilt and became fierce competitors. Years later the auto industry needed a bailout from the U.S. government because they failed to innovate or believe the change from big cars to small, efficient cars was coming.

- As we compare the rules and framework of what's coming with past paradigm shifts and what our thought leaders have told us, a few key predictions emerge:
  - A few top levels will emerge as a trusted go-to source for managing life, business, and interests.
  - More companies will have the ability to participate in communities than in the current fragmented .com space. Because more centralized sources for key themes will emerge, this means it will actually get easier to be connected to the community you want.
  - Search will get easier because you can narrow in on the playing field within which you search. More niche search engines will emerge.
  - Early adopters will capitalize on the loyalty of community followers—members of their organizations or top-level domains—and this access to information will be worth billions to advertisers.
  - The latecomers will quickly jump on the bandwagon and find ways to participate, but the early adopters will already have paved the roads.
  - Cable will disappear—mobile devices, tablets, and the ability to find channels on the expanded Internet will replace traditional television and cable.
  - Movies and all entertainment will change and need to find ways to respond to specific community groups demanding content to make them cry, laugh, think, and be connected in a meaningful way to other people.
  - The shift from technology interfering with direct human interaction will actually change and bolster the desire to be a part of a community—but now a global community empowered by a new Internet.
  - Independent and niche programs, content, and entertainment will emerge—small guys could actually have more power than the big guys.
  - Devices and tools to create content at home by the ampro (amateur professional) will continue to emerge with more and more power.

- Global giants will no longer determine what products to create; consumers will forecast their needs in an online community and savvy companies and entrepreneurs will respond successfully.
- Service providers who create communities and build a following will be more successful than those who continue to just run brochureware on a .com
- .com will ultimately symbolize antiquated or not cool—remember the world before emails—remember when everything was .com?
- A new way of thinking about the Internet and our digital world will emerge and people will rely more on finding what they want when a company has its own top-level domain or belongs to a trusted community's top-level domain.

Chapter Seven

Rewiring the Internet

"This may break the perception of the .com monopoly."

Josh Bourne, Managing Partner, FairWinds Partners

When the new top-level domains launch into action, the entire Internet will be rewired. Throughout the prior chapters, we weaved together predictions from the world's biggest branding companies, the technical specialists, and the organizations that run the Internet to offer a forecasting trend for this new regime based upon expert opinions and beliefs.

A Few Final Conclusions

The official statement from ICANN by Kurt Pritz during the Senate Commerce Subcommittee hearing on December 8, 2011, just a little over a month before the application period opened, included:

> The launch of the new gTLD program was part of ICANN's founding mandate when it was formed by the U.S. government over 12 years ago. That mandate is to introduce competition and choice into the domain name system in a stable and secure

manner. Every reason to believe that the benefits offered by competition in virtually every other market will apply to the introduction of new gTLDs. Expanding the number of TLDs will encourage innovation and result in competition and increased choice for Internet users. The seven years of policy work that led to the formation of the new gTLD program was based upon this principle. In the last decade, the number of domain name registrations has increased nearly tenfold, enabling more than $3 trillion of commerce annually. As with the introduction of any convention, the gTLDs will generate interest, excitement, and, yes, require a period of learning. Internet users have already shown a great adaptability, and they will find value wherever it is created as a result of this program.

The new TLDs that will come in under this program have significantly increased safeguards compared to TLDs that exist today. There will be new and extensive protections to trademark holders including a universal trademark clearinghouse, a rapid take-down process, and new methods of recourse for law enforcement agencies. These new protections, when combined with the distribution of the domain names into many new registries, will sharply reduce pressure for defensive registrations.

New TLDs will also bring better consumer and security protections. Security protection experts develop specific measures to combat malicious conduct and provide law enforcement authorities with more tools to fight malfeasance. These include criminal background checks on applicants, a requirement for DNSSEC deployment, the requirement for maintenance of a thick Whois database, and centralized access for TLD data. What are some of these potential innovations? Here are some published examples. Top brand-type TLDs can diminish consumer confusion and develop consumer awareness around the reliability of the website. This is similar to the trust that your constituents have today when visiting a dot-gov website. Consumers know when they type in senate.gov, they are reaching the domain of the U.S. Senate. Financial industry participants are considering a financial services TLD where banks and financial institutions can offer greater trust to their customers, more secure transactions, and control the data flow for those transactions.

There are new jobs already created and likely more to come. In preparation for the launch of new gTLDs, dozens of small businesses have sprung up to help new TLD applicants understand the opportunities and potential benefits of new TLDs. Lately, innovation has been limited to country-code TLDs, such as dot-co and dot-ly, that are developing business models to meet world demand. These TLDs are not under contract with ICANN and are not required to offer the protections available in the new gTLD program. The important issues under the construction of the gTLD committee have been the subject of discussion, debate, and compromise for the past few years.

Not-for-profit organizations and trademark holders, along with the rest of the ICANN community, provided focus and targeted input into the design of this program. Their input has yielded significant improvements through seven versions of the application. Its emphasis will reach across the spectrum of participants and the program is better for it. Many stakeholders not represented at this table have also participated in the program and are awaiting their opportunity to take part. Thanks for inviting me to testify. I'm happy to answer any questions you might have.

The primary opposition argument was based upon the cost to non-profits and brand owners. The following two arguments were made by Dan Jaffe, Executive Vice President of the Association of National Advertisers, and Angela Williams, the General Counsel of the YMCA.

The NPOC members, like most of not-for-profits, increasingly rely on the Internet to fulfill our missions as well as to raise funds. We share a growing concern that our ability to carry out our collective missions due to the enormous cost and financial burdens of the proposed structure of the new generic top-level domain name program will pose severe hardship and burdens on each of us. The new gTLD program compromises use of the

Internet by increasing the risk of fraud, cybersquatting, and trademark infringement, and by significantly escalating the cost to protect against such unlawful activities.

First, the immediate cost imposed on businesses is likely to be in the multi-billions of dollars. Some have estimated that for a typical company, the cost of acquiring a single, new gTLD and managing it could easily exceed 2 million dollars. Companies that are forced into an auction with another interested applicant will potentially face far higher costs. As many companies have hundreds or even thousands of brands to defend, it is easy to see how these costs would spiral upward.

Even ICANN's own economists recognize an unlimited expansion of gTLDs could cause serious economic harm to marketers. For example, ICANN's own phase two report noted that brand owners may be compelled to file "numerous defensive registrations to protect trademark and intellectual property rights from misuse"—these resources could be far more effectively used for job creation and productive capital investment.

Second, ICANN's protections for consumers in the gTLD program are woefully inadequate. Again, ICANN's own economic experts know that one of the most serious and costly challenges to the unlimited expansion of gTLDs was the harm to consumers from increased cybersquatting and related malware phishing and the unknowing purchase of counterfeit goods.

In 2009, a coalition of law enforcement agencies, including the U.S. Department of Justice and the FBI, issued a set of law enforcement due diligence recommendations for ICANN. These recommendations were intended to help prevent against cyber security threats. However, according to a communiqué from ICANN's own governmental advisory committee dated October 27, 2011, not one of law enforcement's 12 recommendations has been adopted. And yesterday FTC Chairman Jon Leibowitz, testifying before the House Judiciary Sub-Committee, stated that the unlimited gTLD roll out could be a "disaster for business and consumers," and could dramatically increase problems for law enforcement.

Third, we have serious concerns about the potential major conflicts of interest involving both the board and staff of ICANN. It is very troubling that many of the same individuals who approved the unlimited roll out of the gTLD program, including the former chairman, now stand to benefit substantially from the expansion program.

These are not just our concerns. The full European commission and ICANN's own governmental advisory committee have expressed "extreme concern about the inadequacy of the existing rules of ethics and conflicts of interest." We believe that the affirmation of commitments that ICANN agreed to in order to obtain the freedom to manage major functions of the Internet from the Department of Commerce are real commitments. They must not be allowed to become merely meaningless, high sounding platitudes.

This means that all Internet participants, and in particular the Department of Commerce, must take whatever steps are necessary to assure that the top-level domain policy is fully justified on a cost-benefit basis and provides strong and adequate protections for businesses, NGOs, and consumers, thereby furthering the public interest. That is simply not the case today. We hope that this hearing places a spotlight on these issues and will help to begin the process of careful reevaluation of the misguided ICANN top-level domain initiative. Thank you very much for your attention.

The final opposition argument by Esther Dyson, the founding chairman of ICANN from 1998 to 2000, was rooted in complexity, confusion, and the fundamental lack of need:

I'm the only person here talking on behalf of the real public, not on behalf of the large trademark owners, not on behalf of the businesses, not on behalf of government, not on behalf of non-profits, but actually on behalf of the users, who I think stand to be extremely confused if there is a proliferation of top-level domain names.

Either marriott.com and marriott.hotel are the same, in which case, marriott.hotel is simply redundant. Or they're different, in which case it's simply confusing. And multiply that by thousands of different top-level domains, dot-hotel, and then there is hotel.marriott, residenceinn.marriott—it creates a profusion of new things to protect without creating any additional value, because it remains only one Marriott. And that's why I think this whole idea is fundamentally misguided. It's akin to derivatives, which also create great complexity, new transactions, and yes, both derivatives and domain names create opportunities for entrepreneurs, but they don't really create any value for the economy. And that's my problem with this. I don't think any particular domain name is evil or illegal, but it's a big waste.

Finally, you could ask, what should ICANN do and what will happen if we have a lot of new domain names? I studied economics in college and I didn't learn a whole lot there, to be honest, but I did learn how to think. Fundamentally, economics is about math and common sense.

Right now, what we have is an artificially restricted scarcity of domain names. We can enlarge it, in which case it will be artificial and somewhat enlarged, but the same issues will happen. Or we can say, "We really believe in no scarcity at all. Let's have as many domain names as anybody wants." And then you don't really need ICANN, because there is nothing to protect. But in the middle, there is going to be a period of great confusion. In the long run, probably people will start looking for everything through the search engines, and so domain names won't matter.

But I don't think it makes sense to go through a period of several years where there's a profusion of domain names, a profusion of the kinds of costs Angela Williams and Dan Jaffe talked about. It just doesn't make sense. I understand ICANN is not responsible to Congress. I'm not suggesting that you guys do much other than what you are doing here, which is to raise the public's awareness of this issue, and then I hope that ICANN will go back and reconsider and somehow figure out how to actually get real consumers involved and maybe just stick to the international domain names which do make sense and actually are in fact properly regulated largely by other governments. But, in general, I don't see the point of this program. Thank you very much.

So there are the two basic arguments for and against the launch of the TLD. But, now it's gone forward. And we need to predict trends to help guide businesses, large and small, nonprofits, and other organizations to be prepared. Be prepared not just to protect your brand, but be prepared to transition your business strategy and Internet strategy to a new way of thinking. This can be a disruptive innovation to the fundamental way you think about the Internet.

"There are many changes in store for users. The really successful new top-level domains will be the ones that can distinguish themselves. They will succeed not just because they have a great name, but because of what they do with it."

Jeffrey J. Neuman, Vice President, Business Affairs, Enterprise Services, Neustar, Inc.

"I think we can expect certain brands—brands that were born of the Internet—to be amongst the leaders of the revolution that the new gTLDs are bringing. These companies all have very extensive distributed architectures and networks capable of supporting numerous software and platforms, and they have massive resources of technologists. In a way they have a walled garden. But to get into their walled garden, where their infrastructure and technologists are based, you currently have to go to the .com registry. This is a weakness. Their contract for their .com is via a third-party registrar, not directly with the registry, and they pay around $8 a year for what is arguably the most important asset of their business, the domain name which ensures they can be found on the web, that their email works, that e-commerce flows. If brands can control their own top-level domain—the

(continued)

entrance into their walled garden—that's very valuable and interesting for them. It is about the privatization of the domain name system. It gives them the ability to control their destiny and to ensure their visibility and independence from interference and attack. Their new gTLD registry, sited in a jurisdiction of choice, could become one of their most valuable assets."

Nick Wood, Managing Director, Com Laude

"Many companies that are applying for new gTLDs are doing so for defensive reasons only, not because the new gTLD is needed or wanted. They are worried about losing rights in their trademark to bad actors or allowing third parties to manage an important community space like a .bank."

Sarah Deutsch, Vice President and Associate General Counsel,
Verizon Communications

What If You Missed the Boat?

Most important to branding executives and business leaders is what to do if your company didn't apply for a top-level domain. There are a number of important strategies for building the operational plan if you did apply. But since the vast majority of our readers didn't, we want to focus on what to do now. If you did apply and need help, see Chapter One and our website at www.domainnamesrewired.com. Understanding the role of the generics and community sites and looking for opportunities to quickly buy real estate within the generics and community top levels will be more important than ever.

In addition to the defensive/offensive strategy mapped out in Chapter Four, it's time to start evaluating your Internet strategy. First, start with assumptions and evaluate your overall business strategy.

"If you missed the boat and think you should have been on it, then you want to lobby ICANN to open up the second round as soon as possible. If you didn't want to
(*continued*)

> be on the boat, then you must still carefully monitor what is happening. Your domain registration strategy cannot be expanded from a world where there are just under 300 TLD extensions to a world with over 1,000. You really need to think about your branding and communication strategy. The new gTLDs are about disruptive innovation. You can't contain them or eliminate them. You must adapt to them by evolving your thinking."
>
> Nick Wood, Managing Director, Com Laude

Begin with the End in Mind

Coined by Stephen Covey in *The 7 Habits of Highly Effective People*, the statement "Begin with the end in mind" continues to provide guidance for any type of strategy. To build your plan for the next generation of the Internet you have to start with the end in mind. A few starting questions:

- Map the landscape of your competitors' Internet strategy, domains and presence. Then map your entire market industry.
- What aligns with your business strategy?
- Where can you be a market leader in an important new top-level domain?
- What are your short- and long-term goals?
- How does your current Internet strategy work in the new landscape?
- Can you map it out against competitors?
- Do you need disruptive innovation now? Is this the catalyst?
- Can your .com strategy just evolve or do you need to reinvent it?

It's usually a good idea to start any strategy with assumptions. We've mapped out our predictions for how this will play out in Chapter Six so you could use that as a base of assumptions or create your own. But, write them down—what do you assume will happen as the new Internet takes shape? Then continue asking yourself important questions:

- Where will my consumers go if I don't adapt?
- What is my biggest competitive threat? Direct? Indirect?
- What are my strengths and how I can play to those?

- What are my weaknesses and how do I overcome them?
- Do I need help to find answers to these questions? Will I need resources that I don't have?
- What budget is required? Can I cut costs somewhere to cover new costs associated with a changing Internet strategy?
- If this does change everything about the way people use the Internet, how will it impact my bottom line?
- What can I do about it?
- If I had endless financial resources, what would I do?
- Now, how do I bootstrap and do that for less?

Also, remember one important fact. Even if you didn't get a top-level domain, success is wholly dependent upon execution. I can give you the best ideas in the world—tell you about Microsoft, Facebook, or Google—but if you don't believe them and don't build a model to execute around them, they won't work. Lots of great ideas failed at execution. And, failed execution is usually not about having enough money, but about having the right people, the right leadership, process, and incentives.

This is worth repeating: Execution is everything. The team who will execute is everything. You need people on your Internet strategy team who believe in disruptive innovation—who believe in new ways of thinking—who aren't afraid to take risks. There are and always will be good ideas, but doing something with them is a different story. This is why we cannot overemphasize the importance of planning. The next generation of the Internet is coming. You have advance notice to prepare—it's like a massive business tsunami about to change the landscape. It's coming and you need to be prepared defensively and offensively. You have time, but you have to start now. The strategic thinking required to be successful requires a top-notch, fully invested team of internal and external people whose jobs are on the line to figure this out.

So, once you have built your own business strategy to use the next generation of the Internet, let's take a look at a few generalized tools available.

Generic and Community Sites

Once you develop your strategy, survey the landscape of the generic and community sites that impact your industry. Map them out along with your competitors to try and predict what competitors will do and where you want to be. Likewise, map out sites you think will be important to your customers and stakeholders. How will they be using these sites? What can and should you apply for? Community sites may provide a greater badge of authenticity and may be held to a higher standard in the minds of consumers, so if counterfeiting is a problem in your business this is definitely something for you to look to. Of course, once you determine where you want to be, you have to go back to your strategy and figure out how to execute that plan, Securing the real estate is important, but moving consumers is another.

Also, remember to piggyback of what others are doing. Monitor Google, Amazon, and Microsoft, to see what and how they are maneuvering. Where they go, others will follow.

Geographic Sites

Depending upon your business model, geographic sites may be very important. For example, if you are in the restaurant or entertainment business—any business where people still actually go to a physical location—you will want to register on these geographic sites. For example, yourbusiness.nyc. Or, consider partnering with a geographic site to help build a generic such as restaurants.nyc or restaurants.cincinnati. They or local associations may be open to partnering with you if you take a community activist approach. This not only helps you build your strategy, but to be a leader in building the community online.

Backup Plans

Build in backup plans. While there are safeguards in place, if your entire strategy is built around a generic or community and they fail entirely or just fail to generate the critical mass anticipated (such as .tv or .travel), you will want to continue to have other strategies and build plans in tandem with one another. Sometimes you have to throw a lot up and see what sticks and then throw everything you have behind what sticks. Like any uncharted business territory, we can use past experience and similar paradigm shifts for guidance, but we can never be 100 percent certain of what will happen. Accordingly, build in backup plans so that wherever the next generation takes us you are ready.

Acquire or Partner

Of course, if you didn't get in and want to be in quickly, you can acquire a site or a company with a top-level domain that fits your strategy. Alternatively, you can find other domain owners that might partner with you. Use your map of competitors and your industry on the Internet to identify potential partners or acquisition sources. Can you license, collaborate, or in some way leverage your success with someone else's?

Don't Sit on the Sidelines

This next generation of the Internet creates new global opportunities for businesses around the planet to be connected in a deeper way and create a universal language of branding on the Internet. Use this as an opportunity to think about new opportunities and find ways to be engaged. And, if you think a top-level domain is right for you, carefully monitor ICANN. The plan is that if all goes well, they'll do this again.

"With the expectation there will be over 1,000 applications for new gTLDs, trademark owners will need to pay close attention to the changing landscape on many fronts. For example, we may see an emergence of industry-specific top-level domains, many with restricted registration requirements. The National Association of Boards of Pharmacy (NABP) has indicated it may apply for .pharmacy to protect consumers and ensure that only legitimate pharmacies can apply for a second-level domain. This could lead to improvements in consumer trust, as users might count on going to a 'mylocal.pharmacy' domain to find a legitimate pharmacy site, as they might currently visit a '.gov' or '.edu' domain with a higher level of confidence in finding a government or educational institution. However, industry and governments will need to monitor that industry-specific domains do not create a false sense of consumer or regulatory protection that may not otherwise exist."

Claudio Di Gangi, Manager, External Relations, Internet and the Judiciary, International Trademark Association

(continued)

"The reality is that ICANN has made commitments to the governments and the Internet community to thoroughly review the process and make sure there is time to implement changes for the next round of applications. If the first TLD doesn't launch until 2013, then it would seem unlikely that ICANN would be able to complete such a review prior to the evaluation of all of the new gTLD applications and a thorough analysis of what went right and wrong with the process. This could be as late as 2014 and changes have to be implemented based upon what was learned. By the time the policy and implementation changes are made it is at least 2015 to 2016 before this opens up again.

.com is not dead. None of the existing TLDs or country codes is dead. A small business owner should not worry about all the extensions, but really focus on those extensions that affect their immediate business. The days of concern that you have to register in every single typo or formulation of your domain are over or should be over very soon. You have to be selective on the ones that you really believe that if someone else were to have it would create consumer confusion.

For those too late to the game, you will see your competitors using the domain name space in an innovative way. Unfortunately they are going to be faced with a long delay before this opens up again. Three to four years in the Internet business is a game changer."

Jeffrey J. Neuman, Vice President, Business Affairs, Enterprise Services, Neustar, Inc.

"Brand owners should be able to save enormous amounts of money in this next generation of the Internet if they can evolve their defensive strategies. By the time the second application round has closed it won't be necessary to maintain thousands and thousands of defensive domain names just to ensure no one else takes them. Internet users will expect all major trademark owners to have a new gTLD. They won't look for them under.com or the ccTLDs or irrelevant new gTLDs but will go straight for Dot-brand. .Com will remain very valuable in the short term, but in the long term it could well be seen as the untrusted, unregulated, old-school extension where anybody can register anything. Of course there will be short-term

(continued)

uncertainty and increased costs because no right-minded brand owner is going to delete all of their portfolio. However, with 50 new registry launches a month from 2013 onwards, blanket defensive registration will become unaffordable and brand owners, like Internet users, will have to change their thinking."

Nick Wood, Managing Director, Com Laude

"If you didn't apply, you will want to evaluate opportunities to partner with someone who did apply. There will likely be clear strategic applicants with sophisticated plans. They will develop the secondary market for those that didn't apply."

Cynthia Gibson, Executive Vice President Legal Affairs, Scripps Networks Interactive Inc.

"We ran the numbers on how long it will take ICANN to churn through the applications, and then added that to the 12-month review period required by the Government Advisory Committee, plus the time it will take for a new policy development process for a second round of applications, and at this point, it appears that, at the earliest, it will be five to seven years before ICANN can hold a second round."

Josh Bourne, Managing Partner, FairWinds Partners

"Until now most brand owners were relegated to the Intellectual Property Constituency (IPC) playground at ICANN—not the most popular group there. Once brand owners become registry operators, effectively 'owning' Internet real estate and thus contracted parties within ICANN, it's going to be a whole new ballgame of potential influence."

Ellen Shankman, Principal, Ellen B. Shankman & Associates, Rehovot, Israel

A Few Key Predictions

From our interviews and research, we have identified a few key predictions.

Economic Impact

- .com strategies that don't evolve will fail.
- The value of your .com will be diluted.
- Many of the generic TLD businesses will fail and new business models will emerge just as in the dot-com era.
- There will be increased merger and acquisition activity because large companies that did not apply will look for companies that did apply and adopt successful strategies to acquire.
- This will likely spawn innovative activity that may lead to an increase in IPOs of the companies that get it right. IPOs always follow innovative or disruptive technology as a quick and fast way to generate capital and grow at an accelerated rate.
- A flurry of IPOs and mergers and acquisitions could boost global economies.
- There will initially be increased costs to businesses, but those that restructure their approach will realize more economies of scale.
- Businesses will become more fragmented into specific communities. While the global nature of our economy and the impact on the economy proliferates, consumers will function in smaller communities from supporting local businesses to participating in lifestyle-oriented groups with like-minded individuals.
- Businesses will shift how they spend their advertising dollars in an accelerated and dramatic way.
- Big companies will invest and spur innovation to obtain a return on investment.
- Invention and inventors will follow dollars from the large companies, looking to monetize their top-level domain investment.

Societal Impact

- Use of the Internet and online experiences will dramatically change within the first 18 months of the launch.
- Elimination of cable and traditional television will accelerate.
- Advertising trends and shifts toward digital, social, and community will accelerate.
- Consumers and businesses alike will want everything customized and tailored to them and they will want to participate in content creation.
- Mail will continue to disappear in favor of a customized world online. Most businesses may start to charge consumers for delivery

and payment of bills through traditional mail rather than online. Consumers will be incented to do more online.

- Good content, entertainment, and community interaction in a simplified way will be critical to consumers—the companies that build it will succeed and those that don't will fail.
- Brick-and-mortar retailers will need to become an entertainment destination for consumers to continue to come in to the actual store, and they will need to tie their in-store experience to savings when purchasing other products online. Like Apple, the store is so much more than just a store.

Government and Regulatory Impact

- With the expanded pool of registry operators as brand owners, brand owners will have more influence within the ICANN community and have the power to increase protection for brand owners and stop cybersquatters.
- The global economy and connectedness by the Internet will require more countries to participate in anticounterfeiting and protection of intellectual property rights to protect its citizens.
- If companies expand their lobbying effort for worldwide laws and agreements to protect brand rights and stop counterfeiting and cybersquatting, consumers will benefit. This could be the single greatest benefit to consumers that comes from this program—now there is a strong enough lobby to stop counterfeiting on the Internet.

Technological Impact

- There will be new ways of navigating the Internet—accessing communities, apps, and disruptive innovation will result.
- Search won't die, but must evolve. Apps and tools that get people to exactly what they want faster will become more prevalent.
- Search will change and become more focused on specific categories rather than broad universal searching.
- There will be an ever-increasing dependence on customization online.
- Cloud computing will accelerate in a world that is easier to own and maintain top-level domains.
- Disruptive innovators could have dramatic shifts on how traditional businesses distribute their products and services.

How long until all of this happens? Based upon our interviews and research, we believe there is likely a 12- to 18-month adoption window once new top-level domains go live and within three years when the second round of applications is in process, many of these changes will be underway. For businesses, this means mapping your industry and competitors to understand where you fit, and mapping your customers, consumers, vendors, and supply chain to identify new, disruptive thinking and opportunities to give you a leading edge. Of course, you also need to audit your brands and domain names and determine how you cost effectively protect your brand in this new Internet. We detailed the process and steps in Chapter Four. There is no question that opportunity exists on many levels for businesses of all sizes to be a first mover in this next generation of the Internet. As with any emerging trend, we can simply report on it and advise on what we see the leading companies doing. The rest is up to you.

"Opportunity is missed by most people because it is dressed in overalls and looks like work."

Thomas Alva Edison

Chapter Seven Highlights and Concluding Trends

- The debate over the top-level domain program was hotly debated. Just a few weeks before the application period opened, the Senate Commerce Subcommittee called for testimony on the subject.
- Those for the program cited innovation, new opportunities in all languages of the world, and expanding a saturated .com universe as reasons for moving forward.
- Those against said it was too costly for existing brand owners, that no one wanted it or needed it, and it would just confuse everyone.
- Despite the debate, the program has gone forward. The debate will now continue on how to continue to evolve and better protect brand owners and Internet users from the bad actors who cybersquat and counterfeit on the Internet.
- For companies that applied for a top-level domain, there are many new and exciting business models and opportunities for disruptive innovation that will require risk taking, leadership, and methodologies to evolve into a new way of thinking.

- For companies that did not apply, it's time to think carefully about how you can evolve your .com strategy into a new Internet strategy, including use of generic and community sites, geographic sites, acquisitions or partners, and getting fully engaged in what's happening so you can make decisions about applying in the second round, which will likely occur in the next two to three years.
- To summarize all of the predictions that emerged from our thought leaders and research:
  - .com strategies that don't evolve will fail.
  - Many of the generic TLD business will fail and new business models will emerge just as in the dot-com era.
  - There will be increased merger and acquisition activity because large companies that did not apply will look for companies that did apply and adopt successful strategies to acquire.
  - This will likely spawn innovative activity that may lead to an increase in IPOs of the companies that get it right. IPOs always follow innovative or disruptive technology as a quick and fast way to generate capital and grow at an accelerated rate.
  - There will initially be an increased cost to businesses, but those that restructure their approach will realize more economies of scale.
  - Businesses will become more fragmented into specific communities. While the global nature of our economy and the impact on the economy proliferates, consumers will function in smaller communities, from supporting local businesses to participating in lifestyle-oriented groups with like-minded individuals.
  - Big companies will invest and spur innovation to obtain a return on investment.
  - Invention and inventors will follow dollars from the large companies looking to monetize their top-level domain investment.
  - Elimination of cable and traditional television will accelerate. A few sources we trust will emerge as aggregators of content. Consumers will select a handful of sites and apps they trust to manage their entire life and world online.
  - Advertising trends and shifts toward digital, social, and community will accelerate.
  - Consumers and businesses alike will want everything customized and tailored to them and they will want to participate in content creation.

- Mail will continue to disappear in favor of a customized world online. Most businesses may start to charge consumers for delivery and payment of bills that use traditional mail rather than online. Consumers will be incented to do more online.
- Brick-and-mortar retail will need to become an entertainment destination for consumers to continue to come in to the actual store and they will need to tie their in-store experience to savings when purchasing other products online. Like Apple, the store is so much more than just a store.
- If the many brand top-level domain registry operators—now the largest representation of registry operators within ICANN—expand their lobbying effort for worldwide laws and agreements to protect brand rights and stop counterfeiting and cybersquatting, consumers will benefit. This could be the single greatest benefit to consumers that comes from this program—now there is a strong enough lobby to stop counterfeiting on the Internet.
- There will be new ways of navigating the Internet—accessing communities, apps, and disruptive innovation will result. Search won't die, but must evolve. Apps and tools that get people to exactly what they want faster will become more prevalent.
- Disruptive innovators could have dramatic shifts on how traditional businesses distribute their products and services.
- Thinking about brands has to evolve to incorporate a comprehensive Internet, app, digital, interactive, and intellectual property strategy—none of these can operate independently in a *.brand* world.
- While there is a bigger universe to protect, trademark owners have more tools available today than they did in the .com explosion and need to think more strategically about the approach in a return-on-investment methodology rather than just a defensive cost structure in the annual budget.
- There will be opportunities to partner or collaborate to build communities that mean something—especially if you didn't apply for a top-level domain. Who did and might be a good partner for you?
- Companies could actually improve their overall Internet strategy by taking the challenge and hear about brand protection and

turning it into the opportunity to audit, evaluate, and improve the way you build and cultivate your brand identity on the Internet.

- In the short term, there will be confusion and most companies will likely increase their spend on brand protection until they can reengineer the process to efficiently evaluate the return on investment associated with brand protection activities.

- The importance of creating a brand that can be protected in a global community of trademark right holders will become more important than ever. It's no longer just checking to see if it's available on a .com; it's a whole new level of thinking about what you are building, cultivating, and protecting.

- More companies will have the ability to participate in communities than in the current fragmented.com space. Meaning, because more centralized sources for key themes will emerge, it will actually get easier to be connected to the community you want.

- Early adopters will capitalize on the loyalty of community followers—members of their organizations or top-level domains—and this access to information will be worth billions to advertisers.

- The shift from technology interfering with direct human interaction will actually change and bolster the desire to be a part of a community—but now a global community empowered by a new Internet.

- Global giants will no longer determine what products to create. Consumers will forecast their needs in an online community and savvy companies and entrepreneurs will respond successfully.

- .com will ultimately symbolize antiquated or not cool—remember the world before emails?

- A new way of thinking about the Internet and our digital world will emerge and people will rely more on finding what they want when a company has its own top-level domain or belongs to a trusted community top-level domain.

- Big search engines may begin to charge in a different way to use their search engine. Consumers could pay a premium for better search or companies may pay even more for enhanced results.

- Companies that use this change as a way to disruptively innovate their business will succeed while those that resist change will face increasing challenges or fail.

For more information about the expanding internet, go to www.domainnamesrewired.com.

Appendix A

The History and Changing Landscape of the Top-Level Domain

Committed Companies

Even before ICANN started accepting applications for the first round of gTLDs, numerous companies had already committed to purchasing one of the new domains.

Canon

In March 2010, the Japanese printer maker became the first global brand to publicly announce its plans to apply for a brand gTLD as soon as ICANN finalizes the process for doing so. In a statement, the company said, "Canon hopes to globally integrate open communication policies that are intuitive and easier to remember compared with existing domain names such as canon.com. Canon has made the official decision to begin necessary procedures to acquire '.canon' upon the introduction of the new system." Canon has said that it will make full use of the new domain name to increase the convenience and effectiveness of its online communications.

Unicef

The United Nations Children's Fund confirmed publicly that it was planning to apply for a .brand top-level domain. The non-profit was quoted as saying, "Taking the long view, as time goes on, a name such as www.donations.unicef and www.cards.unicef will become more intuitive in a more crowded Internet, and thus more valuable because the name reflects exactly that of an organization and declares what it does." With unscrupulous individuals frequently seeking to capitalize on global tragedies to cheat money out of people through bogus websites, charities could very well see some anti-phishing benefits from having their own sufficiently publicized TLD. Unicef's Chief of IT, Stephen Fridakis, summed it up best when he explained, "There are advantages ranging from brand protection to message validation (email). The costs and migration are significant, but any long-term, comprehensive brand protection strategy should incorporate the acquisition of a gTLD."

Hitachi

In March 2011, Hitachi, Ltd. became another major company to declare publicly that it would apply to operate a new gTLD. Hitachi will operate its gTLD in partnership with a Tokyo company, GMO Registry, established in 2009, to provide all-in-one registry package solutions including application assistance, system architecture, backend operation, and marketing support for new gTLDs.

Other Major Companies

Other major companies that publicly expressed interest in applying prior to the application period include IBM and Nokia. In addition, over 40 applicants have publicly announced their plans to apply for generic-term domains, including: .health, .food, .homes, .hotel, .restaurant, .wine, .love, .film, .health, .mail, .money, and .car. While many kept their plans confidential and very secretive, we now know that more than 36 of the Fortune 100 and half of the leading global brands applied.

Applied-for New gTLD Strings

This list is as of June 13, 2012.

ICANN

String	Applicant	Loc/Reg	Properties	IDN Attributes	Appl. ID
ابوظبي	Abu Dhabi Systems and Information Centre	AE/AP	IDN Geographic	A-label: xn--mgbca7dzdo Script Code: Arab English Meaning: Abu Dhabi – An Emirate of the United Arab Emirates	1-1925-2822
اتصالات	Emirates Telecommunications Corporation (trading as Etisalat) http://www.etisalat.com	AE/AP	IDN	A-label: xn--mgbaakc7dvf Script Code: Arab English Meaning: The word "اتصالات" is Applicant's registered trademark used in 18 countries across Asia, the Middle East and Africa. "اتصالات" is also a word in Arabic language that means "communications."	1-1745-25333
ارامكو	Aramco Services Company http://www.aramcoservices.com	US/NA	IDN	A-label: xn--mgba3a3ejt Script Code: Arab English Meaning: Aramco	1-1961-53268
العليان	Olayan Investments Company Establishment http://olayan.com	LI/EUR	IDN	A-label: xn--mgba7c0bbn0a Script Code: Arab English Meaning: 14(b) Olayan is the family name of the founders of the applicant entity and group of companies, and a recognized brand for a wide variety of products and services offered throughout the world.	1-1017-64718
بازار	CORE Association http://corenic.org	CH/EUR	IDN	A-label: xn--mgbab2bd Script Code: Arab English Meaning: The string means "bazaar" in English.	1-862-50853
بيتك	Kuwait Finance House http://www.kfh.com	KW/AP	IDN	A-label: xn--ngbe9e0a Script Code: Arab English Meaning: The string is used worldwide in relation to the services of the Applicant. The string has always been used as a short name for KFH in all publications. The meaning of the string is "your own "house."	1-2100-57621
شبكة	International Domain Registry Pty. Ltd.	AU/AP	IDN	A-label: xn--ngbc5azd Script Code: Arab English Meaning: Web / Network	1-1926-49360
عرب	League of Arab States http://www.arableagueonline.org	EG/AF	IDN	A-label: xn--ngbrx Script Code: Arab English Meaning: Arab	1-1346-36518
كاثوليك	Pontificium Consilium de Comunicationibus Socialibus (PCCS) (Pontifical Council for Social Communication) http://www.pccsva.org/	VA/EUR	IDN Community	A-label: xn--mgbi4ecexp Script Code: Arab English Meaning: Catholic	1-1311-1455
كوم	VeriSign Sarl http://www.verisigninc.com/en_CH/index.xhtml?loc=en_CH#/site_owners	CH/EUR	IDN	A-label: xn--fhbei Script Code: Arab English Meaning: Transliteration of com	1-1254-25640
كيوتل	Qatar Telecom (Qtel) http://www.qtel.qa	QA/AP	IDN	A-label: xn--pgb3ceoj Script Code: Arab English Meaning: كيوتل is the brand name of Applicant, the primary telecommunications provider in Qatar. The designation is used throughout the country in relation to the services of the Applicant.	1-1928-24515
موبايلي	GreenTech Consultancy Company W.L.L. http://www.greentechwll.com	BH/AP	IDN	A-label: xn--mgbb9fbpob Script Code: Arab English Meaning: Mobily	1-2115-92778
موزايك	Qatar Telecom (Qtel) http://www.qtel.qa	QA/AP	IDN	A-label: xn--mgbv6cfpo Script Code: Arab English Meaning: موزايك is a brand name of Applicant, the primary telecommunications provider in Qatar.	1-1930-13222

String	Applicant	Loc/Reg	Properties	IDN Attributes	Appl. ID
				the Applicant.	
موقع	Suhub Electronic Establishment www.suhub.com.sa	SA/AP	IDN	A-label: xn--4gbrim Script Code: Arab English Meaning: Site	1-1013-15278
همراه	Asia Green IT System Bilgisayar San. ve Tic. Ltd. Sti.	TR/AP	IDN	A-label: xn--mgbt3dhd Script Code: Arab English Meaning: Compeer, comrade, concomitant, along with, together with each other.	1-2134-95773
дети	The Foundation for Network Initiatives "The Smart Internet" http://www.smartinternet.info/	RU/EUR	IDN	A-label: xn--d1acj3b Script Code: Cyrl English Meaning: kids, children	1-1193-2906
католик	Pontificium Consilium de Comunicationibus Socialibus (PCCS) (Pontifical Council for Social Communication) http://www.pccsva.org/	VA/EUR	IDN Community	A-label: xn--80aqecdr1a Script Code: Cyrl English Meaning: Catholic	1-1311-52357
ком	VeriSign Sarl http://www.verisigninc.com/en_CH/index.xhtml?loc=en_CH#/site_owners	CH/EUR	IDN	A-label: xn--j1aef Script Code: Cyrl English Meaning: Transliteration of com	1-1254-23113
москва	Foundation for Assistance for Internet Technologies and Infrastructure Development (FAITID) http://www.faitid.org	RU/EUR	IDN Geographic	A-label: xn--80adxhks Script Code: Cyrl English Meaning: MOSKVA is the full name of the Russian capital - Moscow - in Russian	1-975-90576
онлайн	CORE Association http://corenic.org	CH/EUR	IDN	A-label: xn--80asehdb Script Code: Cyrl English Meaning: online	1-862-29948
орг	Public Interest Registry http://www.pir.org	US/NA	IDN	A-label: xn--c1avg Script Code: Cyrl English Meaning: Org (организация - organization)	1-910-36696
рус	Rusnames Limited	RU/EUR	IDN Community	A-label: xn--p1acf Script Code: Cyrl English Meaning: Means community of Russian speaking who originated in Kiev Rús in the 13 century. This includes but is not limited to residents of Belarus, Kazakhstan, Norway, Russia, Ukraine, and the United States.	1-1957-68557
сайт	CORE Association http://corenic.org	CH/EUR	IDN	A-label: xn--80aswg Script Code: Cyrl English Meaning: site	1-862-90073
कॉम	VeriSign Sarl http://www.verisigninc.com/en_CH/index.xhtml?loc=en_CH#/site_owners	CH/EUR	IDN	A-label: xn--11b4c3d Script Code: Deva English Meaning: Transliteration of com	1-1254-28833
नेट	VeriSign Sarl http://www.verisigninc.com/en_CH/index.xhtml?loc=en_CH#/site_owners	CH/EUR	IDN	A-label: xn--c2br7g Script Code: Deva English Meaning: Transliteration of net	1-1254-86085
संगठन	Public Interest Registry http://www.pir.org	US/NA	IDN	A-label: xn--i1b6b1a6a2e Script Code: Deva English Meaning: Organization (Org)	1-910-41904
一号店	Wal-Mart Stores, Inc.	US/NA	IDN	A-label: xn--4gq48lf9j Script Code: Hans English Meaning: Number One Store	1-1244-37294
世界	Stable Tone Limited	HK/AP	IDN	A-label: xn--rhqv96g Script Code: Hans English Meaning: world, globe, universe (or similar)	1-1708-19635
中信	CITIC Group Corporation http://www.citic.com	CN/AP	IDN	A-label: xn--fiQ64B Script Code: Hans English Meaning: CITIC (China International Trust and Investment Corporation)	1-914-3594
中文网	TLD REGISTRY LIMITED http://internetregistry.info	IE/EUR	IDN	A-label: xn--fiq228c5hs Script Code: Hans English Meaning: website in chinese	1-1939-78147
亚马逊	Amazon EU S.à r.l. http://www.amazon.com/	LU/EUR	IDN	A-label: xn--jlq480n2rg Script Code: Hans English Meaning: Amazon	1-1318-5591
企业	Dash McCook, LLC	US/NA	IDN	A-label: xn--vhquv Script Code: Hans	1-1495-41000

Copyright 2012 Internet Corporation for Assigned Names and Numbers.

String	Applicant	Loc/Reg	Properties	IDN Attributes	Appl. ID
				English Meaning: Enterprise, firm, company.	
佛山	Guangzhou YU Wei Information Technology Co., Ltd.	CN/AP	IDN Geographic	A-label: xn--1qqw23a Script Code: Hans English Meaning: Foshan	1-1121-69393
信息	Afilias Limited	IE/EUR	IDN	A-label: xn--vuq861b Script Code: Hans English Meaning: info	1-868-7047
	Beijing Tele-info Network Technology Co., Ltd. http://www.tele-info.cn	CN/AP	IDN	A-label: xn--vuq861b Script Code: Hans English Meaning: "信息" means knowledge or message in the form suitable for communications, storage, or processing, which is closely related to notions of form, meaning, pattern, perception, representation, and entropy.	1-995-44061
健康	Stable Tone Limited	HK/AP	IDN	A-label: xn--nyqy26a Script Code: Hans English Meaning: healthy	1-1708-88054
八卦	Zodiac Scorpio Limited http://www.zodiac-corp.com/	HK/AP	IDN	A-label: xn--45q11c Script Code: Hans English Meaning: gossip	1-859-69634
公司	Computer Network Information Center of Chinese Academy of Sciences ?China Internet Network Information Center? http://www.cnnic.cn	CN/AP	IDN	A-label: xn--55qx5d Script Code: Hans English Meaning: "公司" means business organization. It is an association or collection of individual real persons and/or other companies. This group usually has a common focus and an aim of gaining profits.	1-932-93337
公益	China Organizational Name Administration Center http://www.conac.cn	CN/AP	IDN	A-label: xn--55qw42g Script Code: Hans English Meaning: public interest	1-922-7037
商城	Zodiac Capricorn Limited http://www.zodiac-corp.com/	HK/AP	IDN	A-label: xn--czru2d Script Code: Hans English Meaning: mall	1-867-66064
商店	Wild Island, LLC	US/NA	IDN	A-label: xn--czrs0t Script Code: Hans English Meaning: Commercial shop or store, selling goods	1-1490-59840
商标	HU YI GLOBAL INFORMATION RESOURCES(HOLDING) COMPANY.HONGKONG LIMITED http://www.8hy.hk	HK/AP	IDN	A-label: xn--czr694b Script Code: Hans English Meaning: Trademark	1-1157-41509
嘉里	Kerry Trading Co. Limited	HK/AP	IDN	A-label: xn--w4rs40l Script Code: Hani English Meaning: Kerry	1-928-57387
嘉里大酒店	Kerry Trading Co. Limited	HK/AP	IDN	A-label: xn--w4r85el8fhu5dnra Script Code: Hani English Meaning: Kerry Hotel(s)	1-928-73202
在线	TLD REGISTRY LIMITED http://internetregistry.info	IE/EUR	IDN	A-label: xn--3ds443g Script Code: Hans English Meaning: online	1-1940-42600
大众汽车	Volkswagen (China) Investment Co., Ltd. http://www.vw.com.cn	CN/AP	IDN Community	A-label: xn--3oq18vl8pn36a Script Code: Hans English Meaning: volkswagon	1-1824-64001
大拿	VeriSign Sarl http://www.verisigninc.com/en_CH/index.xhtml? loc=en_CH#/site_owners	CH/EUR	IDN	A-label: xn--pssy2u Script Code: Hans English Meaning: Transliteration of dot net	1-1254-52569
天主教	Pontificium Consilium de Comunicationibus Socialibus (PCCS) (Pontifical Council for Social Communication) http://www.pccs.va.org/	VA/EUR	IDN Community	A-label: xn--tiq49xqyj Script Code: Hani English Meaning: Catholic	1-1311-58570
娱乐	Will Bloom, LLC	US/NA	IDN	A-label: xn--fjq720a Script Code: Hans English Meaning: Entertainment	1-1491-83816
	Morden Media Limited	KY/EUR	IDN	A-label: xn--fjq720a Script Code: Hans English Meaning: entertainment	1-963-13166

Copyright 2013 Internet Corporation for Assigned Names and Numbers

String	Applicant	Loc/Reg	Properties	IDN Attributes	Appl. ID
家電	Amazon EU S.à r.l. http://www.amazon.com/	LU/EUR	IDN	A-label: xn--fct429k Script Code: Hani English Meaning: Consumer Electronics	1-1318-54339
工行	Industrial and Commercial Bank of China Limited	CN/AP	IDN	A-label: xn--estv75g Script Code: Hans English Meaning: 工行 is a commonly used and wildly recognized Chinese abbreviation of the Industrial and Commercial Bank of China (ICBC). It is an official registered trademark of ICBC.	1-1011-2710
广东	Guangzhou YU Wei Information Technology Co., Ltd.	CN/AP	IDN Geographic	A-label: xn--xhq521b Script Code: Hans English Meaning: Guangdong	1-1121-17301
	Xinhua News Agency Guangdong Branch http://www.gd.xinhua.org	CN/AP	IDN Community Geographic	A-label: xn--xhq521b Script Code: Hans English Meaning: Guangdong	1-1309-35206
广州	Guangzhou YU Wei Information Technology Co., Ltd.	CN/AP	IDN Geographic	A-label: xn--6rtwn Script Code: Hans English Meaning: Guangzhou	1-1121-22691
微博	Tencent Holdings Limited http://tencent.com	CN/AP	IDN	A-label: xn--9krt00a Script Code: Hans English Meaning: Microblogging	1-1313-58483
	Sina Corporation http://www.sina.com.cn	CN/AP	IDN	A-label: xn--9krt00a Script Code: Hans English Meaning: The transliteration of applied-for string in English is "Weibo." "Wei" and "Bo" means "Minute or Small" and "abundant, plentiful, rich," respectively.	1-950-28485
慈善	Excellent First Limited	KY/EUR	IDN	A-label: xn--30rr7y Script Code: Hans English Meaning: charity	1-961-6109
我爱你	Tycoon Treasure Limited	KY/EUR	IDN	A-label: xn--6qq986b3xd Script Code: Hans English Meaning: i love you	1-960-63893
手机	Beijing RITT-Net Technology Development Co., Ltd http://www.rntd.cn	CN/AP	IDN	A-label: xn--kput3i Script Code: Hans English Meaning: Cell	1-1013-60869
手表	Richemont DNS Inc. http://www.richemont.com	CH/EUR	IDN	A-label: xn--kpu716f Script Code: Hans English Meaning: Watches	1-1253-73407
招聘	HU YI GLOBAL INFORMATION RESOURCES (HOLDING) COMPANY. HONGKONG LIMITED http://www.8hy.hk	HK/AP	IDN	A-label: xn--otu796d Script Code: Hans English Meaning: Recruitment	1-1158-95080
政务	China Organizational Name Administration Center http://www.conac.cn	CN/AP	IDN Community	A-label: xn--zfr164b Script Code: Hans English Meaning: government and government affairs	1-922-56316
政府	Net-Chinese Co., Ltd. http://www.netc.tw	TW/AP	IDN	A-label: xn--mxtq1m Script Code: Hani English Meaning: This string indicates public affairs and public sectors including governmental organizations, public institutions, or any related organizations supported by government to provide public services	1-1658-94344
新闻	Xinhua News Agency Guangdong Branch http://www.gd.xinhua.org	CN/AP	IDN	A-label: xn--efvy88h Script Code: Hans English Meaning: news	1-1309-40591
时尚	RISE VICTORY LIMITED	CN/AP	IDN	A-label: xn--9et52u Script Code: Hans English Meaning: vogue, fashion	1-1120-95098
普利司通	Bridgestone Corporation http://www.bridgestone.co.jp	JP/AP	IDN	A-label: xn--kcrx7bb75ajk3b Script Code: Hans English Meaning: 普利司通 are the Chinese characters representing "Bridgestone,"	1-954-90045

Copyright 2012 Internet Corporation for Assigned Names and Numbers

String	Applicant	Loc/Reg	Properties	IDN Attributes	Appl. ID
				meant to be read roughly similar to the pronunciation of "Bridgestone" in English. The string doesn't hold any particular meaning in Chinese.	
机构	Public Interest Registry http://www.pir.org	US/NA	IDN	A-label: xn--nqv7f Script Code: Hans English Meaning: Org (Organization)	1-910-16443
机构体制	Public Interest Registry http://www.pir.org	US/NA	IDN	A-label: xn--tqq33ed31aqia Script Code: Hans English Meaning: Org (Organization / Institution)	1-910-25137
欧莱雅	L'Oréal http://www.loreal.com	FR/EUR	IDN	A-label: xn--dkwm73cwpn Script Code: Hans English Meaning: L'Oréal	1-1302-55079
淡马锡	Temasek Holdings (Private) Limtied http://www.temasek.com.sg	SG/AP	IDN	A-label: xn--b4w605ferd Script Code: Hans English Meaning: temasek – the applicant's main brand in (simplified) Chinese script	1-848-71299
深圳	Guangzhou YU Wei Information Technology Co., Ltd.	CN/AP	IDN Geographic	A-label: xn--fes124c Script Code: Hans English Meaning: Shenzhen	1-1121-82863
游戏	Spring Fields, LLC	US/NA	IDN	A-label: xn--unup4y Script Code: Hans English Meaning: Game(s)	1-1485-72605
点看	VeriSign Sarl http://www.verisigninc.com/en_CH/index.xhtml?loc=en_CH#/site_owners	CH/EUR	IDN	A-label: xn--3pxu8k Script Code: Hans English Meaning: Transliteration of dot com	1-1254-85868
珠宝	Richemont DNS Inc. http://www.richemont.com	CH/EUR	IDN	A-label: xn--pbt977c Script Code: Hans English Meaning: Jewelry	1-1253-4621
盛貿飯店	Shangri La International Hotel Management Limited http://www.shangri-la.com	HK/AP	IDN	A-label: xn--hxt035cmppuel Script Code: Hant English Meaning: Traders Hotel(s)	1-940-75591
盛贸饭店	Shangri La International Hotel Management Limited http://www.shangri-la.com	HK/AP	IDN	A-label: xn--hxt035czzpffl Script Code: Hans English Meaning: Traders Hotel(s)	1-940-43388
移动	Afilias Limited	IE/EUR	IDN	A-label: xn--6frz82g Script Code: Hans English Meaning: Mobile	1-868-82489
网址	HU YI GLOBAL INFORMATION RESOURCES (HOLDING) COMPANY. HONGKONG LIMITED http://www.8hy.hk	HK/AP	IDN	A-label: xn--ses554g Script Code: Hans English Meaning: Netaddress (network address, URL)	1-1159-3507
	Top Level Domain Holdings Limited http://www.tldh.org	VG/EUR	IDN	A-label: xn--ses554g Script Code: Hans English Meaning: website	1-994-51307
网店	Global eCommerce TLD Asia Limited	HK/AP	IDN	A-label: xn--hxt814e Script Code: Hani English Meaning: Webstore. The Registry wishes to apply .店 (.dian) but current rules disallow 1 char IDN TLD & GNSO policy advises against ASCII squatting (.dian is ASCII squatting as 1 char IDN TLDs are not allowed)	1-2102-26509
	Zodiac Libra Limited http://www.zodiac-corp.com/	HK/AP	IDN	A-label: xn--hxt814e Script Code: Hans English Meaning: webshop, e-shop	1-858-36255
网站	RISE VICTORY LIMITED	CN/AP	IDN	A-label: xn--5tzm5g Script Code: Hans English Meaning: website, homepage, portal	1-1120-42188
	Global Website TLD Asia Limited	HK/AP	IDN	A-label: xn--5tzm5g Script Code: Hani English Meaning: Website. Registry wishes to apply .网 (.wang) but current rules disallow 1 char IDN TLD & GNSO policy advises	1-2101-67873

APPENDIX A

String	Applicant	Loc/Reg	Properties	IDN Attributes	Appl. ID
				against ASCII squatting (.wang would be ASCII squatting as 1 char IDN TLDs are not allowed)	
网络	Computer Network Information Center of Chinese Academy of Sciences ?China Internet Network Information Center? http://www.cnnic.cn	CN/AP	IDN	A-label: xn--io0a7i Script Code: Hans English Meaning: The string of "网络" means network. It is a collection of hardware components and computers interconnected by communication channels that allow sharing of resources and information.	1-932-13797
联通	China United Network Communications Corporation Limited http://www.chinaunicom.com	CN/AP	IDN	A-label: xn--8y0a063a Script Code: Hans English Meaning: Unicom	1-996-21855
诺基亚	Nokia Corporation http://www.nokia.com	FI/EUR	IDN	A-label: xn--jlq61u9w7b Script Code: Hans English Meaning: Nokia	1-957-40223
谷歌	Charleston Road Registry Inc.	US/NA	IDN	A-label: xn--flw351e Script Code: Hani English Meaning: Chinese for "Google"	1-1141-36998
购物	Top Level Domain Holdings Limited http://www.tldh.org	VG/EUR	IDN	A-label: xn--g2xx48c Script Code: Hans English Meaning: shopping	1-994-1450
通用电气公司	GE GTLD Holdings LLC	US/NA	IDN	A-label: xn--55qx5d8y0buji4b870u Script Code: Hans English Meaning: Gecompany	1-1330-89853
通販	Amazon EU S.à r.l. http://www.amazon.com/	LU/EUR	IDN	A-label: xn--gk3at1e Script Code: Hani English Meaning: Online Shopping	1-1318-15593
集团	Eagle Horizon Limited	KY/EUR	IDN	A-label: xn--3bst00m Script Code: Hans English Meaning: conglomerate, group	1-962-55795
電訊盈科	PCCW Enterprises Limited www.pccw.com	HK/AP	IDN	A-label: xn--fzys8d69uvgm Script Code: Hant English Meaning: PCCW -- Pacific Century Cyber Works	1-1309-63598
飞利浦	Koninklijke Philips Electronics N.V. http://www.philips.com	NL/EUR	IDN	A-label: xn--kcrx77d1x4a Script Code: Hani English Meaning: Philips	1-1748-14964
食品	Amazon EU S.à r.l. http://www.amazon.com/	LU/EUR	IDN	A-label: xn--jvr189m Script Code: Hani English Meaning: Food	1-1318-83264
餐厅	HU YI GLOBAL INFORMATION RESOURCES (HOLDING) COMPANY. HONGKONG LIMITED http://www.8hy.hk	HK/AP	IDN	A-label: xn--imr513n Script Code: Hans English Meaning: Restaurant	1-1103-5695
香格里拉	Shangri La International Hotel Management Limited http://www.shangri-la.com	HK/AP	IDN	A-label: xn--5su34j936bgsg Script Code: Hani English Meaning: Shangri-La	1-940-19689
香港電訊	PCCW-HKT DataCom Services Limited www.hkt.com	HK/AP	IDN	A-label: xn--j6w470d71issc Script Code: Hant English Meaning: Hong Kong Telecom	1-1309-10813
點看	VeriSign Sarl http://www.verisigninc.com/en_CH/index.xhtml?loc=en_CH#/site_owners	CH/EUR	IDN	A-label: xn--c1yn36f Script Code: Hant English Meaning: Transliteration of dot com	1-1254-86222
닷넷	VeriSign Sarl http://www.verisigninc.com/en_CH/index.xhtml?loc=en_CH#/site_owners	CH/EUR	IDN	A-label: xn--t60b56a Script Code: Hang English Meaning: Transliteration of dot net	1-1254-76331
닷컴	VeriSign Sarl http://www.verisigninc.com/en_CH/index.xhtml?loc=en_CH#/site_owners	CH/EUR	IDN	A-label: xn--mk1bu44c Script Code: Hang English Meaning: Transliteration of dot com	1-1254-16209
삼성	SAMSUNG SDS CO., LTD http://www.sds.samsung.co.kr	KR/AP	IDN	A-label: xn--cg4bki Script Code: Hang English Meaning: The gTLD string is korean name of SAMSUNG.	1-955-42062
קום	VeriSign Sarl http://www.verisigninc.com/en_CH/index.xhtml?	CH/EUR	IDN	A-label: xn--hdb9cza1b Script Code: Hebr	1-1254-29622

Copyright 2012 Internet Corporation for Assigned Names and Numbers

String	Applicant	Loc/Reg	Properties	IDN Attributes	Appl. ID
				English Meaning: Transliteration of com	
みんな	Charleston Road Registry Inc.	US/NA	IDN	**A-label:** xn--q9jyb4c **Script Code:** Jpan **English Meaning:** Japanese for "everyone"	1-1678-4149
グーグル	Charleston Road Registry Inc.	US/NA	IDN	**A-label:** xn--qcka1pmc **Script Code:** Jpan **English Meaning:** Google	1-1099-81471
アマゾン	Amazon EU S.à r.l. http://www.amazon.com/	LU/EUR	IDN	**A-label:** xn--cckwcxetd **Script Code:** Kana **English Meaning:** Amazon	1-1318-83995
クラウド	Amazon EU S.à r.l. http://www.amazon.com/	LU/EUR	IDN	**A-label:** xn--gckr3f0f **Script Code:** Kana **English Meaning:** Cloud	1-1318-69604
コム	VeriSign Sarl http://www.verisigninc.com/en_CH/index.xhtml? loc=en_CH#/site_owners	CH/EUR	IDN	**A-label:** xn--tckwe **Script Code:** Kana **English Meaning:** Transliteration of com	1-1254-37311
ストア	Amazon EU S.à r.l. http://www.amazon.com/	LU/EUR	IDN	**A-label:** xn--cck2b3b **Script Code:** Kana **English Meaning:** Store	1-1318-83013
セール	Amazon EU S.à r.l. http://www.amazon.com/	LU/EUR	IDN	**A-label:** xn--1ck2e1b **Script Code:** Kana **English Meaning:** Sale	1-1318-75179
ファッション	Amazon EU S.à r.l. http://www.amazon.com/	LU/EUR	IDN	**A-label:** xn--bck1b9a5dre4c **Script Code:** Kana **English Meaning:** Fashion	1-1318-40887
ポイント	Amazon EU S.à r.l. http://www.amazon.com/	LU/EUR	IDN	**A-label:** xn--eckvdtc9d **Script Code:** Kana **English Meaning:** Point	1-1318-7184
書籍	Amazon EU S.à r.l. http://www.amazon.com/	LU/EUR	IDN	**A-label:** xn--rovu88b **Script Code:** Kana **English Meaning:** Book	1-1318-52278
AAA	American Automobile Association, Inc. http://www.aaa.com	US/NA			1-1386-27446
AARP	AARP	US/NA			1-1169-4534
ABARTH	Fiat S.p.A. ("società per azioni") http://www.fiatspa.com	IT/EUR			1-2072-28769
ABB	ABB Ltd http://abb.com	CH/EUR			1-1673-93106
ABBOTT	Abbott Laboratories http://www.abbott.com	US/NA			1-1765-99580
ABBVIE	Abbott Laboratories http://www.abbott.com	US/NA			1-1766-21421
ABC	American Broadcasting Companies, Inc.	US/NA			1-1146-98846
ABLE	Able Inc. http://www.able.co.jp/	JP/AP			1-901-17807
ABOGADO	Top Level Domain Holdings Limited http://www.tldh.org	VG/EUR			1-927-56004
ABUDHABI	Abu Dhabi Systems and Information Centre http://adsic.abudhabi.ae	AE/AP	Geographic		1-1924-90958
ACADEMY	Half Oaks, LLC	US/NA			1-1336-51768
ACCENTURE	Accenture Global Services Limited http://www.accenture.com	IE/EUR			1-2024-58277
ACCOUNTANT	dot Accountant Limited	GI/EUR			1-1240-93305
ACCOUNTANTS	Knob Town, LLC	US/NA			1-1340-40734
ACER	Acer Incorporated http://www.acer.com/worldwide/selection.html	TW/AP			1-2038-17410
ACO	ACO Severin Ahlmann GmbH & Co. KG http://www.aco.com	DE/EUR	Community		1-1026-17004
ACTIVE	The Active Network, Inc http://www.activenetwork.com	US/NA			1-1008-95821
ACTOR	United TLD Holdco Ltd. http://unitedtld.com	KY/EUR			1-1255-99377
ADAC	Allgemeiner Deutscher Automobil-Club e.V. (ADAC) http://www.adac.de	DE/EUR	Community		1-1031-24651
ADS	Charleston Road Registry Inc.	US/NA			1-1680-21285
ADULT	ICM Registry AD LLC http://icmregistryad.com	US/NA			1-1107-2377

String	Applicant	Loc/Reg	Properties	IDN Attributes	Appl. ID
AEG	Aktiebolaget Electrolux http://www.electrolux.com	SE/EUR			1-1955-15449
AETNA	Aetna Life Insurance Company http://www.aetna.com	US/NA			1-1850-74225
AFAMILYCOMPANY	Johnson Shareholdings, Inc.	US/NA			1-1248-76254
AFL	Australian Football League http://www.afl.com.au	AU/AP			1-1816-41150
AFRICA	UniForum SA (NPC) trading as Registry.Africa http://www.AfricaInOneSpace.org	ZA/AF	Geographic		1-1243-89583
AFRICAMAGIC	Electronic Media Network Limited (M-Net) http://www.mnet.co.za	ZA/AF			1-1842-12883
AGAKHAN	Fondation Aga Khan (Aga Khan Foundation) Http://www.akdn.org	CH/EUR			1-1013-32567
AGENCY	Steel Falls, LLC	US/NA			1-1339-13106
AIG	American International Group, Inc. http://www.aig.com	US/NA			1-1700-54316
AIGO	aigo Digital Technology Co,Ltd. http://en.aigo.com/	CN/AP			1-942-46156
AIRBUS	Airbus S.A.S. http://www.airbus.com	FR/EUR			1-1671-14472
AIRFORCE	United TLD Holdco Ltd. http://unitedtld.com	KY/EUR			1-1255-29190
AIRTEL	Bharti Airtel Limited http://www.airtel.in	IN/AP			1-1285-61415
AKDN	Fondation Aga Khan (Aga Khan Foundation) Http://www.akdn.org	CH/EUR			1-1013-36598
ALCON	Alcon Laboratories, Inc. http://www.alcon.com	US/NA			1-1959-92494
ALFAROMEO	Fiat S.p.A. ("società per azioni") http://www.fiatspa.com	IT/EUR			1-2068-239
ALIBABA	Alibaba Group Holding Limited http://news.alibaba.com/specials/aboutalibaba/aligroup/index.html	KY/EUR			1-1092-9273
ALIPAY	Alibaba Group Holding Limited http://news.alibaba.com/specials/aboutalibaba/aligroup/index.html	KY/EUR			1-1093-81854
ALLFINANZ	Allfinanz Deutsche Vermögensberatung Aktiengesellschaft http://www.allfinanz-dvag.com	DE/EUR			1-903-89627
ALLFINANZBERATER	Allfinanz Deutsche Vermögensberatung Aktiengesellschaft http://www.allfinanz-dvag.com	DE/EUR			1-903-23146
ALLFINANZBERATUNG	Allfinanz Deutsche Vermögensberatung Aktiengesellschaft http://www.allfinanz-dvag.com	DE/EUR			1-903-86203
ALLSTATE	Allstate Fire and Casualty Insurance Company	US/NA			1-1191-71962
ALLY	Ally Financial Inc. http://www.ally.com	US/NA			1-1963-65104
ALSACE	REGION D ALSACE http://www.region-alsace.eu	FR/EUR	Geographic		1-1825-82923
ALSTOM	ALSTOM http://www.alstom.com	FR/EUR			1-1135-17943
AMAZON	Amazon EU S.à r.l. http://www.amazon.com/	LU/EUR			1-1315-58086
AMERICANEXPRESS	American Express Travel Related Services Company, Inc.	US/NA			1-1305-84307
AMERICANFAMILY	AmFam, Inc. http://www.amfam.com	US/NA			1-1268-37828
AMEX	American Express Travel Related Services Company, Inc.	US/NA			1-1305-26511
AMFAM	AmFam, Inc. http://www.amfam.com	US/NA			1-1268-70134
AMICA	Amica Mutual Insurance Company http://www.amica.com	US/NA			1-1292-16149
AMP	AMP Limited http://www.amp.com.au	AU/AP			1-1709-77926
AMSTERDAM	Gemeente Amsterdam http://www.amsterdam.nl	NL/EUR	Geographic		1-1322-54903
ANALYTICS	Campus IP LLC	US/NA			1-1323-15308
AND	Charleston Road Registry Inc.	US/NA			1-1142-43609
ANDROID	Charleston Road Registry Inc.	US/NA			1-1681-35565
ANQUAN	QIHOO 360 TECHNOLOGY CO. LTD. http://www.360.cn	CN/AP			1-974-71991

Copyright 2012 Internet Corporation for Assigned Names and Numbers

String	Applicant	Loc/Reg	Properties IDN Attributes	Appl. ID
ANSONS	CBM Creative Brands Marken GmbH	CH/EUR		1-1137-82169
ANTHEM	WellPoint, Inc. http://www.wellpoint.com	US/NA		1-1148-6505
ANTIVIRUS	Symantec Corporation	US/NA		1-1027-34295
ANZ	Australia and New Zealand Banking Group Limited http://www.anz.com	AU/AP		1-1814-82061
AOL	AOL Inc. http://corp.aol.com	US/NA		1-1304-6257
APARTMENTS	June Maple, LLC	US/NA		1-1341-21066
	DERApartments, LLC	US/NA		1-909-9646
APP	.APP REGISTRY INC.	KY/EUR		1-1013-7451
	Charleston Road Registry Inc.	US/NA		1-1138-33325
	dot App Limited	GI/EUR		1-1182-25681
	Webera Inc. http://www.radixregistry.com	AE/AP		1-1289-59445
	NU DOT CO LLC	US/NA		1-1296-33564
	Amazon EU S.à r.l. http://www.amazon.com/	LU/EUR		1-1315-63009
	Lone Maple, LLC	US/NA		1-1343-89689
	Dot App LLC http://dotapp.me	US/NA		1-1778-4598
	DotApp Inc. http://www.dotappcommunity.org	US/NA		1-1815-5857
	TRI Ventures, Inc. http://aquent.com	US/NA		1-2039-18233
	Afilias Limited	IE/EUR		1-868-39920
	Merchant Law Group LLP	CA/NA		1-875-87230
	Top Level Domain Holdings Limited http://www.tldh.org	VG/EUR		1-927-15180
APPLE	Apple Inc. http://www.apple.com	US/NA		1-1772-3875
AQUARELLE	Aquarelle.com http://www.aquarelle.com	FR/EUR		1-1685-37800
AQUITAINE	Région d'Aquitaine http://aquitaine.fr/	FR/EUR	Geographic	1-1826-69911
ARAB	League of Arab States http://www.arableagueonline.org	EG/AF		1-1346-3935
ARAMCO	Aramco Services Company http://www.aramcoservices.com	US/NA		1-2034-17082
ARCHI	STARTING DOT http://www.startingdot.com	FR/EUR	Community	1-1000-49620
ARCHITECT	Spring Frostbite, LLC	US/NA		1-1342-7920
ARE	Charleston Road Registry Inc.	US/NA		1-1682-79898
ARMY	United TLD Holdco Ltd. http://unitedtld.com	KY/EUR		1-1255-29986
ART	.ART REGISTRY INC.	KY/EUR		1-1013-98331
	Top Level Design, LLC	US/NA		1-1086-100
	Dadotart, Inc.	US/NA	Community	1-1097-20833
	UK Creative Ideas Limited	IM/EUR		1-1211-27884
	Baxter Tigers, LLC	US/NA		1-1344-70608
	EFLUX.ART, LLC http://www.e-flux.com/	US/NA	Community	1-1675-51302
	Aremi Group S.A.	LU/EUR		1-1844-98392
	Uniregistry, Corp. http://www.uniregistry.com	KY/EUR		1-855-66616
	Merchant Law Group LLP	CA/NA		1-875-17602
	Top Level Domain Holdings Limited http://www.tldh.org	VG/EUR		1-927-15036
ARTE	Association Relative à la Télévision Européenne G.E.I.E. http://www.arte.tv	FR/EUR		1-1882-68650
ASDA	Wal-Mart Stores, Inc.	US/NA		1-1244-58324
ASSOCIATES	Baxter Hill, LLC	US/NA		1-1345-27582

Copyright 2012, Internet Corporation for Assigned Names and Numbers.

String	Applicant	Loc/Reg	Properties IDN Attributes	Appl. ID
ASTRIUM	Astrium SAS http://www.astrium.eads.net	FR/EUR		1-2037-97318
ATHLETA	The Gap, Inc. http://www.gap.com	US/NA		1-925-78912
ATTORNEY	Victor North, LLC	US/NA		1-1348-99321
AUCTION	Sand Galley, LLC	US/NA		1-1347-98883
	Uniregistry, Corp. http://www.uniregistry.com	KY/EUR		1-855-2943
AUDI	AUDI Aktiengesellschaft http://www.audi.de	DE/EUR	Community	1-1079-59916
AUDIBLE	Amazon EU S.à r.l. http://www.amazon.com/	LU/EUR		1-1315-37509
AUDIO	Holly Castle, LLC	US/NA		1-1349-23181
	Uniregistry, Corp. http://www.uniregistry.com	KY/EUR		1-845-89968
AUSPOST	Australian Postal Corporation http://www.auspost.com.au	AU/AP		1-2096-81155
AUTHOR	Amazon EU S.à r.l. http://www.amazon.com/	LU/EUR		1-1315-99563
AUTO	Big Maple, LLC	US/NA		1-1351-20019
	Fegistry, LLC	US/NA		1-1913-24731
	Uniregistry, Corp. http://www.uniregistry.com	KY/EUR		1-855-72019
	Dot Auto LLC	US/NA		1-879-42119
AUTOINSURANCE	Allstate Fire and Casualty Insurance Company	US/NA		1-1191-86372
AUTOS	DERAutos, LLC	US/NA		1-909-92065
AVERY	AVERY DENNISON CORPORATION http://www.averydennison.com	US/NA		1-1015-61446
AVIANCA	Aerovias del Continente Americano S.A. Avianca http://www.avianca.com	CO/LAC		1-1013-56131
AWS	Amazon EU S.à r.l. http://www.amazon.com/	LU/EUR		1-1315-68636
AXA	AXA SA http://www.axa.com	FR/EUR		1-1746-50891
AXIS	Saudi Telecom Company http://www.stc.com.sa	SA/AP		1-1934-72316
AZURE	Microsoft Corporation http://www.microsoft.com	US/NA		1-1129-27259
BABY	DotBaby Inc. http://www.radixregistry.com	AE/AP		1-1054-95858
	Johnson & Johnson Services, Inc.	US/NA		1-1156-50969
	Compact Registry Limited	GI/EUR		1-1216-75929
	Auburn Beach, LLC	US/NA		1-1352-18081
	Charleston Road Registry Inc.	US/NA		1-1417-16218
	Top Level Domain Holdings Limited http://www.tldh.org	VG/EUR		1-927-8340
BAIDU	Baidu, Inc. http://www.baidu.com	CN/AP		1-2088-98525
BANAMEX	Citigroup Inc. http://www.citigroup.com	US/NA		1-2087-76555
BANANAREPUBLIC	The Gap, Inc. http://www.gap.com	US/NA		1-925-89514
BAND	Auburn Hollow, LLC	US/NA		1-1350-42613
	Red Triangle, LLC	US/NA		1-856-54878
BANK	fTLD Registry Services LLC	US/NA	Community	1-1035-13873
	Dotsecure Inc. http://www.radixregistry.com	AE/AP		1-1053-59307
BANQUE	GEXBAN SAS http://www.gexban.net	FR/EUR		1-1762-63932
BAR	United TLD Holdco Ltd. http://unitedtld.com	KY/EUR		1-1255-43729
	Punto 2012 Sociedad Anonima de Capital Variable	MX/LAC	Geographic	1-1870-98363
BARCELONA	Municipi de Barcelona http://www.bcn.cat	ES/EUR	Community Geographic	1-1820-71568

Copyright 2012 Electronic Corporation for Assigned Names and Numbers

String	Applicant	Loc/Reg	Properties IDN Attributes	Appl. ID
BARCLAYCARD	Barclays Bank PLC http://www.barclays.com	GB/EUR		1-1291-89293
BARCLAYS	Barclays Bank PLC http://www.barclays.com	GB/EUR		1-1291-38102
BAREFOOT	Gallo Vineyards, Inc.	US/NA		1-1856-86918
BARGAINS	Half Hallow, LLC	US/NA		1-1354-34421
BASEBALL	MLB Advanced Media DH, LLC	US/NA		1-1246-9615
	Silver Pass, LLC	US/NA		1-1353-23613
BASKETBALL	dot Basketball Limited	GI/EUR		1-1199-43437
	Little Hollow, LLC	US/NA		1-1355-53565
	Fédération Internationale de Basketball (FIBA) www.fiba.com	CH/EUR		1-994-9184
BAUHAUS	Werkhaus GmbH	DE/EUR		1-1947-29466
BAYERN	Bayern Connect GmbH http://www.bayernconnect.com	DE/EUR	Geographic	1-994-73142
BBB	Council of Better Business Bureaus, Inc. http://www.bbb.org	US/NA	Community	1-1974-73400
BBC	British Broadcasting Corporation	GB/EUR		1-981-86291
BBT	BB&T Corporation http://www.bbt.com/	US/NA		1-1860-74210
BBVA	BANCO BILBAO VIZCAYA ARGENTARIA, S.A. http://www.bbva.com	ES/EUR		1-1111-84953
BCG	The Boston Consulting Group, Inc. http://www.bcg.com	US/NA		1-1969-69205
BCN	Municipi de Barcelona http://www.bcn.cat	ES/EUR		1-1820-23404
BEATS	Beats Electronics, LLC http://www.beatsbydre.com	US/NA		1-2048-47049
BEAUTY	L'Oréal http://www.loreal.com	FR/EUR		1-1302-76087
	Romeo Corner	US/NA		1-1356-74155
	Top Level Domain Holdings Limited http://www.tldh.org	VG/EUR		1-927-46801
BEER	Top Level Domain Holdings Limited http://www.tldh.org	VG/EUR		1-927-52478
BEKNOWN	Monster Worldwide, Inc. http://www.about-monster.com	US/NA		1-1800-89636
BENTLEY	Bentley Motors Limited http://www.bentleymotors.com	GB/EUR		1-1096-37266
BERLIN	dotBERLIN GmbH & Co. KG http://www.dotberlin.de	DE/EUR	Community Geographic	1-902-9993
BEST	BestTLD Pty Ltd	AU/AP		1-1705-80521
BESTBUY	BBY Solutions, Inc.	US/NA		1-1908-53104
BET	dot Bet Limited	GI/EUR		1-1201-33931
	Foggy Way, LLC	US/NA		1-1359-21671
	LADBROKES INTERNATIONAL PLC http://www.ladbrokesplc.com	GI/EUR		1-2015-28690
	Afilias Limited	IE/EUR		1-868-21199
BHARTI	Bharti Enterprises (Holding) Private Limited http://bharti.com	IN/AP		1-1287-43279
BIBLE	American Bible Society www.americanbible.org	US/NA		1-994-57975
BID	dot Bid Limited	GI/EUR		1-1227-16477
BIKE	Grand Hollow, LLC	US/NA		1-1357-41903
BING	Microsoft Corporation http://www.microsoft.com	US/NA		1-1129-41416
BINGO	dot Bingo Limited	GI/EUR		1-1207-57645
	Sand Cedar, LLC	US/NA		1-1360-70873
BIO	STARTING DOT http://www.startingdot.com	FR/EUR		1-1000-94806
BLACK	Afilias Limited	IE/EUR		1-868-74058

String	Applicant	Loc/Reg	Properties	IDN Attributes	Appl. ID
BLACKFRIDAY	Uniregistry, Corp. http://www.uniregistry.com	KY/EUR			1-855-24025
BLANCO	BLANCO GmbH + Co KG http://www.blanco-germany.com	DE/EUR			1-1334-26951
BLOCKBUSTER	Dish DBS Corporation http://www.dish.com	US/NA			1-1921-69359
BLOG	BET Inc. http://www.bet.co.jp	JP/AP			1-1013-6634
	Afilias Domains No. 1 Limited http://www.AfiliasDomains1.info	IE/EUR			1-1013-74175
	Top Level Design, LLC	US/NA			1-1086-2781
	Corn Shadow, LLC	US/NA			1-1358-79189
	Personals TLD Inc. http://www.radixregistry.com	AE/AP			1-1661-34613
	Charleston Road Registry Inc.	US/NA			1-1680-47770
	Merchant Law Group LLP	CA/NA			1-875-12119
	PRIMER NIVEL S.A. http://www.1ernivel.co	PA/LAC			1-917-1259
	Top Level Domain Holdings Limited http://www.tldh.org	VG/EUR			1-927-96975
BLOOMBERG	Bloomberg IP Holdings LLC	US/NA			1-1981-76785
BLOOMINGDALES	Macys, Inc. http://www.macysinc.com	US/NA			1-1790-71418
BLUE	Afilias Limited	IE/EUR			1-868-24255
BMS	Bristol-Myers Squibb Company http://www.bms.com	US/NA			1-1799-64357
BMW	Bayerische Motoren Werke Aktiengesellschaft http://www.bmwgroup.com	DE/EUR			1-938-21301
BNL	Banca Nazionale del Lavoro http://www.bnl.it	IT/EUR			1-1257-44806
BNPPARIBAS	BNP Paribas http://www.bnpparibas.com/	FR/EUR			1-1283-71884
BOATS	Black Shadow, LLC	US/NA			1-1362-58076
	DERBoats. LLC	US/NA			1-909-78528
BOEHRINGER	Boehringer Ingelheim Pharma GmbH & Co. KG http://www.boehringer-ingelheim.com	DE/EUR			1-1967-32024
BOFA	NMS Services, Inc.	US/NA			1-1953-47864
BOM	Núcleo de Informação e Coordenação do Ponto BR - NIC.br http://www.nic.br	BR/LAC			1-1119-71934
BOND	Bond University Limited http://www.bond.edu.au	AU/AP			1-2092-96476
BOO	Charleston Road Registry Inc.	US/NA			1-1681-73672
BOOK	R.R. Bowker LLC http://www.bowker.com	US/NA			1-1020-75316
	Top Level Domain Holdings Limited http://www.tldh.org	VG/EUR			1-1038-7319
	Charleston Road Registry Inc.	US/NA			1-1099-17603
	Global Domain Registry Pty Ltd	AU/AP			1-1132-20461
	Bronze Registry Limited	GI/EUR			1-1217-96477
	NU DOT CO LLC	US/NA			1-1296-97422
	Amazon EU S.à r.l. http://www.amazon.com/	LU/EUR			1-1315-44051
	Double Bloom, LLC	US/NA			1-1361-60591
	DotBook, LLC	US/NA			1-2029-6966
BOOKING	Booking.com B.V. http://www.booking.com	NL/EUR			1-1016-80657
BOOTS	THE BOOTS COMPANY PLC http://www.boots.com	GB/EUR			1-1288-319
BOSCH	Robert Bosch GMBH http://www.bosch.com	DE/EUR			1-1945-29108
BOSTIK	Bostik SA http://www.bostik.com	FR/EUR			1-1264-54834
BOSTON	The Boston Globe Newspaper Company Inc. http://www.boston.com	US/NA	Geographic		1-1958-93212
BOT	Amazon EU S.à r.l. http://www.amazon.com/	LU/EUR			1-1315-81832

Copyright 2012 Internet Corporation For Assigned Names and Numbers

String	Applicant	Loc/Reg	Properties IDN Attributes	Appl. ID
BOUTIQUE	Over Galley, LLC	US/NA		1-1363-29181
BOX	NS1 Limited	HK/AP		1-1309-75738
	Amazon EU S.à r.l. http://www.amazon.com/	LU/EUR		1-1315-32664
BRADESCO	Banco Bradesco S.A. http://www.bradesco.com.br	BR/LAC		1-898-653
BRIDGESTONE	Bridgestone Corporation http://www.bridgestone.co.jp	JP/AP		1-954-27550
BROADWAY	Key GTLD Holding Inc	UA/EUR		1-1326-20526
	Goose North, LLC	US/NA		1-1365-11798
	Celebrate Broadway, Inc. www.celebratebroadway.com	US/NA		1-994-4128
BROKER	IG Group Holdings PLC http://www.iggroup.com	GB/EUR		1-1332-82635
	Spring North, LLC	US/NA		1-1364-8001
BROTHER	Brother Industries, Ltd. http://www.brother.co.jp	JP/AP		1-944-92379
BRUSSELS	DNS.be vzw http://www.dns.be	BE/EUR	Geographic	1-1867-3276
BUDAPEST	Top Level Domain Holdings Limited http://www.tldh.org	VG/EUR	Geographic	1-1037-50753
BUGATTI	Bugatti International SA http://www.bugatti.com	LU/EUR	Community	1-1004-9564
BUICK	General Motors LLC http://www.gm.com	US/NA		1-1968-75588
BUILD	Plan Bee LLC	US/NA		1-888-47096
BUILDERS	Atomic Madison, LLC	US/NA		1-1366-121
BUSINESS	Spring Cross, LLC	US/NA		1-1367-68057
BUY	Charleston Road Registry Inc.	US/NA		1-1141-30048
	dot Buy Limited	GI/EUR		1-1213-57533
	Amazon EU S.à r.l. http://www.amazon.com/	LU/EUR		1-1315-53217
	Bitter Sunset, LLC	US/NA		1-1368-92181
	PVT Registry, LLC	US/NA		1-1694-75318
BUZZ	DOTSTRATEGY CO.	US/NA		1-1133-77383
BWAY	Key GTLD Holding Inc	UA/EUR		1-1326-61800
BZH	Association www.bzh http://www.pointbzh.com	FR/EUR	Community	1-989-18963
CAB	Half Sunset, LLC	US/NA		1-1371-6431
CADILLAC	General Motors LLC http://www.gm.com	US/NA		1-1979-22841
CAFE	Pioneer Canyon, LLC	US/NA		1-1370-88467
	Punto 2012 Sociedad Anonima de Capital Variable	MX/LAC		1-1868-50221
CAL	Charleston Road Registry Inc.	US/NA		1-1680-27519
CALL	Amazon EU S.à r.l. http://www.amazon.com/	LU/EUR		1-1315-29734
CALVINKLEIN	PVH gTLD Holdings LLC http://www.pvh.com	US/NA		1-998-12980
CAM	dot Agency Limited	GI/EUR		1-1234-83704
	United TLD Holdco Ltd. http://unitedtld.com	KY/EUR		1-1255-75865
	AC Webconnecting Holding B.V. http://acwebconnecting.com/	NL/EUR		1-882-71415
CAMERA	Atomic Maple, LLC	US/NA		1-1372-58656
CAMP	Delta Dynamite, LLC	US/NA		1-1373-83008
CANALPLUS	CANAL+ FRANCE http://www.canalplus.fr	FR/EUR		1-1751-49374
CANCERRESEARCH	Australian Cancer Research Foundation http://www.acrf.com.au	AU/AP		1-2027-17584
CANON	Canon Inc. http://canon.jp	JP/AP		1-919-80835

String	Applicant	Loc/Reg	Properties	IDN Attributes	Appl. ID
CAPETOWN	UniForum SA (NPC) trading as ZA Central Registry http://www.Registry.net.za	ZA/AF	Geographic		1-1864-98622
	Delta Mill, LLC	US/NA			1-1375-20218
CAPITAL					
CAPITALONE	Capital One Financial Corporation	US/NA			1-1267-72259
CAR	Charleston Road Registry Inc.	US/NA			1-1683-84431
CARAVAN	Caravan International, Inc.	US/NA			1-1847-21047
CARDS	Foggy Hollow, LLC	US/NA			1-1376-34668
CARE	Goose Cross	US/NA			1-1374-92093
CAREER	dotCareer LLC	US/NA			1-907-61259
CAREERS	Wild Corner, LLC	US/NA			1-1378-74207
CAREMORE	WellPoint, Inc. http://www.wellpoint.com	US/NA			1-1148-58828
CARINSURANCE	Allstate Fire and Casualty Insurance Company	US/NA			1-1191-70059
CARS	Koko Castle, LLC	US/NA			1-1377-8759
	Uniregistry, Corp. http://www.uniregistry.com	KY/EUR			1-845-37810
	DERCars, LLC	US/NA			1-909-45636
CARTIER	Richemont DNS Inc. http://www.richemont.com	CH/EUR			1-1253-32739
CASA	Top Level Domain Holdings Limited http://www.tldh.org	VG/EUR			1-1038-47257
	Go Daddy East, LLC http://www.godaddy.com	US/NA			1-1109-26787
	Extra Way, LLC	US/NA			1-1379-61100
CASE	Fiat Industrial S.p.A (società per azioni) http://www.fiatindustrial.com	IT/EUR			1-2050-40761
CASEIH	Fiat Industrial S.p.A (società per azioni) http://www.fiatindustrial.com	IT/EUR			1-2051-20058
CASH	Delta Lake, LLC	US/NA			1-1381-76948
CASHBACKBONUS	Discover Financial Services https://www.discover.com/	US/NA			1-1439-20671
CASINO	dot Casino Limited	GI/EUR			1-1203-44541
	Binky Sky, LLC	US/NA			1-1382-33633
	Afilias Limited	IE/EUR			1-868-87246
	dotBeauty LLC	US/NA			1-907-62211
CATALONIA	Generalitat de Catalunya http://www.gencat.cat	ES/EUR	Geographic		1-1821-72640
CATERING	New Falls. LLC	US/NA			1-1380-59591
CATHOLIC	Pontificium Consilium de Comunicationibus Socialibus (PCCS) (Pontifical Council for Social Communication) http://www.pccsva.org/	VA/EUR	Community		1-1311-76497
CBA	COMMONWEALTH BANK OF AUSTRALIA http://www.commbank.com.au	AU/AP			1-1672-4934
CBN	The Christian Broadcasting Network, Inc. http://www.cbn.com	US/NA			1-1980-27252
CBRE	CBRE, Inc. http://www.cbre.com	US/NA			1-2116-80094
CBS	CBS Domains Inc.	US/NA			1-869-11721
CEB	The Corporate Executive Board Company http://www.executiveboard.com/	US/NA			1-1773-64649
CENTER	Tin Mill, LLC	US/NA			1-1383-13918
CEO	CEOTLD Pty Ltd	AU/AP			1-1706-31908
CERN	European Organization for Nuclear Research ("CERN") http://cern.ch	CH/EUR			1-1082-60500
CFA	CFA Institute https://www.cfainstitute.org	US/NA			1-1877-69334
CFD	IG Group Holdings PLC http://www.iggroup.com	GB/EUR			1-2041-62930

String	Applicant	Loc/Reg	Properties	IDN Attributes	Appl. ID
CHANEL	Chanel International B.V. http://www.chanel.com	NL/EUR			1-1757-70300
CHANGIAIRPORT	Changi Airport Group (Singapore) Pte. Ltd http://www.changiairportgroup.com/cag/	SG/AP			1-2095-13299
CHANNEL	Charleston Road Registry Inc.	US/NA			1-1139-20196
CHARITY	Spring Registry Limited	GI/EUR			1-1241-87032
	Corn Lake, LLC	US/NA			1-1384-49318
CHARTIS	American International Group, Inc. http://www.aig.com	US/NA			1-1700-49793
CHASE	JPMorgan Chase & Co. http://www.jpmorganchase.com	US/NA			1-1190-39893
CHAT	IM TLD Inc. http://www.radixregistry.com	AE/AP			1-1064-17982
	dot Chat Limited	GI/EUR			1-1237-60534
	Top Level Spectrum, Inc. http://www.toplevelspectrum.com	US/NA			1-1279-42610
	Sand Fields, LLC	US/NA			1-1385-24288
CHATR	Rogers Communications Partnership http://www.rogers.com	CA/NA			1-1036-98768
CHEAP	Sand Cover, LLC	US/NA			1-1388-22552
CHESAPEAKE	Afterdot LLC	US/NA			1-908-25012
CHEVROLET	General Motors LLC http://www.gm.com	US/NA			1-1978-45010
CHEVY	General Motors LLC http://www.gm.com	US/NA			1-1971-57604
CHINTAI	CHINTAI Corporation http://chintai.jp/	JP/AP			1-901-295
CHK	Afterdot LLC	US/NA			1-908-49076
CHLOE	Richemont DNS Inc. http://www.richemont.com	CH/EUR			1-1253-90467
CHRISTMAS	Uniregistry, Corp. http://www.uniregistry.com	KY/EUR			1-855-47142
CHROME	Charleston Road Registry Inc.	US/NA			1-1683-38963
CHRYSLER	Chrysler Group LLC. http://www.chryslergroupllc.com	US/NA			1-2057-24195
CHURCH	Holly Fileds, LLC	US/NA			1-1387-59691
	Life Covenant Church, Inc.	US/NA			1-886-42389
CIALIS	Eli Lilly and Company http://www.lilly.com	US/NA			1-1018-47836
CIMB	CIMB Group Sdn Bhd http://www.cimb.com	MY/AP			1-1719-49476
CIPRIANI	Hotel Cipriani Srl http://www.hotelcipriani.com	IT/EUR			1-1837-53838
CIRCLE	Amazon EU S.à r.l. http://www.amazon.com/	LU/EUR			1-1315-92803
CISCO	Cisco Technology, Inc. http://www.cisco.com/	US/NA			1-1788-37128
CITADEL	Citadel Domain LLC	US/NA			1-1848-15726
CITI	Citigroup Inc. http://www.citigroup.com	US/NA			1-2086-70305
CITIC	CITIC Group Corporation http://www.citic.com	CN/AP			1-914-86033
CITY	DotCity Inc. http://www.radixregistry.com	AE/AP			1-1066-67099
	Snow Sky, LLC	US/NA			1-1389-12139
	TLD REGISTRY LIMITED http://internetregistry.info	IE/EUR			1-1938-29030
CITYEATS	Lifestyle Domain Holdings, Inc.	US/NA			1-1326-83809
CLAIMS	Black Corner, LLC	US/NA			1-1390-429
CLEANING	Fox Shadow, LLC	US/NA			1-1391-32771
CLICK	DotClick Inc. http://www.radixregistry.com	AE/AP			1-1068-4952

Copyright ...

String	Applicant	Loc/Reg	Properties	IDN Attributes	Appl. ID
	Uniregistry, Corp. http://www.uniregistry.com	KY/EUR			1-845-44500
CLINIC	Goose Park, LLC	US/NA			1-1392-58392
CLINIQUE	ELC Online Inc. http://elcompanies.com	US/NA			1-1962-86087
CLOTHING	Steel Lake, LLC	US/NA			1-1394-96113
CLOUD	Symantec Corporation	US/NA			1-1027-19707
	Top Level Domain Holdings Limited http://www.tldh.org	VG/EUR			1-1038-9346
	Charleston Road Registry Inc.	US/NA			1-1099-17190
	Amazon EU S.à r.l. http://www.amazon.com/	LU/EUR			1-1315-79670
	Dash Cedar, LLC	US/NA			1-1393-18458
	ARUBA S.p.A. http://www.aruba.it/	IT/EUR			1-1669-75338
	CloudNames AS http://cloudnames.com	NO/EUR			1-1747-41841
CLUB	Koko Manor, LLC	US/NA			1-1396-86079
	.CLUB DOMAINS, LLC http://rdotclub.com	US/NA			1-864-71021
	Merchant Law Group LLP	CA/NA			1-875-24017
CLUBMED	Club Méditerranée S.A. http://www.clubmed.com	FR/EUR			1-2079-28620
COACH	Koko Island, LLC	US/NA			1-1397-64766
	Coach, Inc. http://www.coach.com	US/NA			1-1880-48905
CODES	Puff Willow, LLC	US/NA			1-1398-14114
COFFEE	Trixy Cover, LLC	US/NA			1-1401-49222
COLLEGE	Binky Edge, LLC	US/NA			1-1400-95244
	XYZ.COM LLC	US/NA			1-2137-73069
COLOGNE	NetCologne Gesellschaft für Telekommunikation mbH http://www.netcologne.de	DE/EUR		Geographic	1-860-75931
COMCAST	Comcast IP Holdings I, LLC	US/NA			1-1170-7009
COMMBANK	COMMONWEALTH BANK OF AUSTRALIA http://www.commbank.com.au	AU/AP			1-1672-79914
COMMUNITY	Fox Orchard, LLC	US/NA			1-1402-32002
COMPANY	Silver Avenue, LLC	US/NA			1-1399-64977
COMPARE	iSelect Ltd http://www.iselect.com.au/	AU/AP			1-1088-79872
COMPUTER	Pine Mill, LLC	US/NA			1-1405-67595
COMSEC	VeriSign, Inc. http://www.verisigninc.com	US/NA			1-1145-38018
CONDOS	Pine House, LLC	US/NA			1-1404-98894
CONNECTORS	MiTek USA, Inc. http://www.mii.com	US/NA			1-1085-40392
CONSTRUCTION	Fox Dynamite, LLC	US/NA			1-1403-98045
	Dot Construction, LLC	US/NA			1-871-10185
CONSULTING	Pixie Station, LLC	US/NA			1-1406-80949
CONTACT	Top Level Spectrum, Inc. http://www.toplevelspectrum.com	US/NA			1-1279-75341
CONTRACTORS	Magic Woods, LLC	US/NA			1-1408-96304
COOKING	Top Level Domain Holdings Limited http://www.tldh.org	VG/EUR			1-1110-51672
COOKINGCHANNEL	Lifestyle Domain Holdings, Inc.	US/NA			1-1326-51959
COOL	Koko Lake, LLC	US/NA			1-1409-69124
CORP	Charleston Road Registry Inc.	US/NA			1-1139-21220
	NU DOT CO LLC	US/NA			1-1296-53960

Copyright 2012 Internet Corporation for Assigned Names and Numbers

String	Applicant	Loc/Reg	Properties	IDN Attributes	Appl. ID
	Cotton Fields, LLC	US/NA			1-1407-41397
	PROC Registry, LLC	US/NA			1-1693-13474
	DOTCORP LIMITED	HK/AP			1-2066-18958
	Dot Registry LLC	US/NA	Community		1-880-39342
CORSICA	Collectivité Territoriale de Corse http://www.corse.fr	FR/EUR	Community		1-937-68428
COUNTRY	Top Level Domain Holdings Limited http://www.tldh.org	VG/EUR			1-1038-69660
	Uniregistry, Corp. http://www.uniregistry.com	KY/EUR			1-845-1644
COUPON	Top Level Domain Holdings Limited http://www.tldh.org	VG/EUR			1-1038-45713
	Amazon EU S.à r.l. http://www.amazon.com/	LU/EUR			1-1315-85731
COUPONS	Black Island, LLC	US/NA			1-1413-96740
	Coupons.com Incorporated	US/NA			1-1668-71698
COURSES	OPEN UNIVERSITIES AUSTRALIA PTY LTD http://www.open.edu.au	AU/AP			1-1327-45933
CPA	Top Level Domain Holdings Limited http://www.tldh.org	VG/EUR			1-1038-40570
	Charleston Road Registry Inc.	US/NA			1-1138-86970
	Trixy Canyon	US/NA			1-1411-59458
	CPA AUSTRALIA LTD http://www.cpaaustralia.com.au/cps/rde/xchg	AU/AP	Community		1-1744-1971
	American Institute of Certified Public Accountants http://www.aicpa.org	US/NA			1-1910-48133
	American Institute of Certified Public Accountants http://www.aicpa.org	US/NA	Community		1-1911-56672
CREDIT	Snow Shadow, LLC	US/NA			1-1410-93823
CREDITCARD	Binky Frostbite, LLC	US/NA			1-1412-63109
CREDITUNION	CUNA Performance Resources, LLC	US/NA			1-1130-18309
CRICKET	Top Level Domain Holdings Limited http://www.tldh.org	VG/EUR			1-1038-10584
	dot Cricket Limited	GI/EUR			1-1205-96748
	Little Cover, LLC	US/NA			1-1414-81052
CROWN	Crown Equipment Corporation http://www.crown.com	US/NA			1-1277-15200
CRS	Federated Co operatives Limited http://www.coopconnection.ca	CA/NA			1-2046-93306
CRUISE	Viking River Cruises (Bermuda) Ltd. http://www.vikingrivercruises.com	US/NA			1-1691-43949
	Cruise Lines International Association Inc. http://www.cruising.org	US/NA			1-1852-14467
CRUISES	Spring Way, LLC	US/NA			1-1415-46513
CSC	Alliance-One Services, Inc. http://www.csc.com/alliance-one	US/NA			1-1674-60067
CUISINELLA	SALM S.A.S.	FR/EUR			1-1114-58195
CYMRU	Nominet UK http://www.nominet.org.uk	GB/EUR	Geographic		1-1105-16488
CYOU	Beijing Gamease Age Digital Technology Co., Ltd. http://www.changyou.com/	CN/AP			1-1659-50039
DABUR	Dabur India Limited http://www.dabur.com	IN/AP			1-1804-73491
DAD	Charleston Road Registry Inc.	US/NA			1-1682-14122
DANCE	United TLD Holdco Ltd. http://unitedtld.com	KY/EUR			1-1255-69937
DATA	Romeo Birch, LLC	US/NA			1-1605-75916
	Dish DBS Corporation http://www.dish.com	US/NA			1-2009-38008
	Top Level Domain Holdings Limited http://www.tldh.org	VG/EUR			1-927-73627
DATE	dot Date Limited	GI/EUR			1-1247-30301
DATING	Pine Fest, LLC	US/NA			1-1416-56404

String	Applicant	Loc/Reg	Properties	IDN Attributes	Appl. ID
DATSUN	NISSAN MOTOR CO., LTD. http://www.nissan-global.com/	JP/AP			1-1023-6629
DAY	Charleston Road Registry Inc.	US/NA			1-1139-19523
DCLK	Charleston Road Registry Inc.	US/NA			1-1141-22713
DDS	Top Level Domain Holdings Limited http://www.tldh.org	VG/EUR			1-1038-5963
	Charleston Road Registry Inc.	US/NA			1-1138-74264
DEAL	Amazon EU S.à r.l. http://www.amazon.com/	LU/EUR			1-1315-35975
	Uniregistry, Corp. http://www.uniregistry.com	KY/EUR			1-855-23694
DEALER	Dealer Dot Com, Inc. http://www.dealer.com	US/NA			1-993-62521
DEALS	DotDeals Inc. http://www.radixregistry.com	AE/AP			1-1056-93782
	Top Level Domain Holdings Limited http://www.tldh.org	VG/EUR			1-1110-25638
	Sand Sunset, LLC	US/NA			1-1419-43874
DEGREE	Puff House, LLC	US/NA			1-1418-57248
DELIVERY	dot Delivery Limited	GI/EUR			1-1220-89939
	Steel Station, LLC	US/NA			1-1420-57575
DELL	Dell Inc.	US/NA			1-1094-11981
DELMONTE	Del Monte International GmbH	MC/EUR			1-929-51262
DELOITTE	Deloitte Touche Tohmatsu http://www.deloitte.com/global	US/NA			1-1944-83205
DELTA	Delta Air Lines, Inc. http://www.delta.com	US/NA			1-1259-75287
DEMOCRAT	United TLD Holdco Ltd. http://unitedtld.com	KY/EUR			1-1255-25868
DENTAL	Tin Birch, LLC	US/NA			1-1421-91857
DENTIST	Outer Lake, LLC	US/NA			1-1422-97537
DESI	Afilias Domains No. 4 Limited, http://www.AfiliasDomains4.info	IE/EUR			1-1013-78434
	Desi Networks LLC	US/NA			1-870-27617
DESIGN	STARTING DOT http://www.startingdot.com	FR/EUR			1-1000-71907
	BET Inc. http://www.bet.co.jp	JP/AP			1-1013-4245
	Top Level Domain Holdings Limited http://www.tldh.org	VG/EUR			1-1038-80812
	Top Level Design, LLC	US/NA			1-1086-90196
	NU DOT CO LLC	US/NA			1-1296-10164
	Black Avenue, LLC	US/NA			1-1425-38025
	Design Trend Registry Inc.	CA/NA			1-2082-69005
	Uniregistry, Corp. http://www.uniregistry.com	KY/EUR			1-845-26161
DEUTSCHEPOST	Deutsche Post AG http://www.dp-dhl.com/de.html	DE/EUR			1-1075-11927
DEV	Charleston Road Registry Inc.	US/NA			1-1138-73066
	Amazon EU S.à r.l. http://www.amazon.com/	LU/EUR			1-1316-95567
DHL	Deutsche Post AG http://www.dp-dhl.com/de.html	DE/EUR			1-1075-45896
DIAMONDS	John Edge, LLC	US/NA			1-1428-32844
DIET	dot Diet Limited	GI/EUR			1-1225-36982
	Pioneer Hill, LLC	US/NA			1-1426-25607
	Uniregistry, Corp. http://www.uniregistry.com	KY/EUR			1-845-21294
DIGIKEY	Digi-Key Corporation http://www.digikey.com/	US/NA			1-976-58323
DIGITAL	Dash Park, LLC	US/NA			1-1427-39640

Copyright 2012 Internet Corporation for Assigned Names and Numbers

String	Applicant	Loc/Reg	Properties IDN Attributes	Appl. ID
DIRECT	Half Trail, LLC	US/NA		1-1424-94823
	Dish DBS Corporation http://www.dish.com	US/NA		1-2007-43424
DIRECTORY	Extra Madison, LLC	US/NA		1-1432-79618
DISCOUNT	Holly Hill, LLC	US/NA		1-1431-6328
	Dot Discount, LLC	US/NA		1-856-55254
DISCOVER	Discover Financial Services https://www.discover.com/	US/NA		1-1423-36348
DISH	Dish DBS Corporation http://www.dish.com	US/NA		1-1919-18145
DIY	Lifestyle Domain Holdings, Inc.	US/NA		1-1326-57740
	Charleston Road Registry Inc.	US/NA		1-1678-58300
DNB	The Dun & Bradstreet Corporation http://ww.dnb.com	US/NA		1-1832-141
DNP	Dai Nippon Printing Co., Ltd. http://www.dnp.co.jp/eng/	JP/AP		1-948-69611
DOCOMO	NTT DOCOMO, INC. http://www.nttdocomo.co.jp	JP/AP		1-1100-83885
DOCS	Microsoft Corporation http://www.microsoft.com	US/NA		1-1129-14280
	Charleston Road Registry Inc.	US/NA		1-1682-12856
DOCTOR	DotMedico TLD Inc. http://www.radixregistry.com	AE/AP		1-1060-13366
	Brice Trail, LLC	US/NA		1-1430-52453
	The Medical Registry Limited http://www.thedoctorregistry.com	US/NA		1-2026-56939
DODGE	Chrysler Group LLC. http://www.chryslergrouplc.com	US/NA		1-2054-9171
DOG	Top Level Domain Holdings Limited http://www.tldh.org	VG/EUR		1-1038-63631
	Charleston Road Registry Inc.	US/NA		1-1140-60957
	Koko Mill, LLC	US/NA		1-1429-22494
DOHA	The Supreme Council of Information and Communication Technology "ictQATAR" http://www.ict.gov.qa	QA/AP	Geographic	1-1150-50794
DOMAINS	Sugar Cross, LLC	US/NA		1-1433-39728
DOOSAN	Doosan Corporation http://www.doosan.com	KR/AP		1-1855-76721
DOT	Charleston Road Registry Inc.	US/NA		1-1140-12803
	Dish DBS Corporation http://www.dish.com	US/NA		1-2005-70840
DOTAFRICA	DotConnectAfrica Trust http://www.dotconnectafrica.org	MU/AF	Geographic	1-1165-42560
DOWNLOAD	dot Support Limited	GI/EUR		1-1210-70457
DRIVE	Charleston Road Registry Inc.	US/NA		1-1138-62581
	Amazon EU S.à r.l. http://www.amazon.com/	LU/EUR		1-1316-37524
DSTV	MultiChoice Africa (Proprietary) Limited http://www.multichoice.co.za	ZA/AF		1-1899-97050
DTV	Dish DBS Corporation http://www.dish.com	US/NA		1-2084-81667
DUBAI	Dubai eGovernment Department http://www.deg.gov.ae	AE/AP	Geographic	1-1838-15469
DUCK	Johnson Shareholdings, Inc.	US/NA		1-1248-11973
DUNLOP	The Goodyear Tire & Rubber Company http://www.goodyear.com	US/NA		1-1885-14876
DUNS	The Dun & Bradstreet Corporation http://ww.dnb.com	US/NA		1-1832-42386
DUPONT	E.I. du Pont de Nemours and Company http://www.dupont.com	US/NA		1-1300-88322
DURBAN	UniForum SA (NPC) trading as ZA Central Registry http://www.Registry.net.za	ZA/AF	Geographic	1-1864-63608
DVAG	Deutsche Vermögensberatung Aktiengesellschaft DVAG http://www.dvag.com	DE/EUR		1-904-62612

Copyright © 2013 John Wiley & Sons, Inc. All rights reserved.

APPENDIX A

String	Applicant	Loc/Reg	Properties	IDN Attributes	Appl. ID
DVR	Hughes Satellite Systems Corporation http://www.hughes.com	US/NA			1-2000-89466
DWG	Autodesk, Inc. http://www.autodesk.com	US/NA			1-1889-53120
EARTH	Charleston Road Registry Inc.	US/NA			1-1140-20623
	Interlink Co., Ltd. http://www.interlink.or.jp/	JP/AP			1-901-26957
EAT	Charleston Road Registry Inc.	US/NA			1-1139-37354
ECO	Top Level Domain Holdings Limited http://www.tldh.org	VG/EUR			1-1039-91823
	Little Birch, LLC	US/NA			1-1434-1370
	Planet Dot Eco, LLC http://planetdoteco.com	US/NA			1-1710-92415
	Big Room Inc. http://www.bigroom.ca	CA/NA	Community		1-912-59314
ECOM	Ecommerce Inc. http://www.ecommerce.com	US/NA			1-2016-12429
EDEKA	EDEKA Verband kaufmännischer Genossenschaften e.V. http://www.edeka.de	DE/EUR	Community		1-1297-3451
EDUCATION	Brice Way, LLC	US/NA			1-1435-73490
EMAIL	Spring Madison, LLC	US/NA			1-1438-98374
EMERCK	Merck KGaA http://www.merckgroup.com	DE/EUR			1-980-60636
EMERSON	Emerson Electric Co. http://www.Emerson.com	US/NA			1-1299-23169
ENERGY	dot Energy Limited	GI/EUR			1-1221-4047
	Binky Birch, LLC	US/NA			1-1437-42738
ENGINEER	United TLD Holdco Ltd. http://unitedtld.com	KY/EUR			1-1255-37010
ENGINEERING	Romeo Canyon	US/NA			1-1436-74788
ENTERPRISES	Snow Oaks, LLC	US/NA			1-1440-71720
EPOST	Deutsche Post AG http://www.dp-dhl.com/de.html	DE/EUR			1-1075-2496
EPSON	Seiko Epson Corporation http://www.epson.jp/	JP/AP			1-936-24218
EQUIPMENT	Corn Station, LLC	US/NA			1-1442-68106
ERICSSON	Telefonaktiebolaget L M Ericsson http://ericsson.com	SE/EUR			1-1798-68430
ERNI	ERNI Group Holding AG http://www.erni.ch	CH/EUR			1-949-56474
ESQ	Charleston Road Registry Inc.	US/NA			1-1140-98965
EST	Charleston Road Registry Inc.	US/NA			1-1681-86067
ESTATE	Trixy Park, LLC	US/NA			1-1441-44965
ESURANCE	Esurance Insurance Company	US/NA			1-1987-61342
ETISALAT	Emirates Telecommunications Corporation (trading as Etisalat) http://www.etisalat.com	AE/AP			1-1743-35887
EUROVISION	European Broadcasting Union (EBU) http://www.ebu.ch	CH/EUR			1-1083-6576
EUS	Puntueus Fundazioa http://www.puntueus.org/	ES/EUR	Community		1-1293-15788
EVENTS	Pioneer Maple, LLC	US/NA			1-1443-27992
EVERBANK	EverBank https://www.everbank.com	US/NA			1-2136-22895
EXCHANGE	Spring Falls, LLC	US/NA			1-1445-68403
EXPERT	Magic Pass, LLC	US/NA			1-1444-46322
	Red Circle, LLC	US/NA			1-1970-27496
EXPOSED	Victor Beach, LLC	US/NA			1-1446-82057
EXPRESS	Sea Sunset, LLC	US/NA			1-1447-46365
	Express LLC	US/NA			1-1690-33371

Copyright 2013 Internet Corporation for Assigned Names and Numbers

String	Applicant	Loc/Reg	Properties IDN Attributes	Appl. ID
	Express LLC http://www.express.com	US/NA		1-1690-33371
EXTRASPACE	Extra Space Storage LLC http://www.extraspace.com	US/NA		1-1688-1352
FAGE	FAGE Dairy Industry S.A. http://www.fage.gr	GR/EUR		1-2125-19961
FAIL	Atomic Pipe, LLC	US/NA		1-1448-73190
FAIRWINDS	FairWinds Partners, LLC	US/NA		1-1173-27755
FAITH	dot Faith Limited	GI/EUR		1-1228-92789
FAMILY	Bitter Galley, LLC	US/NA		1-1450-96002
	Charleston Road Registry Inc.	US/NA		1-1683-11222
	Uniregistry, Corp. http://www.uniregistry.com	KY/EUR		1-845-55827
FAN	Goose Glen, LLC	US/NA		1-1449-26710
FANS	Asiamix Digital Limited	HK/AP		1-1711-46810
FARM	Just Maple, LLC	US/NA		1-1451-8324
FARMERS	Farmers Insurance Exchange http://www.farmers.com	US/NA		1-1801-23208
FASHION	Top Level Domain Holdings Limited http://www.tldh.org	VG/EUR		1-1039-98979
	Diamond Registry Limited	GI/EUR		1-1224-46400
	Big Dynamite, LLC	US/NA		1-1455-48217
	Uniregistry, Corp. http://www.uniregistry.com	KY/EUR		1-845-22951
FAST	Amazon EU S.à r.l. http://www.amazon.com/	LU/EUR		1-1316-97653
FEDEX	Federal Express Corporation http://www.fedex.com/	US/NA		1-1896-90293
FEEDBACK	Top Level Spectrum, Inc. http://www.toplevelspectrum.com	US/NA		1-1279-54497
FERRARI	Fiat S.p.A. ("società per azioni") http://www.fiatspa.com	IT/EUR		1-2071-48444
FERRERO	Ferrero Trading Lux S.A. http://www.ferrero.com	LU/EUR		1-1126-78849
FIAT	Fiat S.p.A. ("società per azioni") http://www.fiatspa.com	IT/EUR		1-2067-46114
FIDELITY	Fidelity Brokerage Services LLC https://www.fidelity.com/	US/NA		1-1845-19586
FIDO	Rogers Communications Partnership http://www.rogers.com	CA/NA		1-1036-80240
FILM	Charleston Road Registry Inc.	US/NA		1-1138-87772
	Outer Avenue, LLC	US/NA		1-1452-20905
	Motion Picture Domain Registry Pty Ltd	AU/AP		1-1802-37358
FINAL	Núcleo de Informação e Coordenação do Ponto BR - NIC.br http://www.nic.br	BR/LAC		1-1119-72288
FINANCE	Cotton Cypress, LLC	US/NA		1-1454-18725
FINANCIAL	Just Cover, LLC	US/NA		1-1453-71764
FINANCIALAID	Rezolve Group, Inc. http://www.rezolvegroup.com/	US/NA		1-1846-66020
FINISH	Reckitt Benckiser N.V. http://www.rb.com	NL/EUR		1-1258-76523
FIRE	Amazon EU S.à r.l. http://www.amazon.com/	LU/EUR		1-1315-94280
FIRESTONE	Bridgestone Corporation http://www.bridgestone.co.jp	JP/AP		1-954-87942
FIRMDALE	Firmdale Holdings Limited http://WWW.FIRMDALEHOTELS.COM	GB/EUR		1-1818-23087
FISH	Fox Woods, LLC	US/NA		1-1459-49079
	Dot Club LLC	US/NA		1-856-22387
FISHING	Top Level Domain Holdings Limited http://www.tldh.org	VG/EUR		1-1039-82031
	United TLD Holdco Ltd. http://unitedtld.com	KY/EUR		1-1255-72432

Copyright 2012 Internet Corporation for Assigned Names and Numbers

String	Applicant	Loc/Reg	Properties	IDN Attributes	Appl. ID
FIT	Top Level Domain Holdings Limited http://www.tldh.org	VG/EUR			1-1039-18316
	Platinum Registry Limited	GI/EUR			1-1229-33615
FITNESS	Brice Orchard, LLC	US/NA			1-1457-79967
FLICKR	Yahoo! Domain Services Inc.	US/NA			1-1168-54294
FLIGHTS	Fox Station, LLC	US/NA			1-1460-3791
FLIR	FLIR Systems, Inc. http://www.flir.com	US/NA			1-1272-48294
FLORIST	Half Cypress, LLC	US/NA			1-1456-34878
FLOWERS	Top Level Domain Holdings Limited http://www.tldh.org	VG/EUR			1-1039-50712
	Fern Willow, LLC	US/NA			1-1458-34042
	Piper Ventures, LLC	US/NA			1-1534-89307
	Uniregistry, Corp. http://www.uniregistry.com	KY/EUR			1-845-21975
FLS	FLSmidth A/S http://www.flsmidth.com	DK/EUR			1-911-22365
FLSMIDTH	FLSmidth A/S http://www.flsmidth.com	DK/EUR			1-911-91166
FLY	Charleston Road Registry Inc.	US/NA			1-1141-48206
FOO	Charleston Road Registry Inc.	US/NA			1-1681-22593
FOOD	Lifestyle Domain Holdings, Inc.	US/NA			1-1326-50608
	Wild Orchard, LLC	US/NA			1-1462-36448
	Dot Food, LLC	US/NA			1-1975-66983
FOODNETWORK	Lifestyle Domain Holdings, Inc.	US/NA			1-1326-10877
FOOTBALL	dot Football Limited	GI/EUR			1-1185-40986
	Foggy Farms, LLC	US/NA			1-1463-19656
FORD	Ford Motor Company http://www.ford.com	US/NA			1-1310-12426
FOREX	IG Group Holdings PLC http://www.iggroup.com	GB/EUR			1-2043-82969
FORSALE	Sea Oaks, LLC	US/NA			1-1461-35653
	DERForsale, LLC	US/NA			1-909-18178
FORUM	dot Forum Limited	GI/EUR			1-1212-56127
	June Hollow, LLC	US/NA			1-1464-71170
	Fegistry, LLC	US/NA			1-1913-92671
FOUNDATION	John Dale, LLC	US/NA			1-1468-64201
FOX	FOX Registry, LLC	US/NA			1-1167-1880
FREE	Top Level Domain Holdings Limited http://www.tldh.org	VG/EUR			1-1039-66889
	Charleston Road Registry Inc.	US/NA			1-1141-1851
	Amazon EU S.à r.l. http://www.amazon.com/	LU/EUR			1-1316-21923
	Over Keep, LLC	US/NA			1-1465-93738
	Uniregistry, Corp. http://www.uniregistry.com	KY/EUR			1-845-38175
FRESENIUS	Fresenius Immobilien-Verwaltungs-GmbH	DE/EUR			1-916-50890
FRL	Metaregistrar B.V. http://www.metaregistrar.com	NL/EUR	Geographic		1-1312-75662
FROGANS	OP3FT http://www.op3ft.org/	FR/EUR			1-1270-9301
FRONTDOOR	Lifestyle Domain Holdings, Inc.	US/NA			1-1326-50203
FRONTIER	Frontier Communications Corporation http://www.ftr.com	US/NA			1-2106-18801
FTR	Frontier Communications Corporation http://www.ftr.com	US/NA			1-2105-39700
FUJITSU	Fujitsu Limited http://www.fujitsu.com/	JP/AP			1-1722-42216

Copyright 2013 Internet Corporation for Assigned Names and Numbers

String	Applicant	Loc/Reg	Properties	IDN Attributes	Appl. ID
FUJIXEROX	Xerox DNHC LLC http://www.xerox.com/	US/NA			1-1046-39945
FUN	DOTSTRATEGY CO.	US/NA			1-1133-86731
	Oriental Trading Company, Inc. http://www.orientaltrading.com	US/NA			1-1274-35353
	Charleston Road Registry Inc.	US/NA			1-1680-35845
FUND	John Castle, LLC	US/NA			1-1467-34522
FURNITURE	Lone Fields, LLC	US/NA			1-1466-60532
	Uniregistry, Corp. http://www.uniregistry.com	KY/EUR			1-845-27313
FUTBOL	Atomic Falls, LLC	US/NA			1-1469-89174
FYI	Silver Tigers, LLC	US/NA			1-1579-33517
	Charleston Road Registry Inc.	US/NA			1-1683-65308
GAL	Asociación puntoGAL http://www.puntogal.org	ES/EUR	Community		1-1278-425
GALLERY	Sugar House, LLC	US/NA			1-1471-10955
GALLO	Gallo Vineyards, Inc.	US/NA			1-1983-39264
GALLUP	Gallup, Inc. http://www.gallup.com	US/NA			1-1124-66954
GAME	Charleston Road Registry Inc.	US/NA			1-1138-34539
	Dot Game Limited	GI/EUR			1-1177-24251
	Amazon EU S.à r.l. http://www.amazon.com/	LU/EUR			1-1316-7998
	Beijing Gamease Age Digital Technology Co., Ltd. http://www.changyou.com	CN/AP			1-1660-73645
	Uniregistry, Corp. http://www.uniregistry.com	KY/EUR			1-855-17500
GAMES	Foggy Beach, LLC	US/NA			1-1470-40168
GAP	The Gap, Inc. http://www.gap.com	US/NA			1-925-90449
GARDEN	Top Level Domain Holdings Limited http://www.tldh.org	VG/EUR			1-1039-6355
	Brice Maple, LLC	US/NA			1-1472-69003
	Uniregistry, Corp. http://www.uniregistry.com	KY/EUR			1-845-21873
GARNIER	L'Oréal http://www.loreal.com	FR/EUR			1-1301-51077
GAY	Top Level Domain Holdings Limited http://www.tldh.org	VG/EUR			1-1039-47682
	Top Level Design, LLC	US/NA			1-1086-79087
	United TLD Holdco Ltd. http://unitedtld.com	KY/EUR			1-1255-4825
	dotgay llc http://dotgay.com	US/NA	Community		1-1713-23699
GBIZ	Charleston Road Registry Inc.	US/NA			1-1683-16092
GCC	GCCIX WLL http://www.gccix.net	BH/AP			1-1936-21010
GDN	Guardian News and Media Limited http://www.guardian.co.uk	GB/EUR			1-1729-48006
	Joint Stock Company "Navigation-information systems" http://www.nis-glonass.ru	RU/EUR			1-1866-26783
GEA	GEA Group Aktiengesellschaft http://www.geagroup.com	DE/EUR	Community		1-1337-68453
GECOMPANY	GE GTLD Holdings LLC	US/NA			1-1330-33640
GED	GED Domains LLC	US/NA			1-1155-50524
GENT	COMBELL GROUP NV/SA http://www.combell.com	BE/EUR	Geographic		1-1679-97532
GENTING	Resorts World Inc Pte. Ltd. http://www.genting.com	HK/AP			1-2073-97647
GEORGE	Wal-Mart Stores, Inc.	US/NA			1-1244-15683
GGEE	GMO Internet, Inc. http://www.gmo.jp/en/	JP/AP			1-1734-71117

String	Applicant	Loc/Reg	Properties	IDN Attributes	Appl. ID
GIFT	Dot Gift Limited	GI/EUR			1-1218-92007
	Uniregistry, Corp. http://www.uniregistry.com	KY/EUR			1-855-85881
GIFTS	Goose Sky, LLC	US/NA			1-1474-76888
	Lucy Ventures, LLC	US/NA			1-1541-3638
GIVES	United TLD Holdco Ltd. http://unitedtld.com	KY/EUR			1-1255-39674
GIVING	Giving Limited http://www.justgiving.com	GB/EUR			1-1284-21841
GLADE	Johnson Shareholdings, Inc.	US/NA			1-1248-47766
GLASS	Black Cover, LLC	US/NA			1-1475-74719
GLE	Charleston Road Registry Inc.	US/NA			1-1099-85478
GLEAN	Lifestyle Domain Holdings, Inc.	US/NA			1-1326-78708
GLOBAL	Goose Falls, LLC	US/NA			1-1473-54534
	CloudNames AS http://cloudnames.com	NO/EUR			1-1747-40234
GLOBALX	GlobalX Information Services Pty Limited http://www.globalx.com.au/	AU/AP			1-952-84372
GLOBO	Globo Comunicação e Participações S.A http://globo.com	BR/LAC			1-1151-96871
GMAIL	Charleston Road Registry Inc.	US/NA			1-1099-70123
GMBH	TLDDOT GmbH http://www.dotgmbh.de	DE/EUR	Community		1-1273-63351
	NU DOT CO LLC	US/NA			1-1296-52581
	Extra Dynamite, LLC	US/NA			1-1477-91047
	Charleston Road Registry Inc.	US/NA			1-1682-34664
	GMBH Registry, LLC	US/NA			1-1693-16758
	InterNetWire Web-Development GmbH	DE/EUR			1-1952-21459
GMC	General Motors LLC http://www.gm.com/	US/NA			1-1843-37097
GMO	GMO Internet, Inc. http://www.gmo.jp/en/	JP/AP			1-1657-61205
GMX	1&1 Mail & Media GmbH http://www.web.de	DE/EUR			1-1256-36701
GODADDY	Go Daddy East, LLC http://www.godaddy.com	US/NA			1-1109-42895
GOLD	WGC (IOM) Limited http://www.gold.org	GB/EUR			1-1143-36731
	June Edge, LLC	US/NA			1-1478-71326
GOLDPOINT	YODOBASHI CAMERA CO.,LTD. http://www.yodobashi.co.jp	JP/AP			1-1809-71826
GOLF	Gold Registry Limited	GI/EUR			1-1184-54304
	Lone falls, LLC	US/NA			1-1476-38656
	Fegistry, LLC	US/NA			1-1913-58763
	Dot-Golf LLC http://www.dotgolf.co	US/NA			1-900-40419
GOO	Charleston Road Registry Inc.	US/NA			1-1142-62939
	NTT Resonant Inc. http://www.nttr.co.jp/	JP/AP			1-1810-48580
GOODHANDS	Allstate Fire and Casualty Insurance Company	US/NA			1-1191-24980
GOODYEAR	The Goodyear Tire & Rubber Company http://www.goodyear.com	US/NA			1-1886-86906
GOOG	Charleston Road Registry Inc.	US/NA			1-1099-4940
GOOGLE	Charleston Road Registry Inc.	US/NA			1-1099-35758
GOP	Republican State Leadership Committee, Inc. RSLC.COM	US/NA			1-994-50847
GOT	Amazon EU S.à r.l. http://www.amazon.com/	LU/EUR			1-1316-81180
GOTV	MultiChoice Africa (Proprietary) Limited http://www.multichoice.co.za	ZA/AF			1-1900-14953

Copyright 2012 Internet Corporation for Assigned Names and Numbers

String	Applicant	Loc/Reg	Properties	IDN Attributes	Appl. ID
GRAINGER	Grainger Registry Services, LLC	US/NA			1-1006-23981
GRAPHICS	Over Madison, LLC	US/NA			1-1479-5306
GRATIS	Pioneer Tigers, LLC	US/NA			1-1481-2922
	Uniregistry, Corp. http://www.uniregistry.com	KY/EUR			1-845-42772
GREE	GREE, Inc. http://www.gree.co.jp/	JP/AP	Community		1-1042-13015
GREEN	Top Level Domain Holdings Limited http://www.tldh.org	VG/EUR			1-1039-46343
	United TLD Holdco Ltd. http://unitedtld.com	KY/EUR			1-1255-2257
	Afilias Limited	IE/EUR			1-868-24661
	DotGreen Community, Inc. http://www.dotgreen.org	US/NA			1-884-75541
GRIPE	Corn Sunset, LLC	US/NA			1-1486-63504
GROCERY	Safeway Inc.	US/NA			1-1189-31055
	Wal-Mart Stores, Inc. http://www.walmartstores.com	US/NA			1-2064-74519
GROUP	Top Level Design, LLC	US/NA			1-1086-21577
	Tucows TLDs Inc. http://www.tucowsinc.com	CA/NA			1-1171-93026
	NU DOT CO LLC	US/NA			1-1296-48207
	Amazon EU S.à r.l. http://www.amazon.com/	LU/EUR			1-1316-84755
	Romeo Town, LLC	US/NA			1-1482-30833
GUARDIAN	The Guardian Life Insurance Company of America	US/NA			1-1298-37058
	Guardian News and Media Limited http://www.guardian.co.uk	GB/EUR			1-1728-88967
GUARDIANLIFE	The Guardian Life Insurance Company of America	US/NA			1-1298-7305
GUARDIANMEDIA	Guardian News and Media Limited http://www.guardian.co.uk	GB/EUR			1-1731-48782
GUCCI	Guccio Gucci S.p.a.	IT/EUR			1-951-28008
GUGE	Charleston Road Registry Inc.	US/NA			1-1099-76403
GUIDE	Top Level Domain Holdings Limited http://www.tldh.org	VG/EUR			1-1039-17716
	Snow Moon, LLC	US/NA			1-1484-33046
GUITARS	Uniregistry, Corp. http://www.uniregistry.com	KY/EUR			1-855-34620
GURU	Pioneer Cypress, LLC	US/NA			1-1487-73268
HAIR	Your Hair Limited	GB/EUR			1-1013-46158
	L'Oréal http://www.loreal.com	FR/EUR			1-1302-98299
HALAL	Asia Green IT System Bilgisayar San. ve Tic. Ltd. Sti.	TR/AP	Community		1-2131-60793
HAMBURG	Hamburg Top-Level-Domain GmbH http://www.dothamburg.de	DE/EUR	Community Geographic		1-1134-57974
HANGOUT	Charleston Road Registry Inc.	US/NA			1-1678-13168
HAUS	Pixie Edge, LLC	US/NA			1-1488-15641
HBO	HBO Registry Services, Inc.	US/NA			1-1783-76510
HDFC	HOUSING DEVELOPMENT FINANCE CORPORATION LIMITED http://www.hdfc.com	IN/AP			1-1859-23172
HDFCBANK	HDFC Bank Limited http://www.hdfcbank.com	IN/AP			1-1307-93169
HEALTH	dot Health Limited	GI/EUR			1-1178-3236
	Goose Fest, LLC	US/NA			1-1489-82287
	DotHealth, LLC http://www.dothealthgtld.com	US/NA			1-1684-6394
	Afilias Limited	IE/EUR			1-868-3442
HEALTHCARE	Silver Glen, LLC	US/NA			1-1492-32589

String	Applicant	Loc/Reg	Properties IDN Attributes	Appl. ID
HEART	American Heart Association, Inc. http://www.heart.org	US/NA		1-1483-85325
HEINZ	ProMark Brands Inc.	US/NA		1-941-50387
HELP	Pioneer Gardens, LLC	US/NA		1-1499-91633
	Dot Tech LLC	US/NA		1-1670-92378
	Uniregistry, Corp. http://www.uniregistry.com	KY/EUR		1-845-3403
HELSINKI	City of Helsinki	FI/EUR	Geographic	1-1865-66478
HERE	Charleston Road Registry Inc.	US/NA		1-1140-20987
HERMES	HERMES INTERNATIONAL http://www.hermes.com	FR/EUR		1-1136-8758
HGTV	Lifestyle Domain Holdings, Inc.	US/NA		1-1326-4851
HILTON	HLT Stakis IP Limited	US/NA		1-1876-7694
HIPHOP	Uniregistry, Corp. http://www.uniregistry.com	KY/EUR		1-855-7383
HISAMITSU	Hisamitsu Pharmaceutical Co.,Inc. http://www.hisamitsu.co.jp/	JP/AP		1-935-57258
HITACHI	Hitachi, Ltd. http://www.hitachi.co.jp	JP/AP		1-1024-52378
HIV	dotHIV gemeinnuetziger e.V. http://www.dothiv.org	DE/EUR		1-971-90747
HKT	PCCW-HKT DataCom Services Limited www.hkt.com	HK/AP		1-1309-96306
HOCKEY	dot Hockey Limited	GI/EUR		1-1204-89680
	Half Willow, LLC	US/NA		1-1493-98462
HOLDINGS	John Madison, LLC	US/NA		1-1496-1524
HOLIDAY	Goose Woods, LLC	US/NA		1-1497-56699
HOME	.HOME REGISTRY INC.	KY/EUR		1-1013-95616
	DotHome Inc. http://www.radixregistry.com	AE/AP		1-1049-60075
	Go Daddy East, LLC http://www.godaddy.com	US/NA		1-1109-77450
	Charleston Road Registry Inc.	US/NA		1-1139-16944
	Lifestyle Domain Holdings, Inc.	US/NA		1-1326-24627
	Baxter Pike, LLC	US/NA		1-1494-83305
	DotHome / CGR E-Commerce Ltd http://dothome.net	CY/AP		1-2021-47438
	Uniregistry, Corp. http://www.uniregistry.com	KY/EUR		1-845-48417
	Merchant Law Group LLP	CA/NA		1-875-27253
	Dot Home LLC	US/NA		1-907-28623
	Top Level Domain Holdings Limited http://www.tldh.org	VG/EUR		1-927-70273
HOMEDEPOT	Homer TLC, Inc. http://www.homedepot.com/	US/NA		1-1095-1782
HOMEGOODS	The TJX Companies, Inc. http://www.tjx.com	US/NA		1-1764-99491
HOMES	DERHomes, LLC	US/NA		1-909-196
HOMESENSE	The TJX Companies, Inc. http://www.tjx.com	US/NA		1-1764-22954
HONDA	Honda Motor Co., Ltd. http://www.honda.co.jp/	JP/AP		1-1923-79996
HONEYWELL	Honeywell GTLD LLC	US/NA		1-1517-81574
HORSE	Top Level Domain Holdings Limited http://www.tldh.org	VG/EUR		1-927-86049
HOSPITAL	Ruby Pike, LLC	US/NA		1-1505-15195
HOST	DotHost Inc. http://www.radixregistry.com	AE/AP		1-1061-73671
HOSTING	Dottransfer Inc. http://www.radixregistry.com	AE/AP		1-1286-14385

Copyright 2012 Internet Corporation for Assigned Names and Numbers

String	Applicant	Loc/Reg	Properties IDN Attributes	Appl. ID
	Uniregistry, Corp. http://www.uniregistry.com	KY/EUR		1-855-76484
HOT	Amazon EU S.à r.l. http://www.amazon.com/	LU/EUR		1-1316-38620
	Auburn Hill, LLC	US/NA		1-1498-82780
	dotHot LLC	US/NA		1-907-22514
HOTEIS	Despegar Online SRL http://www.despegar.com	UY/LAC		1-1249-87712
HOTEL	HOTEL Top-Level-Domain S.a.r.l http://www.dothotel.info	LU/EUR	Community	1-1032-95136
	DotHotel Inc. http://www.radixregistry.com	AE/AP		1-1059-97519
	dot Hotel Limited	GI/EUR		1-1181-77853
	Despegar Online SRL http://www.despegar.com	UY/LAC		1-1249-36568
	Spring McCook, LLC	US/NA		1-1500-16803
	Fegistry, LLC	US/NA		1-1913-57874
	Top Level Domain Holdings Limited http://www.tldh.org	VG/EUR		1-927-25198
HOTELES	Despegar Online SRL http://www.despegar.com	UY/LAC		1-1249-1940
HOTELS	Booking.com B.V. http://www.booking.com	NL/EUR		1-1016-75482
HOTMAIL	Microsoft Corporation http://www.microsoft.com	US/NA		1-1129-32525
HOUSE	Sugar Park, LLC	US/NA		1-1506-83794
HOW	Charleston Road Registry Inc.	US/NA		1-1682-29920
HSBC	HSBC Holdings PLC http://www.hsbc.com	GB/EUR		1-1689-20699
HTC	HTC corporation http://www.htc.com	TW/AP		1-1658-26594
HUGHES	Hughes Satellite Systems Corporation http://www.hughes.com	US/NA		1-1997-46911
HYATT	Hyatt GTLD, L.L.C.	US/NA		1-965-48449
HYUNDAI	Hyundai Motor Company http://www.hyundai.com	KR/AP		1-1922-62743
IBM	International Business Machines Corporation http://www.ibm.com	US/NA		1-992-57662
ICBC	Industrial and Commercial Bank of China Limited	CN/AP		1-1010-74163
ICE	IntercontinentalExchange, Inc. http://www.theice.com	US/NA		1-1965-44528
ICU	One.com A/S http://www.one.com	DK/EUR		1-979-15291
IDN	Nameshop http://nameshop.in	IN/AP		1-1873-71868
IEEE	IEEE Global LLC	US/NA	Community	1-966-50066
IFM	ifm electronic gmbh	DE/EUR		1-1740-10420
IINET	Connect West Pty. Ltd. http://www.connectwest.net.au	AU/AP		1-1164-13371
IKANO	Ikano S.A. http://www.ikano.lu	LU/EUR	Community	1-1002-9044
IMAMAT	Fondation Aga Khan (Aga Khan Foundation) Http://www.akdn.org	CH/EUR		1-1013-17019
IMDB	Amazon EU S.à r.l. http://www.amazon.com/	LU/EUR		1-1315-27811
IMMO	STARTING DOT http://www.startingdot.com	FR/EUR	Community	1-1000-62742
	Top Level Domain Holdings Limited http://www.tldh.org	VG/EUR		1-1037-6617
	Auburn Bloom, LLC	US/NA		1-1511-99612
	dotimmobilie GmbH http://www.dotimmobilie.de	DE/EUR		1-1761-46474
IMMOBILIEN	United TLD Holdco Ltd. http://unitedtld.com	KY/EUR		1-1255-76933
INC	C.V. TLDcare	NL/EUR		1-1112-96698

Copyright 2013 Amazon Corporation. All rights reserved.

String	Applicant	Loc/Reg	Properties IDN Attributes	Appl. ID
INC	C.V. TLDcare	NL/EUR		1-1112-96698
	Charleston Road Registry Inc.	US/NA		1-1142-83944
	Baxter Sunset, LLC	US/NA		1-1271-68369
	NU DOT CO LLC	US/NA		1-1296-44261
	GTLD Limited	HK/AP		1-1309-22501
	CNI Registry, LLC	US/NA		1-1692-77224
	Uniregistry, Corp. http://www.uniregistry.com	KY/EUR		1-855-4741
	Afilias Limited	IE/EUR		1-868-6380
	Dot Registry LLC	US/NA	Community	1-880-35979
	GMO Registry, Inc. http://www.gmoregistry.com	JP/AP		1-890-52980
	Top Level Domain Holdings Limited http://www.tldh.org	VG/EUR		1-927-63223
INDIANS	Reliance Industries Limited http://www.ril.com	IN/AP		1-1308-78414
INDUSTRIES	Outer House, LLC	US/NA		1-1510-3058
INFINITI	NISSAN MOTOR CO., LTD. http://www.nissan-global.com/	JP/AP		1-1022-99709
INFOSYS	Infosys Limited http://www.infosys.com/	IN/AP		1-1792-59978
INFY	Infosys Limited http://www.infosys.com/	IN/AP		1-1792-97165
ING	Charleston Road Registry Inc.	US/NA		1-1683-75852
INK	Top Level Design, LLC	US/NA		1-1086-41069
INSTITUTE	Outer Maple, LLC	US/NA		1-1514-76062
INSURANCE	fTLD Registry Services LLC	US/NA	Community	1-1035-75923
	Dotfresh Inc. http://www.radixregistry.com	AE/AP		1-1063-32835
	Progressive Casualty Insurance Company http://www.Progressive.com	US/NA		1-1269-14573
	Auburn Park, LLC	US/NA		1-1512-20834
INSURE	Pioneer Willow, LLC	US/NA		1-1516-617
INTEL	Intel Corporation	US/NA		1-1695-84442
INTERNATIONAL	Wild Way, LLC	US/NA		1-1513-9603
INTUIT	Intuit Administrative Services, Inc.	US/NA		1-1281-62880
INVESTMENTS	Holly Glen, LLC	US/NA		1-1521-75718
IPIRANGA	Ipiranga Produtos de Petroleo S.A. http://www.ipiranga.com.br	BR/LAC		1-1047-90306
IRA	Fidelity Brokerage Services LLC https://www.fidelity.com/	US/NA		1-1845-3627
IRISH	Dot-Irish LLC http://www.dotirish.com	US/NA		1-899-83326
ISELECT	iSelect Ltd http://www.iselect.com.au/	AU/AP		1-1088-54663
ISLAM	Asia Green IT System Bilgisayar San. ve Tic. Ltd. Sti.	TR/AP	Community	1-2130-23450
ISMAILI	Fondation Aga Khan (Aga Khan Foundation) Http://www.akdn.org	CH/EUR	Community	1-1013-63095
IST	Istanbul Metropolitan Municipality http://www.ibb.gov.tr	TR/AP	Geographic	1-896-64208
ISTANBUL	Istanbul Metropolitan Municipality http://www.ibb.gov.tr	TR/AP	Geographic	1-896-81048
ITAU	Itau Unibanco Holding S.A. http://www.itau.com	BR/LAC		1-876-18413
ITV	ITV Services Limited	GB/EUR		1-978-21016
IVECO	Fiat Industrial S.p.A (società per azioni) http://www.fiatindustrial.com	IT/EUR		1-2053-96234
IWC	Richemont DNS Inc. http://www.richemont.com	CH/EUR		1-1253-3840
JAGUAR	Jaguar Cars Limited http://www.jaguar.com	GB/EUR		1-2033-3936

Copyright 2013 Internet Corporation for Assigned Names and Numbers.

String	Applicant	Loc/Reg	Properties	IDN	Attributes	Appl. ID
JAVA	Oracle Corporation http://www.oracle.com	US/NA				1-1785-88138
JCB	JCB Co., Ltd. http://www.jcbcorporate.com	JP/AP				1-1806-69861
JCP	JCP Media, Inc.	US/NA				1-1897-48644
JEEP	Chrysler Group LLC. http://www.chryslergroupllc.com	US/NA				1-2056-76990
JETZT	New TLD Company AB	SE/EUR				1-1758-31045
JEWELRY	Richemont DNS Inc. http://www.richemont.com	CH/EUR				1-1253-11362
	Wild Bloom, LLC	US/NA				1-1520-93221
JIO	Affinity Names, Inc.	US/NA				1-1013-15809
JLC	Richemont DNS Inc. http://www.richemont.com	CH/EUR				1-1253-23191
JLL	Jones Lang LaSalle Incorporated http://www.joneslanglasalle.com	US/NA				1-1250-4137
JMP	Matrix IP LLC	US/NA				1-1323-79639
JNJ	Johnson & Johnson Services, Inc.	US/NA				1-1156-43157
JOBURG	UniForum SA (NPC) trading as ZA Central Registry http://www.Registry.net.za	ZA/AF	Geographic			1-1864-76634
JOT	Amazon EU S.à r.l. http://www.amazon.com/	LU/EUR				1-1316-47849
JOY	Amazon EU S.à r.l. http://www.amazon.com/	LU/EUR				1-1316-61557
JPMORGAN	JPMorgan Chase & Co. http://www.jpmorganchase.com	US/NA				1-1190-27386
JPMORGANCHASE	JPMorgan Chase & Co. http://www.jpmorganchase.com	US/NA				1-1190-16643
JPRS	Japan Registry Services Co., Ltd. http://jprs.co.jp/	JP/AP				1-913-735
JUEGOS	Goose Gardens, LLC	US/NA				1-1522-61364
	Uniregistry, Corp. http://www.uniregistry.com	KY/EUR				1-845-92261
JUNIPER	JUNIPER NETWORKS, INC. http://www.juniper.net	US/NA				1-1937-57060
JUSTFORU	Safeway Inc.	US/NA				1-1189-43551
KAUFEN	United TLD Holdco Ltd. http://unitedtld.com	KY/EUR				1-1255-46630
KDDI	KDDI CORPORATION http://global.kddi.com/	JP/AP				1-1306-80495
KERASTASE	L'Oréal http://www.loreal.com	FR/EUR				1-1301-47281
KERRYHOTELS	Kerry Trading Co. Limited	HK/AP				1-928-47602
KERRYLOGISITICS	Kerry Trading Co. Limited	HK/AP				1-928-31367
KERRYPROPERTIES	Kerry Trading Co. Limited	HK/AP				1-928-12798
KETCHUP	ProMark Brands Inc.	US/NA				1-941-54947
KFH	Kuwait Finance House http://www.kfh.com	KW/AP				1-2099-6189
KIA	KIA MOTORS CORPORATION http://www.kia.co.kr/	KR/AP				1-1737-31984
KID	Charleston Road Registry Inc.	US/NA				1-1141-94472
KIDS	DotKids Foundation Limited	HK/AP	Community			1-1309-46695
	Amazon EU S.à r.l. http://www.amazon.com/	LU/EUR				1-1316-67680
KIEHLS	L'Oréal http://www.loreal.com	FR/EUR				1-1301-10203
KIM	Afilias Limited	IE/EUR				1-868-81619
KINDER	Ferrero Trading Lux S.A. http://www.ferrero.com	LU/EUR				1-1126-16883
KINDLE	Amazon EU S.à r.l. http://www.amazon.com/	LU/EUR				1-1315-18526

Copyright 2013 John Wiley & Sons, Inc. for assigned TLDs and Numbers

String	Applicant	Loc/Reg	Properties	IDN Attributes	Appl. ID
KITCHEN	Just Goodbye, LLC	US/NA			1-1526-71442
KIWI	DOT KIWI LIMITED http://www.dot-kiwi.com	NZ/AP			1-853-70338
KOELN	NetCologne Gesellschaft für Telekommunikation mbH http://www.netcologne.de	DE/EUR	Geographic		1-860-46860
KOMATSU	Komatsu Ltd. http://www.komatsu.co.jp	JP/AP			1-946-52298
KONAMI	KONAMI CORPORATION http://www.konami.co.jp/	JP/AP			1-1117-18023
KONE	KONE Corporation http://www.kone.com/	FI/EUR			1-1263-47652
KOSHER	Kosher Marketing Assets LLC	US/NA			1-1013-67544
KPMG	KPMG International Cooperative (KPMG International Genossenschaft)	NL/EUR			1-1091-69197
KPN	Koninklijke KPN N.V. http://www.kpn.com	NL/EUR			1-1667-96713
KRD	KRG Department of Information Technology http://www.krgit.org	IQ/AP			1-1260-38811
KRED	KredTLD Pty Ltd	AU/AP			1-1707-1944
KSB	KSB Aktiengesellschaft http://www.ksb.com/	DE/EUR			1-984-8485
KUOKGROUP	Kerry Trading Co. Limited	HK/AP			1-928-30883
KYKNET	Electronic Media Network Limited (M-Net) http://www.mnet.co.za	ZA/AF			1-1901-94916
KYOTO	Academic Institution: Kyoto Jyoho Gakuen http://www.kcg.edu/	JP/AP	Geographic		1-1716-31099
LACAIXA	CAIXA D'ESTALVIS I PENSIONS DE BARCELONA http://www.lacaixa.com	ES/EUR			1-1835-20716
LADBROKES	LADBROKES INTERNATIONAL PLC http://www.ladbrokesplc.com	GI/EUR			1-1823-86614
LAMBORGHINI	Automobili Lamborghini S.p.A. http://www.lamborghini.com	IT/EUR	Community		1-1261-2722
LAMER	ELC Online Inc. http://elcompanies.com	US/NA			1-1964-45137
LANCASTER	LANCASTER	FR/EUR			1-854-19943
LANCIA	Fiat S.p.A. ("società per azioni") http://www.fiatspa.com	IT/EUR			1-2070-21096
LANCOME	L'Oréal http://www.loreal.com	FR/EUR			1-1301-74397
LAND	Pine Moon, LLC	US/NA			1-1525-41533
LANDROVER	Land Rover http://www.landrover.com	GB/EUR			1-2032-73816
LANXESS	LANXESS Corporation http://lanxess.us/	US/NA			1-1754-39601
LASALLE	Jones Lang LaSalle Incorporated http://www.joneslanglasalle.com	US/NA			1-1250-96768
LAT	ECOM-LAC Federación de Latinoamérica y el Caribe para Internet y el Comercio Electrónico http://www.ecomlac.org	UY/LAC			1-943-512
LATINO	Top Level Domain Holdings Limited http://www.tldh.org	VG/EUR			1-1038-32393
	Dish DBS Corporation http://www.dish.com	US/NA			1-2008-77299
LATROBE	La Trobe University http://www.latrobe.edu.au	AU/AP			1-2074-51517
LAW	Dotmaker Inc. http://www.radixregistry.com	AE/AP			1-1055-21389
	Silver Registry Limited	GI/EUR			1-1183-17612
	NU DOT CO LLC	US/NA			1-1296-62922
	Corn Dynamite, LLC	US/NA			1-1523-55821
	Merchant Law Group LLP	CA/NA			1-875-2472
	Top Level Domain Holdings Limited http://www.tldh.org	VG/EUR			1-927-20582
LAWYER	Atomic Station, LLC	US/NA			1-1531-96078
	Top Level Domain Holdings Limited http://www.tldh.org	VG/EUR			1-927-4468
LDS	IRI Domain Management, LLC ("Applicant") http://notapplicable.info	US/NA	Community		1-1098-21368

String	Applicant	Loc/Reg	Properties IDN Attributes	Appl. ID
LEASE	Victor Trail, LLC	US/NA		1-1540-49920
LECLERC	A.C.D. LEC Association des Centres Distributeurs Edouard Leclerc http://www.mouvement-leclerc.com	FR/EUR	Community	1-1251-68491
LEFRAK	LeFrak Organization, Inc. http://lefrak.com	US/NA		1-1907-30970
LEGAL	Blue Falls, LLC	US/NA		1-1536-79233
	PRIMER NIVEL S.A. http://www.1ernivel.co	PA/LAC		1-917-16797
LEGO	LEGO Juris A/S http://www.LEGO.com	DK/EUR		1-1795-41858
LEXUS	TOYOTA MOTOR CORPORATION http://www.toyota.co.jp	JP/AP		1-1717-84290
LGBT	Afilias Limited	IE/EUR		1-868-8822
LIAISON	Liaison Technologies, Incorporated http://www.liaison.com	US/NA		1-1904-8749
LIDL	Schwarz Domains und Services GmbH & Co. KG	DE/EUR		1-1123-60314
LIFE	Trixy Oaks, LLC	US/NA		1-1535-64595
	Xiamen 35.com Technology Co.,Ltd http://www.35.com	CN/AP		1-1861-18909
	CompassRose.Life Inc.	CA/NA		1-927-66189
LIFEINSURANCE	American Council of Life Insurers http://www.acli.com	US/NA		1-1160-79590
LIFESTYLE	Lifestyle Domain Holdings, Inc.	US/NA		1-1326-24715
LIGHTING	John McCook, LLC	US/NA		1-1539-6233
LIKE	Amazon EU S.à r.l. http://www.amazon.com/	LU/EUR		1-1316-52467
LILLY	Eli Lilly and Company http://www.lilly.com	US/NA		1-1018-57217
LIMITED	Big Fest, LLC	US/NA		1-1542-96415
LIMO	Hidden Frostbite, LLC	US/NA		1-1543-47454
LINCOLN	Ford Motor Company http://www.ford.com	US/NA		1-1666-99781
LINDE	Linde Aktiengesellschaft http://www.linde.com	DE/EUR		1-1793-71500
LINK	Uniregistry, Corp. http://www.uniregistry.com	KY/EUR		1-855-72194
LIPSY	Lipsy Ltd http://www.lipsy.co.uk	GB/EUR		1-1319-371
LIVE	Microsoft Corporation http://www.microsoft.com	US/NA		1-1129-83871
	Half Woods, LLC	US/NA		1-1545-55209
	Charleston Road Registry Inc.	US/NA		1-1680-95108
LIVESTRONG	Lance Armstrong Foundation http://www.livestrong.org	US/NA		1-2090-26288
LIVING	Lifestyle Domain Holdings, Inc.	US/NA		1-1326-92909
	Outer Way, LLC	US/NA		1-1547-37710
LIXIL	JS Group Corporation http://www.jsgc.co.jp	JP/AP		1-969-63512
LLC	myLLC GmbH http://www.myLLC.info	DE/EUR		1-1013-43904
	Top Level Design, LLC	US/NA		1-1086-42934
	NU DOT CO LLC	US/NA		1-1296-44333
	Charleston Road Registry Inc.	US/NA		1-1417-41320
	Foggy North, LLC	US/NA		1-1546-93002
	LLC Registry, LLC	US/NA		1-1692-61931
	Afilias Limited	IE/EUR		1-868-65445
	Dot Registry LLC	US/NA	Community	1-880-17627
	Top Level Domain Holdings Limited http://www.tldh.org	VG/EUR		1-927-11663
LLP	myLLP GmbH http://www.myLLP.info	DE/EUR		1-1013-89480

168

String	Applicant	Loc/Reg	Properties	IDN Attributes	Appl. ID
	Charleston Road Registry Inc.	US/NA			1-1142-52922
	PLL Registry, LLC	US/NA			1-1693-56810
	Dot Registry LLC	US/NA	Community		1-880-35508
LOAN	dot Loan Limited	GI/EUR			1-1222-21097
LOANS	Dotserve Inc. http://www.radixregistry.com	AE/AP			1-1065-49761
	June Woods, LLC	US/NA			1-1544-18264
LOCKER	Dish DBS Corporation http://www.dish.com	US/NA			1-2013-75702
LOCUS	Locus Analytics LLC	US/NA			1-1890-88961
LOFT	Annco, Inc. http://www.loft.com	US/NA			1-1161-52785
LOL	Charleston Road Registry Inc.	US/NA			1-1681-93347
	Uniregistry, Corp. http://www.uniregistry.com	KY/EUR			1-855-10958
LONDON	Dot London Domains Limited http://www.londonandpartners.com/	GB/EUR	Geographic		1-1252-62369
LOREAL	L'Oréal http://www.loreal.com	FR/EUR			1-1301-87539
LOTTE	Lotte Holdings Co., Ltd. http://www.lotte.co.jp	JP/AP			1-1863-52010
LOTTO	Afilias Limited	IE/EUR			1-868-7904
LOVE	Sierra Registry Limited http://www.famousfourmedia.com	GI/EUR			1-1230-19511
	Richemont DNS Inc. http://www.richemont.com	CH/EUR			1-1253-49828
	Hidden Cypress, LLC	US/NA			1-1549-37731
	Charleston Road Registry Inc.	US/NA			1-1678-55117
	Uniregistry, Corp. http://www.uniregistry.com	KY/EUR			1-855-55170
	Merchant Law Group LLP	CA/NA			1-875-6276
	Top Level Domain Holdings Limited http://www.tldh.org	VG/EUR			1-927-91932
LPL	LPL Holdings, Inc.	US/NA			1-1144-53270
LPLFINANCIAL	LPL Holdings, Inc.	US/NA			1-1144-82616
LTD	myLTD GmbH http://www.myLTD.info	DE/EUR			1-1013-19866
	NU DOT CO LLC	US/NA			1-1296-16820
	Over Corner, LLC	US/NA			1-1550-65638
	LTD Registry, LLC	US/NA			1-1694-79399
	C.V. TLDcare	NL/EUR			1-1714-80638
	Afilias Limited	IE/EUR			1-868-84727
	Dot Registry LLC	US/NA			1-880-44249
LTDA	DOMAIN ROBOT SERVICOS DE HOSPEDAGEM NA INTERNET LTDA http://www.myLTDA.com.br	BR/LAC			1-1013-35966
LUNDBECK	H. Lundbeck A/S http://www.lundbeck.com	DK/EUR			1-2077-4329
LUPIN	LUPIN LIMITED http://www.lupinworld.com	IN/AP			1-1325-70178
LUXE	Top Level Domain Holdings Limited http://www.tldh.org	VG/EUR			1-1037-14905
LUXURY	Luxury Partners, LLC	US/NA			1-1265-36346
	Dash Tigers, LLC	US/NA			1-1551-91953
MACYS	Macys, Inc. http://www.macysinc.com	US/NA			1-1790-19744
MADRID	Comunidad de Madrid http://www.madrid.org	ES/EUR	Community Geographic		1-1742-48964
MAIF	Mutuelle Assurance Instituteur France (MAIF) http://www.maif.fr	FR/EUR			1-1819-55314
MAIL	Afilias Domains No. 2 Limited, http://www.AfiliasDomains2.info	IE/EUR			1-1013-47551
	Charleston Road Registry Inc.	US/NA			1-1141-82929
	1&1 Mail & Media GmbH http://www.web.de	DE/EUR			1-1256-50020

Copyright 2012 Internet Corporation for Assigned Names and Numbers

String	Applicant	Loc/Reg	Properties	IDN Attributes	Appl. ID
	Amazon EU S.à r.l. http://www.amazon.com/	LU/EUR			1-1316-17384
	Victor Dale, LLC	US/NA			1-1548-63140
	WhitePages TLD LLC	US/NA			1-1906-88399
	GMO Registry, Inc. http://www.gmoregistry.com	JP/AP			1-890-53570
MAISON	Victor Frostbite, LLC	US/NA			1-1552-8006
MAKEUP	L'Oréal http://www.loreal.com	FR/EUR			1-1302-1511
MAN	MAN SE	DE/EUR			1-1869-92391
MANAGEMENT	John Goodbye, LLC	US/NA			1-1555-40996
MANGO	PUNTO FA S.L. http://www.mango.com	ES/EUR			1-1784-26967
MAP	United TLD Holdco Ltd. http://unitedtld.com	KY/EUR			1-1255-71670
	Amazon EU S.à r.l. http://www.amazon.com/	LU/EUR			1-1316-5335
	Charleston Road Registry Inc.	US/NA			1-1417-46480
MARKET	Victor Way, LLC	US/NA			1-1553-52336
MARKETING	Tucows TLDs Inc. http://www.tucowsinc.com	CA/NA			1-1171-71619
	Fern Pass, LLC	US/NA			1-1557-30317
	Uniregistry, Corp. http://www.uniregistry.com	KY/EUR			1-855-23003
MARKETS	IG Group Holdings PLC http://www.iggroup.com	GB/EUR			1-2042-29017
MARRIOTT	Marriott Worldwide Corporation http://www.marriott.com/default.mi	US/NA			1-1242-18450
MARSHALLS	The TJX Companies, Inc. http://www.tjx.com	US/NA			1-1764-97027
MASERATI	Fiat S.p.A. ("società per azioni") http://www.fiatspa.com	IT/EUR			1-2069-31888
MATRIX	L'Oréal http://www.loreal.com	FR/EUR			1-1301-37991
MATTEL	Mattel Sites, Inc.	US/NA			1-2089-2530
MAYBELLINE	L'Oréal http://www.loreal.com	FR/EUR			1-1301-95720
MBA	Your Dot Phd, Inc. http://yourdotphd.com	US/NA			1-1076-76766
	Lone Hollow, LLC	US/NA			1-1556-47497
MCD	Charleston Road Registry Inc.	US/NA			1-1678-4292
	McDonald's Corporation http://mcdonalds.com	US/NA			1-1787-49234
MCDONALDS	McDonald's Corporation http://mcdonalds.com	US/NA			1-1787-26554
MCKINSEY	McKinsey Holdings, Inc. http://www.mckinsey.com	US/NA			1-1782-78035
MED	Charleston Road Registry Inc.	US/NA			1-1139-2965
	HEXAP SAS http://www.hexap.com	FR/EUR	Community		1-1192-28569
	DocCheck AG	DE/EUR	Community		1-1320-21500
	Medistry LLC	US/NA			1-907-38758
MEDIA	Tucows TLDs Inc. http://www.tucowsinc.com	CA/NA			1-1171-56570
	Grand Glen, LLC	US/NA			1-1560-69674
	Uniregistry, Corp. http://www.uniregistry.com	KY/EUR			1-855-44456
MEDICAL	Steel Hill, LLC	US/NA			1-1561-23663
MEET	Afilias Limited	IE/EUR			1-868-85241
MELBOURNE	The Crown in right of the State of Victoria, represented by its Department of Business and Innovation http://www.dbi.vic.gov.au	AU/AP	Geographic		1-1918-10194
MEME	Charleston Road Registry Inc.	US/NA			1-1680-9209

Copyright 2012 Internet Corporation for Assigned Names and Numbers

String	Applicant	Loc/Reg	Properties	IDN Attributes	Appl. ID
MEMORIAL	Dog Beach, LLC	US/NA			1-1563-40885
	dotCOOL, Inc.	US/NA			1-2108-24342
	Afilias Limited	IE/EUR			1-868-46640
MEN	Exclusive Registry Limited	GI/EUR			1-1215-86537
MENU	Wedding TLD2, LLC	US/NA			1-856-30202
MEO	PT Comunicacoes S.A. http://www.telecom.pt	PT/EUR			1-1811-10837
MERCK	Merck Registry Holdings, Inc.	US/NA			1-1702-28003
	Merck Registry Holdings, Inc.	US/NA	Community		1-1702-73085
	Merck KGaA http://www.merckgroup.com	DE/EUR	Community		1-980-7217
MERCKMSD	MSD Registry Holdings, Inc.	US/NA			1-1704-28482
METLIFE	MetLife Services and Solutions, LLC http://www.metlife.com	US/NA			1-1774-89667
MIAMI	Top Level Domain Holdings Limited http://www.tldh.org	VG/EUR	Geographic		1-1039-76209
MICROSOFT	Microsoft Corporation http://www.microsoft.com	US/NA			1-1129-74317
MIH	Myriad International Holdings B.V. http://www.mih.com	NL/EUR			1-1770-66709
MII	MiTek USA, Inc. http://www.mii.com	US/NA			1-1085-30851
MINI	Bayerische Motoren Werke Aktiengesellschaft http://www.bmwgroup.com	DE/EUR			1-938-68005
MINT	Intuit Administrative Services, Inc.	US/NA			1-1509-35084
MIT	Massachusetts Institute of Technology	US/NA			1-986-42582
MITEK	MiTek USA, Inc. http://www.mii.com	US/NA			1-1085-77906
MITSUBISHI	Mitsubishi Corporation http://www.mitsubishicorp.com	JP/AP			1-1195-88153
MLB	MLB Advanced Media DH, LLC	US/NA			1-1246-40551
MLS	The Canadian Real Estate Association http://www.crea.ca	CA/NA			1-1828-26452
	The Canadian Real Estate Association http://www.crea.ca	CA/NA	Community		1-1888-47714
	Afilias Limited	IE/EUR			1-868-71271
MMA	MMA IARD http://www.mma.fr	FR/EUR	Community		1-1727-80321
MNET	Electronic Media Network Limited (M-Net) http://www.mnet.co.za	ZA/AF			1-1779-67877
MOBILE	Amazon EU S.à r.l. http://www.amazon.com/	LU/EUR			1-1316-6133
	Pixie North, LLC	US/NA			1-1566-85057
	Dish DBS Corporation http://www.dish.com	US/NA			1-2012-89566
MOBILY	GreenTech Consultancy Company W.L.L. http://www.greentechwll.com	BH/AP			1-2114-81237
MODA	United TLD Holdco Ltd. http://unitedtld.com	KY/EUR			1-1255-64246
MOE	Interlink Co., Ltd. http://www.interlink.or.jp/	JP/AP			1-901-45839
MOI	Amazon EU S.à r.l. http://www.amazon.com/	LU/EUR			1-1316-70032
MOM	Charleston Road Registry Inc.	US/NA			1-1139-52584
	United TLD Holdco Ltd. http://unitedtld.com	KY/EUR			1-1255-96181
	Uniregistry, Corp. http://www.uniregistry.com	KY/EUR			1-855-75369
MONASH	Monash University http://monash.edu/	AU/AP			1-1153-75618
MONEY	dot Money Limited	GI/EUR			1-1179-41884
	Outer McCook, LLC	US/NA			1-1567-79679
MONSTER	Monster Worldwide, Inc. http://www.about-monster.com	US/NA			1-1697-33789

String	Applicant	Loc/Reg	Properties	IDN Attributes	Appl. ID
	Monster, Inc. http://www.monsterproducts.com	US/NA			1-1851-68583
MONTBLANC	Richemont DNS Inc. http://www.richemont.com	CH/EUR			1-1253-99008
MOPAR	Chrysler Group LLC. http://www.chryslergroupllc.com	US/NA			1-2060-34064
MORMON	IRI Domain Management, LLC ("Applicant") http://notapplicable.info	US/NA			1-1098-52000
MORTGAGE	Outer Gardens, LLC	US/NA			1-1564-75367
MOSCOW	Foundation for Assistance for Internet Technologies and Infrastructure Development (FAITID) http://www.faitid.org	RU/EUR	Geographic		1-975-59500
MOTO	Charleston Road Registry Inc.	US/NA			1-1138-87257
	United TLD Holdco Ltd. http://unitedtld.com	KY/EUR			1-1255-15838
MOTORCYCLES	DERMotorcycles, LLC	US/NA			1-909-56431
MOV	Charleston Road Registry Inc.	US/NA			1-1142-23068
MOVIE	Charleston Road Registry Inc.	US/NA			1-1140-55599
	dot Movie Limited	GI/EUR			1-1180-29599
	Webdeus Inc. http://www.radixregistry.com	AE/AP			1-1290-2671
	NU DOT CO LLC	US/NA			1-1296-23277
	Amazon EU S.à r.l. http://www.amazon.com/	LU/EUR			1-1316-44615
	New Frostbite, LLC	US/NA			1-1570-42842
	Motion Picture Domain Registry Pty Ltd	AU/AP			1-1803-2593
	Dish DBS Corporation http://www.dish.com	US/NA			1-1920-39242
MOVISTAR	Telefónica S.A. http://telefonica.com	ES/EUR			1-1791-84637
MOZAIC	Qatar Telecom (Qtel) http://www.qtel.qa	QA/AP			1-1929-6005
MRMUSCLE	Johnson Shareholdings, Inc.	US/NA			1-1248-61894
MRPORTER	Richemont DNS Inc. http://www.richemont.com	CH/EUR			1-1253-4861
MSD	MSD Registry Holdings, Inc.	US/NA			1-1704-5879
MTN	MTN Dubai Limited https://www.mtn.com	AE/AP			1-2140-13825
MTPC	Mitsubishi Tanabe Pharma Corporation http://www.mt-pharma.co.jp/e	JP/AP			1-988-84412
MTR	MTR Corporation Limited http://www.mtr.com.hk	HK/AP			1-2028-44295
MULTICHOICE	MultiChoice Africa (Proprietary) Limited http://www.multichoice.co.za	ZA/AF			1-1777-3550
MUSIC	DotMusic Inc. http://www.radixregistry.com	AE/AP			1-1058-25065
	DotMusic / CGR E-Commerce Ltd http://music.us	CY/AP	Community		1-1115-14110
	dot Music Limited	GI/EUR			1-1175-68062
	Amazon EU S.à r.l. http://www.amazon.com/	LU/EUR			1-1316-18029
	Victor Cross	US/NA			1-1571-12951
	Charleston Road Registry Inc.	US/NA			1-1680-18593
	.music LLC http://www.farfurther.com	US/NA	Community		1-959-51046
	Entertainment Names Inc.	VG/EUR			1-994-99764
MUTUAL	Northwestern Mutual MU TLD Registry, LLC	US/NA			1-1187-18162
MUTUALFUNDS	Fidelity Brokerage Services LLC https://www.fidelity.com/	US/NA			1-1845-68316
MUTUELLE	Fédération Nationale de la Mutualité Française http://www.mutualite.fr	FR/EUR			1-1752-85513
MZANSIMAGIC	Electronic Media Network Limited (M-Net) http://www.mnet.co.za	ZA/AF			1-1892-31276
NAB	National Australia Bank Limited http://www.nab.com.au	AU/AP			1-1724-35592

Copyright 2012 Garden Corporation for Assigned Names and Numbers

String	Applicant	Loc/Reg	Properties	IDN Attributes	Appl. ID
NADEX	IG Group Holdings PLC http://www.iggroup.com	GB/EUR			1-2044-88394
NAGOYA	GMO Registry, Inc. http://gmoregistry.com/	JP/AP	Geographic		1-1725-26914
NASPERS	Intelprop (Proprietary) Limited	ZA/AF			1-1769-30581
NATIONWIDE	Nationwide Mutual Insurance Company http://www.nationwide.com	US/NA			1-1878-48436
NATURA	NATURA COSMÉTICOS S.A. http://www.natura.net	BR/LAC			1-1781-73309
NAVY	United TLD Holdco Ltd. http://unitedtld.com	KY/EUR			1-1255-53893
NBA	NBA REGISTRY, LLC	US/NA			1-1763-23748
NEC	NEC Corporation http://www.nec.co.jp	JP/AP			1-1665-55096
NETAPORTER	Richemont DNS Inc. http://www.richemont.com	CH/EUR			1-1253-52208
NETBANK	COMMONWEALTH BANK OF AUSTRALIA http://www.commbank.com.au	AU/AP			1-1672-75814
NETFLIX	Netflix, Inc. http://www.netflix.com	US/NA			1-1333-56033
NETWORK	Trixy Manor, LLC	US/NA			1-1572-10553
NEUSTAR	NeuStar, Inc. http://www.neustar.biz	US/NA			1-863-45071
NEW	Charleston Road Registry Inc.	US/NA			1-1682-52941
NEWHOLLAND	Fiat Industrial S.p.A (società per azioni) http://www.fiatindustrial.com	IT/EUR			1-2052-3417
NEWS	DotNews Inc. http://www.radixregistry.com	AE/AP			1-1057-44086
	dot News Limited	GI/EUR			1-1172-3099
	Amazon EU S.à r.l. http://www.amazon.com/	LU/EUR			1-1316-26110
	Hidden Bloom, LLC	US/NA			1-1573-27315
	Uniregistry, Corp. http://www.uniregistry.com	KY/EUR			1-855-42105
	Merchant Law Group LLP	CA/NA			1-875-79821
	PRIMER NIVEL S.A. http://www.1ernivel.co	PA/LAC			1-917-11894
NEXT	Next plc http://www.next.co.uk	GB/EUR			1-1154-86661
NEXTDIRECT	Next plc http://www.next.co.uk	GB/EUR			1-1154-75728
NEXUS	Charleston Road Registry Inc.	US/NA			1-1099-20038
NFL	NFL Reg Ops LLC	US/NA			1-1118-57681
NGO	Public Interest Registry http://www.pir.org	US/NA	Community		1-910-97160
NHK	Japan Broadcasting Corporation (NHK) http://www.nhk.or.jp/	JP/AP			1-905-1298
NICO	DWANGO Co., Ltd. http://info.dwango.co.jp/	JP/AP			1-1805-20663
NIKE	NIKE, Inc.	US/NA			1-1395-25808
NIKON	NIKON CORPORATION http://www.nikon.com	JP/AP			1-1808-6217
NINJA	United TLD Holdco Ltd. http://unitedtld.com	KY/EUR			1-1255-70047
NISSAN	NISSAN MOTOR CO., LTD. http://www.nissan-global.com/	JP/AP			1-1021-24248
NISSAY	Nippon Life Insurance Company http://www.nissay.co.jp/english/	JP/AP			1-2093-82497
NOKIA	Nokia Corporation http://www.nokia.com	FI/EUR			1-957-83376
NORTHLANDINSURANCE	Travelers TLD, LLC	US/NA			1-1966-24162
NORTHWESTERNMUTUAL	Northwestern Mutual Registry, LLC	US/NA			1-1186-85299
NORTON	Symantec Corporation	US/NA			1-1027-83460

Copyright 2012 Internet Corporation for Assigned Names and Numbers

String	Applicant	Loc/Reg	Properties	IDN Attributes	Appl. ID
NOW	Starbucks (HK) Limited www.pccw.com	HK/AP			1-1309-93271
	Amazon EU S.à r.l. http://www.amazon.com/	LU/EUR			1-1316-48771
	Grand Turn, LLC	US/NA			1-1575-53902
	XYZ.COM LLC	US/NA			1-2138-10969
	Global Top Level ApS	DK/EUR			1-861-67658
	One.com A/S http://www.one.com	DK/EUR			1-979-89214
NOWRUZ	Asia Green IT System Bilgisayar San. ve Tic. Ltd. Sti.	TR/AP			1-2132-15133
NOWTV	Starbucks (HK) Limited www.pccw.com	HK/AP			1-1309-12985
NRA	NRA Holdings Company, INC. http://www.NRA.org	US/NA			1-1013-27442
NRW	Minds + Machines GmbH http://www.mindsandmachines.de	DE/EUR	Geographic		1-994-3470
NTT	NIPPON TELEGRAPH AND TELEPHONE CORPORATION	JP/AP			1-920-75151
NYC	The City of New York by and through the New York City Department of Information Technology & Telecommunications http://www.nyc.gov	US/NA	Geographic		1-1715-21938
OBI	OBI Group Holding GmbH http://www.obi.de	DE/EUR			1-1739-45800
OBSERVER	Guardian News and Media Limited http://www.guardian.co.uk	GB/EUR			1-1732-536
OFF	Johnson Shareholdings, Inc.	US/NA			1-1248-7515
OFFICE	Microsoft Corporation http://www.microsoft.com	US/NA			1-1129-34449
OKINAWA	BusinessRalliart inc. http://www.eigyo.jp/	JP/AP	Geographic		1-1147-43520
OLAYAN	Olayan Investments Company Establishment http://olayan.com	LI/EUR			1-1017-44037
OLAYANGROUP	Olayan Investments Company Establishment http://olayan.com	LI/EUR			1-1017-54910
OLDNAVY	The Gap, Inc. http://www.gap.com	US/NA			1-925-60784
OLLO	Dish DBS Corporation http://www.dish.com	US/NA			1-2010-64737
OLYMPUS	Olympus Corporation http://www.olympus.co.jp	JP/AP			1-953-77745
OMEGA	The Swatch Group Ltd http://www.swatchgroup.com/	CH/EUR			1-2122-64214
ONE	DotAbout Inc. http://www.radixregistry.com	AE/AP			1-1073-19391
	One.com A/S http://www.one.com	DK/EUR			1-979-77610
ONG	Public Interest Registry http://www.pir.org	US/NA	Community		1-910-64447
ONL	I-REGISTRY Ltd., Niederlassung Deutschland http://www.i-registry.com	DE/EUR			1-1003-27595
ONLINE	I-REGISTRY Ltd., Niederlassung Deutschland http://www.i-registry.com	DE/EUR			1-1003-97300
	DotOnline Inc. http://www.radixregistry.com	AE/AP			1-1070-97873
	Tucows TLDs Inc. http://www.tucowsinc.com	CA/NA			1-1171-72107
	Bitter Frostbite, LLC	US/NA			1-1574-83272
	Namecheap Inc. http://www.namecheap.com/	US/NA			1-2091-95954
	Dot Online LLC	US/NA			1-856-67717
ONYOURSIDE	Nationwide Mutual Insurance Company http://www.nationwide.com	US/NA			1-2083-37948
OOO	INFIBEAM INCORPORATION LIMITED http://www.infibeam.com	IN/AP			1-1950-81778
OPEN	American Express Travel Related Services Company, Inc.	US/NA			1-1305-8942
ORACLE	Oracle Corporation http://www.oracle.com	US/NA			1-1785-25388
ORANGE	Orange Brand Services Limited http://www.orange.com	GB/EUR			1-958-59844

Copyright 2013 Internet Corporation for Assigned Names and Numbers.

String	Applicant	Loc/Reg	Properties IDN Attributes	Appl. ID
ORGANIC	Afilias Limited	IE/EUR		1-868-66930
ORIENTEXPRESS	Orient-Express Hotels Ltd. http://www.orient-express.com	GB/EUR		1-1836-78507
ORIGINS	ELC Online Inc. http://elcompanies.com	US/NA		1-1898-34084
OSAKA	Interlink Co., Ltd. http://www.interlink.or.jp/	JP/AP	Community Geographic	1-901-9391
	GMO Registry, Inc. http://gmoregistry.com/	JP/AP	Geographic	1-921-91127
OTSUKA	Otsuka Holdings Co., Ltd. http://www.otsuka.com	JP/AP		1-906-65402
OTT	Dish DBS Corporation http://www.dish.com	US/NA		1-2006-79052
OVERHEIDNL	ministery of the Interior and Kingdom Relations	NL/EUR		1-2124-3690
OVH	OVH SAS http://www.ovh.com	FR/EUR	Community	1-1074-68417
PAGE	Charleston Road Registry Inc.	US/NA		1-1682-55525
PAMPEREDCHEF	The Pampered Chef, Ltd. http://www.pamperedchef.com	US/NA		1-2062-64273
PANASONIC	Panasonic Corporation http://panasonic.co.jp	JP/AP		1-915-75941
PANERAI	Richemont DNS Inc. http://www.richemont.com	CH/EUR		1-1253-69999
PARIS	City of Paris http://www.paris.fr/	FR/EUR	Community Geographic	1-1087-47153
PARS	Asia Green IT System Bilgisayar San. ve Tic. Ltd. Sti.	TR/AP	Community	1-2127-79611
PARTNERS	Magic Glen, LLC	US/NA		1-1576-29395
PARTS	Sea Goodbye, LLC	US/NA		1-1577-85976
PARTY	Blue Sky Registry Limited	GI/EUR		1-1214-59403
	Oriental Trading Company, Inc. http://www.orientaltrading.com	US/NA		1-1274-20024
PASSAGENS	Despegar Online SRL http://www.despegar.com	UY/LAC		1-1249-57355
	Patagonia, inc. http://www.patagonia.com/	US/NA		1-1084-78254
PATAGONIA				
PATCH	AOL Inc. http://corp.aol.com	US/NA		1-1304-25192
PAY	Amazon EU S.à r.l. http://www.amazon.com/	LU/EUR		1-1317-64413
	DOTPAY SA http://www.dotpay.ch	CH/EUR		1-1750-33973
PAYU	MIH PayU B.V. http://www.payu.eu	NL/EUR		1-1776-5924
PCCW	PCCW Enterprises Limited www.pccw.com	HK/AP		1-1309-16706
PERSIANGULF	Asia Green IT System Bilgisayar San. ve Tic. Ltd. Sti.	TR/AP		1-2128-55439
PET	Charleston Road Registry Inc.	US/NA		1-1678-92681
	Afilias Limited	IE/EUR		1-868-95281
PETS	John Island, LLC	US/NA		1-1578-44109
PFIZER	Pfizer Inc. http://www.pfizer.com/home/	US/NA		1-1827-93225
PHARMACY	National Association of Boards of Pharmacy http://www.nabp.net	US/NA	Community	1-1040-55064
PHD	Your Dot Phd, inc. http://yourdotphd.com	US/NA		1-1076-91066
	Charleston Road Registry Inc.	US/NA		1-1142-85390
PHILIPS	Koninklijke Philips Electronics N.V. http://www.philips.com	NL/EUR		1-1748-81516
PHONE	Wild Frostbite, LLC	US/NA		1-1582-80831
	Dish DBS Corporation http://www.dish.com	US/NA		1-2011-80942
PHOTO	Uniregistry, Corp. http://www.uniregistry.com	KY/EUR		1-845-871
PHOTOGRAPHY	Top Level Design, LLC	US/NA		1-1086-52200

Copyright 2012 Internet Corporation for Assigned Names and Numbers.

String	Applicant	Loc/Reg	Properties IDN Attributes	Appl. ID
	Sugar Glen, LLC	US/NA		1-1581-70192
PHOTOS	Sea Corner, LLC	US/NA		1-1580-67148
PHYSIO	PhysBiz Pty Ltd http://www.dotphysio.com	AU/AP		1-967-85854
PIAGET	Richemont DNS Inc. http://www.richemont.com	CH/EUR		1-1253-59416
PICS	Uniregistry, Corp. http://www.uniregistry.com	KY/EUR		1-845-88170
PICTET	Pictet Europe S.A. http://www.pictet.com	LU/EUR		1-1314-50545
PICTURES	Foggy Sky, LLC	US/NA		1-1585-29698
PID	Top Level Spectrum, Inc. http://www.toplevelspectrum.com	US/NA		1-1279-3321
PIN	Amazon EU S.à r.l. http://www.amazon.com/	LU/EUR		1-1317-59644
PING	DotPing Inc. http://www.radixregistry.com	IN/AP		1-1069-35959
	Ping Registry Provider, Inc. http://www.ping.com/	US/NA		1-1833-90242
PINK	Afilias Limited	IE/EUR		1-868-27848
PIONEER	Pioneer Corporation http://pioneer.jp	JP/AP		1-934-72221
PIPERLIME	The Gap, Inc. http://www.gap.com	US/NA		1-925-92730
PITNEY	Pitney Bowes Inc. http://www.pb.com	US/NA		1-1677-22680
PIZZA	Foggy Moon, LLC	US/NA		1-1583-6697
	Asiamix Digital Limited	HK/AP		1-1711-63214
	Uniregistry, Corp. http://www.uniregistry.com	KY/EUR		1-845-62256
	Top Level Domain Holdings Limited http://www.tldh.org	VG/EUR		1-927-3932
PLACE	Snow Galley, LLC	US/NA		1-1584-14507
	1589757 Alberta Ltd.	CA/NA		1-1976-9220
PLAY	Entertainment TLD Inc. http://www.radixregistry.com	AE/AP		1-1067-89443
	Star Registry Limited	GI/EUR		1-1231-63687
	Amazon EU S.à r.l. http://www.amazon.com/	LU/EUR		1-1317-97559
	Charleston Road Registry Inc.	US/NA		1-1683-17546
PLAYSTATION	Sony Computer Entertainment Inc. http://www.scei.co.jp	JP/AP		1-1738-53001
PLUMBING	Spring Tigers, LLC	US/NA		1-1586-62771
PLUS	Charleston Road Registry Inc.	US/NA		1-1140-91567
	Sugar Mill, LLC	US/NA		1-1589-56456
PNC	PNC Domain Co., LLC http://www.pnc.com	US/NA		1-1909-74251
POHL	Deutsche Vermögensberatung Aktiengesellschaft DVAG http://www.dvag.com	DE/EUR		1-904-3406
POKER	Afilias Domains No. 5 Limited http://www.AfiliasDomains5.info	IE/EUR		1-1013-94737
	dot Poker Limited	GI/EUR		1-1202-1720
	Binky Mill, LLC	US/NA		1-1587-4615
	Dot Poker LLC	US/NA		1-1696-52899
POLITIE	Politie Nederland http://www.vtspn.nl/	NL/EUR		1-1736-17699
POLO	Ralph Lauren Corporation http://www.ralphlauren.com	US/NA		1-1125-1032
PORN	ICM Registry PN LLC http://wwwicmregistrypn.com	US/NA		1-1108-8653
PRAMERICA	Prudential Financial, Inc. http://www.prudential.com/	US/NA		1-1329-24914
PRAXI	Praxi S.p.A. http://www.praxi.com	IT/EUR		1-873-25989
PRESS	DotPress Inc.	AE/AP		1-1062-36956

String	Applicant	Loc/Reg	Properties	IDN Attributes	Appl. ID
PRIME	Amazon EU S.à r.l. http://www.amazon.com/	LU/EUR			1-1315-6810
PROD	Charleston Road Registry Inc.	US/NA			1-1680-83223
PRODUCTIONS	Magic Birch, LLC	US/NA			1-1590-83448
PROF	Charleston Road Registry Inc.	US/NA			1-1417-94253
PROGRESSIVE	Progressive Casualty Insurance Company http://www.Progressive.com	US/NA			1-1269-35396
PROMO	Phenomena Group Oy http://www.phenomena.com	FI/EUR			1-973-2576
PROPERTIES	Big Pass, LLC	US/NA			1-1588-73251
PROPERTY	Steel Goodbye, LLC	US/NA			1-1592-63879
	Uniregistry, Corp. http://www.uniregistry.com	KY/EUR			1-845-65560
	Top Level Domain Holdings Limited http://www.tldh.org	VG/EUR			1-927-66497
PROTECTION	Symantec Corporation	US/NA			1-1027-42662
PRU	Prudential Financial, Inc. http://www.prudential.com/	US/NA			1-1329-41024
PRUDENTIAL	Prudential Financial, Inc. http://www.prudential.com/	US/NA			1-1329-43577
PUB	United TLD Holdco Ltd. http://unitedtld.com	KY/EUR			1-1255-25091
PWC	PwC Business Trust http://www.pwc.com	US/NA			1-1891-70526
QPON	dotCOOL, Inc.	US/NA			1-2107-33929
QTEL	Qatar Telecom (Qtel) http://www.qtel.qa	QA/AP			1-1931-31184
QUEBEC	PointQuébec Inc http://www.pointquebec.org	CA/NA	Community	Geographic	1-1663-45909
QUEST	Quest ION Limited http://www.qigroup.com	HK/AP			1-1817-89377
QVC	QVC, Inc. http://www.qvc.com	US/NA			1-877-83686
RACING	Premier Registry Limited	GI/EUR			1-1200-70811
	Black Orchard, LLC	US/NA			1-1594-21696
	Uniregistry, Corp. http://www.uniregistry.com	KY/EUR			1-855-75445
RADIO	European Broadcasting Union (EBU) http://www.ebu.ch	CH/EUR	Community		1-1083-39123
	Tin Dale, LLC	US/NA			1-1593-8224
	Afilias Limited	IE/EUR			1-868-75631
	BRS MEDIA, Inc.	US/NA			1-994-75477
RAID	Johnson Shareholdings, Inc.	US/NA			1-1248-89181
RAM	Chrysler Group LLC. http://www.chryslergroupllc.com	US/NA			1-2055-15880
READ	Amazon EU S.à r.l. http://www.amazon.com/	LU/EUR			1-1317-97509
REALESTATE	New North, LLC	US/NA			1-1597-13898
	Uniregistry, Corp. http://www.uniregistry.com	KY/EUR			1-845-86924
	dotRealEstate LLC	US/NA			1-907-1363
	Top Level Domain Holdings Limited http://www.tldh.org	VG/EUR			1-927-76919
REALTOR	Real Estate Domains LLC	US/NA			1-907-41079
REALTY	Dash Bloom, LLC	US/NA			1-1598-77594
	Fegistry, LLC	US/NA			1-1913-14988
RECIPES	Grand Island, LLC	US/NA			1-1603-97736
RED	Steel Keep, LLC	US/NA			1-1595-97277
	Afilias Limited	IE/EUR			1-868-93793
REDKEN	L'Oréal	FR/EUR			1-1301-62660

Copyright 2013 Internet Corporation for Assigned Names and Numbers

String	Applicant	Loc/Reg	Properties IDN Attributes	Appl. ID
REDKEN	L'Oréal http://www.loreal.com	FR/EUR		1-1301-62660
REDSTONE	Redstone Haute Couture Co., Ltd. http://www.iredstone.com/indexEn.html	CN/AP		1-1321-41821
REDUMBRELLA	Travelers TLD, LLC	US/NA		1-1894-74544
REHAB	United TLD Holdco Ltd. http://unitedtld.com	KY/EUR		1-1255-34333
REISE	dotreise GmbH http://www.dotreise.de	DE/EUR		1-892-71956
REISEN	New Cypress, LLC	US/NA		1-1606-68851
REIT	National Association of Real Estate Investment Trusts, Inc. http://www.nareit.com/	US/NA	Community	1-1760-71167
RELIANCE	Reliance Industries Limited http://www.ril.com	IN/AP		1-1308-77805
REN	Beijing Qianxiang Wangjing Technology Development Co., Ltd. http://www.renren.com	CN/AP		1-924-11693
RENT	Pearl Town, LLC	US/NA		1-1604-36499
	DERRent, LLC	US/NA		1-909-9048
RENTALS	Big Hollow,LLC	US/NA		1-1600-90191
REPAIR	Lone Sunset, LLC	US/NA		1-1611-39225
REPORT	Binky Glen, LLC	US/NA		1-1615-74729
REPUBLICAN	United TLD Holdco Ltd. http://unitedtld.com	KY/EUR		1-1255-42012
REST	Punto 2012 Sociedad Anonima de Capital Variable	MX/LAC		1-1712-32476
RESTAURANT	Top Level Domain Holdings Limited http://www.tldh.org	VG/EUR		1-1110-95066
	dot Restaurant Limited	GI/EUR		1-1219-75721
	Snow Avenue, LLC	US/NA		1-1610-3807
	Uniregistry, Corp. http://www.uniregistry.com	KY/EUR		1-845-64388
RETIREMENT	Fidelity Brokerage Services LLC https://www.fidelity.com/	US/NA		1-1845-17694
REVIEW	Top Level Domain Holdings Limited http://www.tldh.org	VG/EUR		1-1037-71433
	dot Review Limited	GI/EUR		1-1208-90224
REVIEWS	Extra Cover, LLC	US/NA		1-1607-34771
REXROTH	Bosch Rexroth AG http://www.boschrexroth.com	DE/EUR		1-1943-50410
RICH	I-REGISTRY Ltd., Niederlassung Deutschland http://www.i-registry.com	DE/EUR		1-1003-1483
RICHARDLI	Pacific Century Asset Management (HK) Limited	HK/AP		1-1309-98748
RICOH	Ricoh Company, Ltd. http://www.ricoh.co.jp/	JP/AP		1-1101-5912
RIGHTATHOME	Johnson Shareholdings, Inc.	US/NA		1-1248-60975
RIL	Reliance Industries Limited http://www.ril.com	IN/AP		1-1308-43524
RIO	Empresa Municipal de Informática SA - IPLANRIO http://www.rio.rj.gov.br/web/iplanrio	BR/LAC	Geographic	1-1151-10158
RIP	United TLD Holdco Ltd. http://unitedtld.com	KY/EUR		1-1255-57953
	dotRIP LIMITED	NZ/AP		1-1854-53707
	Nevaeh Ventures Inc	CA/NA		1-865-67813
RMIT	Royal Melbourne Institute of Technology http://www.rmit.edu.au/	AU/AP		1-2135-63522
ROCHER	Ferrero Trading Lux S.A. http://www.ferrero.com	LU/EUR		1-1126-33363
ROCKS	Ruby Moon, LLC	US/NA		1-1131-85666
ROCKWOOL	Rockwool International A/S http://www.rockwool.com/	DK/EUR		1-1759-59728
RODEO	Top Level Domain Holdings Limited http://www.tldh.org	VG/EUR		1-1110-28830
ROGERS	Rogers Communications Partnership http://www.rogers.com	CA/NA		1-1036-55073

String	Applicant	Loc/Reg	Properties IDN Attributes	Appl. ID
ROMA	Top Level Domain Holdings Limited http://www.tldh.org	VG/EUR	Geographic	1-927-80477
ROOM	Amazon EU S.à r.l. http://www.amazon.com/	LU/EUR		1-1317-22695
RSVP	Charleston Road Registry Inc.	US/NA		1-1683-44078
RUGBY	dot Rugby Limited	GI/EUR		1-1206-66762
	Atomic Cross, LLC	US/NA		1-1612-2805
	IRB Strategic Developments Limited www.irb.com	IE/EUR		1-994-63638
RUHR	regiodot GmbH & Co. KG http://www.regiodot.de	DE/EUR		1-1753-50246
RUN	dot Run Limited	GI/EUR		1-1232-61938
	Snow Park, LLC	US/NA		1-1616-69474
RWE	RWE AG http://www.rwe.com	DE/EUR		1-1756-92979
RYUKYU	BusinessRalliart inc. http://www.elgyo.jp/	JP/AP	Geographic	1-1147-46178
SAARLAND	dotSaarland GmbH http://www.nic-saarland.de	DE/EUR	Geographic	1-893-50963
SAFE	Amazon EU S.à r.l. http://www.amazon.com/	LU/EUR		1-1317-39217
SAFETY	Safety Registry Services, LLS	US/NA		1-1007-20096
SAFEWAY	Safeway Inc.	US/NA		1-1189-49480
SAKURA	SAKURA Internet Inc. http://www.sakura.ad.jp	JP/AP		1-1163-37277
SALE	Top Level Domain Holdings Limited http://www.tldh.org	VG/EUR		1-1110-17668
	dot Sale Limited	GI/EUR		1-1235-38087
	Half Bloom, LLC	US/NA		1-1617-57149
	Dot-Sale LLC http://www.saledomain.name	US/NA		1-1984-65341
	Uniregistry, Corp. http://www.uniregistry.com	KY/EUR		1-855-27044
SALON	Aesthetics Practitioners Advisory Network Pty Ltd http://www.apanetwork.com/	AU/AP		1-1028-58177
	L'Oréal http://www.loreal.com	FR/EUR		1-1302-58142
	Outer Orchard, LLC	US/NA		1-1618-18834
	DaySmart Software http://www.daysmart.com	US/NA		1-939-82184
SAMSCLUB	Wal-Mart Stores, Inc.	US/NA		1-1244-43641
SAMSUNG	SAMSUNG SDS CO., LTD http://www.sds.samsung.co.kr	KR/AP		1-955-67484
SANDVIK	Sandvik AB http://www.sandvik.com/	SE/EUR		1-1941-6798
SANDVIKCOROMANT	Sandvik AB http://www.sandvik.com/	SE/EUR		1-2075-66439
SANOFI	Sanofi http://www.sanofi.com/	FR/EUR		1-1872-16158
SAP	SAP AG http://www.sap.com	DE/EUR		1-1735-78954
SAPO	PT Comunicacoes S.A. http://www.telecom.pt	PT/EUR		1-1839-70998
SAPPHIRE	MiTek USA, Inc. http://www.mii.com	US/NA		1-1085-70653
SARL	mySARL GmbH http://www.mySARL.info	DE/EUR		1-1013-83132
	Delta Orchard, LLC	US/NA		1-1624-75239
SAS	Research IP LLC	US/NA		1-1323-55150
	SAS AB (publ) http://www.sasgroup.net	SE/EUR		1-1794-37473
SAVE	Amazon EU S.à r.l. http://www.amazon.com/	LU/EUR		1-1317-82096
	Uniregistry, Corp. http://www.uniregistry.com	KY/EUR		1-855-45602

Copyright 2012 Internet Corporation for Assigning Names and Numbers

String	Applicant	Loc/Reg	Properties	IDN Attributes	Appl. ID
SAXO	Saxo Bank A/S http://www.saxobank.com	DK/EUR			1-1043-58809
SBI	STATE BANK OF INDIA http://www.sbi.co.in	IN/AP			1-1029-42857
SBS	SPECIAL BROADCASTING SERVICE CORPORATION http://www.sbs.com.au	AU/AP			1-1080-34634
SCA	SVENSKA CELLULOSA AKTIEBOLAGET SCA (publ) http://www.sca.com	SE/EUR			1-1149-58739
SCB	The Siam Commercial Bank Public Company Limited ("SCB") http://www.scb.co.th	TH/AP			1-1197-50009
SCHAEFFLER	Schaeffler Technologies AG & Co. KG http://www.schaeffler.com	DE/EUR			1-1749-12808
SCHMIDT	SALM S.A.S.	FR/EUR			1-1114-79381
SCHOLARSHIPS	Scholarships.com, LLC http://www.scholarships.com	US/NA			1-1116-65830
SCHOOL	Top Level Domain Holdings Limited http://www.tldh.org	VG/EUR			1-1110-66434
	Little Galley, LLC	US/NA			1-1622-67844
	Fegistry, LLC	US/NA			1-1913-18850
	Uniregistry, Corp. http://www.uniregistry.com	KY/EUR			1-845-60801
SCHULE	Outer Moon, LLC	US/NA			1-1627-1624
SCHWARZ	Schwarz Domains und Services GmbH & Co. KG	DE/EUR			1-1123-39254
SCHWARZGROUP	Schwarz Domains und Services GmbH & Co. KG	DE/EUR			1-1123-12611
SCIENCE	Top Level Domain Holdings Limited http://www.tldh.org	VG/EUR			1-1110-8071
	dot Science Limited	GI/EUR			1-1238-98669
SCJOHNSON	Johnson Shareholdings, Inc.	US/NA			1-1248-67439
SCOR	SCOR SE	FR/EUR			1-1875-27045
SCOT	Dot Scot Registry Limited http://www.dot-scot.org	GB/EUR	Community Geographic		1-1741-29613
SEARCH	Charleston Road Registry Inc.	US/NA			1-1141-50966
	dot Now Limited	GI/EUR			1-1209-16177
	Amazon EU S.à r.l. http://www.amazon.com/	LU/EUR			1-1317-13549
	Bitter McCook, LLC	US/NA			1-1626-61742
SEAT	SEAT, S.A. (Sociedad Unipersonal) http://www.seat.es	ES/EUR			1-1879-27918
SECURE	Amazon EU S.à r.l. http://www.amazon.com/	LU/EUR			1-1317-98508
	Artemis Internet Inc. https://www.artemisinternet.com	US/NA			1-1796-18939
SECURITY	Symantec Corporation	US/NA			1-1027-69486
	Fern Trail, LLC	US/NA			1-1625-43519
	Defender Security Company http://www.defenderdirect.com	US/NA			1-2058-59499
SEEK	Seek Limited http://www.seek.com.au	AU/AP			1-2098-16297
SELECT	iSelect Ltd http://www.iselect.com.au/	AU/AP			1-1088-97737
SENER	Sener Ingeniería y Sistemas, S.A. http://www.sener.es	ES/EUR			1-1044-53079
SERVICES	Fox Castle, LLC	US/NA			1-1628-41321
SES	SES http://www.ses.com	LU/EUR			1-1122-77859
SEVEN	Seven West Media Ltd http://www.sevenwestmedia.com.au	AU/AP			1-2094-72761
SEW	SEW-EURODRIVE GmbH & Co KG http://www.sew-eurodrive.com/	DE/EUR			1-849-59039
SEX	ICM Registry SX LLC http://www.icmregistrysx.com	US/NA			1-1106-79501
	Internet Marketing Solutions Limited	VG/EUR			1-2113-59868
SEXY	Uniregistry, Corp. http://www.uniregistry.com	KY/EUR			1-855-58140

String	Applicant	Loc/Reg	Properties IDN Attributes	Appl. ID
SFR	Societe Francaise du Radiotelephone - SFR http://www.sfr.com	FR/EUR		1-1686-61159
SHANGRILA	Shangri7La International Hotel Management Limited http://www.shangri-la.com	HK/AP		1-940-76333
SHARP	Sharp Corporation http://www.sharp.co.jp	JP/AP		1-1733-97084
SHAW	Shaw Cablesystems G.P. http://www.shaw.ca	CA/NA		1-1013-60745
SHELL	Shell Information Technology International Inc http://www.shell.com	US/NA		1-1090-40748
SHIA	Asia Green IT System Bilgisayar San. ve Tic. Ltd. Sti.	TR/AP	Community	1-2129-23641
SHIKSHA	Afilias Limited	IE/EUR		1-868-35885
SHOES	Binky Galley, LLC	US/NA		1-1630-4186
SHOP	DotShop Inc. http://www.radixregistry.com	AE/AP		1-1051-32260
	Charleston Road Registry Inc.	US/NA		1-1138-5993
	Dot Shop Limited	GI/EUR		1-1176-45062
	Amazon EU S.à r.l. http://www.amazon.com/	LU/EUR		1-1317-37897
	Sugar Maple, LLC	US/NA		1-1632-57390
	Commercial Connect LLC http://www.dotShop.com	US/NA	Community	1-1830-1672
	BEIJING JINGDONG 360 DU E-COMMERCE LTD http://www.360buy.com	CN/AP		1-889-24496
	GMO Registry, Inc. http://www.gmoregistry.com	JP/AP	Community	1-890-52063
	GMO Registry, Inc. http://www.gmoregistry.com	JP/AP		1-890-65213
SHOPPING	Sea Tigers, LLC	US/NA		1-1631-16988
	Uniregistry, Corp. http://www.uniregistry.com	KY/EUR		1-845-21316
SHOPYOURWAY	Shop Your Way, Inc. http://ShopYourWay.com	US/NA		1-1767-1759
SHOUJI	QIHOO 360 TECHNOLOGY CO. LTD. http://www.360.cn	CN/AP		1-974-38448
SHOW	Amazon EU S.à r.l. http://www.amazon.com/	LU/EUR		1-1317-52877
	Charleston Road Registry Inc.	US/NA		1-1417-47872
	Snow Beach, LLC	US/NA		1-1633-36635
	Zodiac Aries Limited http://www.zodiac-corp.com/	HK/AP		1-866-43988
SHOWTIME	CBS Domains Inc.	US/NA		1-869-34582
SHRIRAM	Shriram Capital Ltd. http://shriramcapital.com	IN/AP		1-1857-52823
SILK	Amazon EU S.à r.l. http://www.amazon.com/	LU/EUR		1-1315-37701
SINA	Sina Corporation http://www.sina.com.cn	CN/AP		1-950-30912
SINGLES	Fern Madison, LLC	US/NA		1-1634-15520
SITE	DotSite Inc. http://www.radixregistry.com	AE/AP		1-1048-46315
	Top Level Domain Holdings Limited http://www.tldh.org	VG/EUR		1-1110-76338
	Corn Mill, LLC	US/NA		1-1637-12997
	Charleston Road Registry Inc.	US/NA		1-1681-36344
	Interlink Co., Ltd. http://www.interlink.or.jp/	JP/AP		1-901-58689
SKI	STARTING DOT http://www.startingdot.com	FR/EUR	Community	1-1000-18032
	Wild Lake, LLC	US/NA		1-1636-27531
SKIN	L'Oréal http://www.loreal.com	FR/EUR		1-1302-80853
SKOLKOVO	Fund for Development of the Center for Elaboration and Commercialization of New Technologies http://www.sk.ru	RU/EUR		1-1166-4783

Copyright 2013 Internet Corporation for Assigned Names and Numbers.

String	Applicant	Loc/Reg	Properties	IDN Attributes	Appl. ID
SKY	Sky IP International Ltd, a company incorporated in England and Wales, operating via its registered Swiss branch http://www.sky.com/	CH/EUR			1-991-90219
SKYDRIVE	Microsoft Corporation http://www.microsoft.com	US/NA			1-1129-63735
SKYPE	Microsoft Corporation http://www.microsoft.com	US/NA			1-1129-38236
SLING	Hughes Satellite Systems Corporation http://www.hughes.com	US/NA			1-1999-59552
SMART	Smart Communications, Inc. (SMART) http://www.smart.com.ph	PH/AP			1-2139-55785
SMILE	Amazon EU S.à r.l. http://www.amazon.com/	LU/EUR			1-1317-10329
SNCF	Société Nationale des Chemins de fer Francais S N C F http://www.sncf.com	FR/EUR			1-1871-30331
SOCCER	Top Level Domain Holdings Limited http://www.tldh.org	VG/EUR			1-1110-28392
	dot Soccer Limited	GI/EUR			1-1196-35744
	Foggy Shadow, LLC	US/NA			1-1635-18982
	Soccer United Marketing, LLC http://www.sumworld.com	US/NA			1-1905-88711
SOCIAL	United TLD Holdco Ltd. http://unitedtld.com	KY/EUR			1-1255-66111
SOFTBANK	SOFTBANK CORP. http://www.softbank.co.jp/	JP/AP			1-1807-31061
SOFTWARE	Over Birch, LLC	US/NA			1-1621-97265
SOHU	Sohu.com Limited http://www.sohu.com	CN/AP			1-933-39092
SOLAR	Ruby Town, LLC	US/NA			1-1623-664
SOLUTIONS	Silver Cover, LLC	US/NA			1-1620-15722
SONG	Amazon EU S.à r.l. http://www.amazon.com/	LU/EUR			1-1317-53837
SONY	Sony Corporation http://www.sony.net	JP/AP			1-999-76968
SOY	Charleston Road Registry Inc.	US/NA			1-1139-58678
SPA	Top Level Domain Holdings Limited http://www.tldh.org	VG/EUR			1-1110-73648
	Asia Spa and Wellness Promotion Council Limited www.aswpc.org	MY/AP		Community	1-1309-81322
	Foggy Sunset, LLC	US/NA			1-1619-92115
SPACE	DotSpace Inc. http://www.radixregistry.com	AE/AP			1-1072-65736
SPIEGEL	SPIEGEL-Verlag Rudolf Augstein GmbH & Co. KG http://www.spiegelgruppe.de	DE/EUR			1-997-40034
SPORT	SportAccord http://www.sportaccord.com	CH/EUR		Community	1-1012-71460
	dot Sport Limited	GI/EUR			1-1174-59954
SPORTS	Steel Edge, LLC	US/NA			1-1614-27785
SPOT	Charleston Road Registry Inc.	US/NA			1-1139-66836
	Dotspot LLC	US/NA			1-1303-82330
	Amazon EU S.à r.l. http://www.amazon.com/	LU/EUR			1-1317-50025
SPREADBETTING	IG Group Holdings PLC http://www.iggroup.com	GB/EUR			1-2045-23929
SRL	mySRL GmbH http://www.mySRL.info	DE/EUR			1-1013-93642
	Charleston Road Registry Inc.	US/NA			1-1681-77547
SRT	Chrysler Group LLC. http://www.chryslergroupllc.com	US/NA			1-2059-70151
STADA	STADA Arzneimittel AG http://www.stada.de	DE/EUR		Community	1-1089-42298
STAPLES	Staples, Inc. http://www.staples.com/	US/NA			1-1954-61706
STAR	Star India Private Limited http://www.startv.com/	IN/AP			1-2109-49205
STARHUB	StarHub Limited http://www.starhub.com	SG/AP			1-1127-53723

APPENDIX A

String	Applicant	Loc/Reg	Properties	IDN Attributes	Appl. ID
STATEBANK	STATE BANK OF INDIA http://www.sbi.co.in	IN/AP			1-1029-24289
STATEFARM	State Farm Mutual Automobile Insurance Company http://www.statefarm.com	US/NA			1-1034-97709
STATOIL	Statoil ASA http://www.statoil.com	NO/EUR			1-1335-37595
STC	Saudi Telecom Company http://www.stc.com.sa	SA/AP			1-1927-64607
STCGROUP	Saudi Telecom Company http://www.stc.com.sa	SA/AP			1-1932-58265
STOCKHOLM	Stockholms kommun http://www.international.stockholm.se	SE/EUR	Geographic		1-1078-1796
STORAGE	Extra Beach, LLC	US/NA			1-1613-64465
	Self Storage Company LLC	US/NA			1-1687-62688
STORE	DotStore Inc. http://www.radixregistry.com	AE/AP			1-1052-82517
	Top Level Domain Holdings Limited http://www.tldh.org	VG/EUR			1-1110-26809
	Amazon EU S.à r.l. http://www.amazon.com/	LU/EUR			1-1317-24947
	Sand Dale, LLC	US/NA			1-1609-60839
	Charleston Road Registry Inc.	US/NA			1-1681-60225
	Dot Store Group LLC http://www.thedotstore.com	US/NA			1-1789-97294
	Uniregistry, Corp. http://www.uniregistry.com	KY/EUR			1-855-18880
STREAM	dot Stream Limited	GI/EUR			1-1881-96350
	Hughes Satellite Systems Corporation http://www.hughes.com	US/NA			1-2002-31471
STROKE	American Heart Association, Inc. http://www.heart.org	US/NA			1-1483-31708
STUDIO	Namesphere Limited	HK/AP			1-1309-22538
	Spring Goodbye, LLC	US/NA			1-1608-9291
STUDY	OPEN UNIVERSITIES AUSTRALIA PTY LTD http://www.open.edu.au	AU/AP			1-2031-1961
STYLE	Top Level Design, LLC	US/NA			1-1086-6187
	Top Level Domain Holdings Limited http://www.tldh.org	VG/EUR			1-1110-21114
	Binky Moon, LLC	US/NA			1-1602-30813
	Evolving Style Registry Inc.	CA/NA			1-2081-48775
	Uniregistry, Corp. http://www.uniregistry.com	KY/EUR			1-845-11507
SUCKS	Top Level Spectrum, Inc. http://www.toplevelspectrum.com	US/NA			1-1279-43617
	Dog Bloom, LLC	US/NA			1-1596-35125
	Vox Populi Registry Inc.	CA/NA			1-2080-92776
SUPERSPORT	SuperSport International Holdings Limited http://www.supersport.com	ZA/AF			1-1780-12497
SUPPLIES	Atomic Fields, LLC	US/NA			1-1601-42282
SUPPLY	Half Falls, LLC	US/NA			1-1591-23028
SUPPORT	Grand Orchard, LLC	US/NA			1-1568-22230
SURF	Top Level Domain Holdings Limited http://www.tldh.org	VG/EUR			1-1110-69902
SURGERY	Tin Avenue, LLC	US/NA			1-1569-96051
SUZUKI	SUZUKI MOTOR CORPORATION http://www.globalsuzuki.com	JP/AP			1-1858-80460
SVR	SVR GROUP http://www.labo-svr.com	FR/EUR			1-970-69510
SWATCH	The Swatch Group Ltd http://www.swatchgroup.com/	CH/EUR			1-2121-49660
SWIFTCOVER	Swiftcover Insurance Services Limited http://www.swiftcover.com	GB/EUR			1-1834-24645

Copyright 2012 by ICANN Corporation for Assigned Names and Numbers

Appendix A 183

String	Applicant	Loc/Reg	Properties IDN Attributes	Appl. ID
SWISS	Swiss Confederation http://www.uvek.admin.ch/index.html?lang=en	CH/EUR	Community	1-1328-58462
	Swiss International Air Lines Ltd. http://www.swiss.com	CH/EUR		1-1831-36248
SYDNEY	State of New South Wales, Department of Premier and Cabinet http://www.dpc.nsw.gov.au	AU/AP	Geographic	1-1917-99809
SYMANTEC	Symantec Corporation	US/NA		1-1027-75900
SYSTEMS	Dash Cypress, LLC	US/NA		1-1565-27165
TAB	Tabcorp Holdings Limited http://www.tabcorp.com.au/	AU/AP		1-2078-73725
TAIPEI	Taipei City Government http://www.taipei.gov.tw	TW/AP	Geographic	1-1946-86958
TALK	Amazon EU S.à r.l. http://www.amazon.com/	LU/EUR		1-1317-29107
	Charleston Road Registry Inc.	US/NA		1-1417-17579
TAOBAO	Alibaba Group Holding Limited http://news.alibaba.com/specials/aboutalibaba/aligroup/index.html	KY/EUR		1-1041-74793
TARGET	Target Domain Holdings, LLC	US/NA		1-1188-55951
TATA	TATA SONS LIMITED http://www.tata.com	IN/AP		1-1720-93817
TATAMOTORS	Tata Motors Ltd http://www.tatamotors.com	IN/AP		1-2148-25869
TATAR	Limited Liability Company "Coordination Center of Regional Domain of Tatarstan Republic"	RU/EUR	Community	1-1664-2308
TATTOO	Uniregistry, Corp. http://www.uniregistry.com	KY/EUR		1-845-15798
TAX	Storm Orchard, LLC	US/NA		1-1562-9879
TAXI	Taxi Pay GmbH http://www.taxi.eu	DE/EUR	Community	1-1025-18840
	dot Taxi Limited	GI/EUR		1-1239-50781
	Pine Falls, LLC	US/NA		1-1558-74769
TCI	Asia Green IT System Bilgisayar San. ve Tic. Ltd. Sti.	TR/AP		1-2133-18206
TDK	TDK Corporation http://www.global.tdk.com/	JP/AP		1-901-92814
TEAM	Charleston Road Registry Inc.	US/NA		1-1141-13949
	Atomic Lake, LLC	US/NA		1-1559-19356
	Uniregistry, Corp. http://www.uniregistry.com	KY/EUR		1-855-72897
	Afilias Limited	IE/EUR		1-868-34317
TECH	Top Level Domain Holdings Limited http://www.tldh.org	VG/EUR		1-1110-23787
	NU DOT CO LLC	US/NA		1-1296-83792
	Lone Moon, LLC	US/NA		1-1554-19894
	Dot Tech LLC	US/NA		1-1670-76346
	Charleston Road Registry Inc.	US/NA		1-1678-63859
	Uniregistry, Corp. http://www.uniregistry.com	KY/EUR		1-855-90632
TECHNOLOGY	Auburn Falls	US/NA		1-1639-5968
TELECITY	TelecityGroup International Limited http://www.telecitygroup.com	GB/EUR		1-1113-2279
TELEFONICA	Telefónica S.A. http://telefonica.com	ES/EUR		1-1791-89073
TEMASEK	Temasek Holdings (Private) Limtied http://www.temasek.com.sg	SG/AP		1-848-96376
TENNIS	dot Tennis Limited	GI/EUR		1-1198-18833
	Cotton Bloom, LLC	US/NA		1-1640-29241
	TENNIS AUSTRALIA LTD http://www.tennis.com.au	AU/AP	Community	1-1723-69677
	Washington Team Tennis, LLC http://www.washingtonkasties.com	US/NA		1-2036-18560
TERRA	Telefónica S.A. http://telefonica.com	ES/EUR		1-1791-91793
TEVA	Teva Pharmaceutical Industries Limited	IL/AP		1-1081-27807

Copyright © The Internet Corporation for Assigned Names and Numbers

String	Applicant	Loc/Reg	Properties	IDN Attributes	Appl. ID
THAI	Better Living Management Company Limited	TH/AP	Community		1-2112-4478
THD	Homer TLC, Inc. http://www.homedepot.com/	US/NA			1-1095-68549
THEATER	Key GTLD Holding Inc	UA/EUR			1-1326-97308
	Blue Tigers, LLC	US/NA			1-1641-67063
THEATRE	Key GTLD Holding Inc	UA/EUR			1-1326-3558
THEGUARDIAN	Guardian News and Media Limited http://www.guardian.co.uk	GB/EUR			1-1730-23038
THEHARTFORD	Hartford Fire Insurance Company http://www.thehartford.com	US/NA			1-982-27770
TIAA	Teachers Insurance and Annuity Association of America http://www.tiaa-cref.org	US/NA			1-1501-39101
TICKETS	Tickets TLD LLC	US/NA			1-1013-4506
	dot Tickets Limited	GI/EUR			1-1233-26032
	Atomic McCook, LLC	US/NA			1-1638-77826
	Shubert Internet, Inc.	US/NA			1-1973-48269
	Accent Media Limited	GB/EUR			1-2155-24150
TIENDA	Victor Manor, LLC	US/NA			1-1646-17411
TIFFANY	Tiffany and Company http://international.tiffany.com/	US/NA			1-1266-93721
TIPS	Corn Willow, LLC	US/NA			1-1644-52968
TIRES	Dog Edge, LLC	US/NA			1-1645-45928
	The Goodyear Tire & Rubber Company http://www.goodyear.com	US/NA			1-1884-1217
	Bridgestone Americas Tire Operations, LLC http://BridgestoneTire.com	US/NA			1-2123-56973
TIROL	punkt Tirol GmbH http://www.tirol.com	AT/EUR	Community Geographic		1-1703-3426
TJMAXX	The TJX Companies, Inc. http://www.tjx.com	US/NA			1-1764-20650
TJX	The TJX Companies, Inc. http://www.tjx.com	US/NA			1-1764-49592
TKMAXX	The TJX Companies, Inc. http://www.tjx.com	US/NA			1-1764-51316
TMALL	Alibaba Group Holding Limited http://news.alibaba.com/specials/aboutalibaba/aligroup/index.html	KY/EUR			1-1041-11077
TODAY	Pearl Woods, LLC	US/NA			1-1643-67659
TOKYO	GMO Registry, Inc. http://www.gmoregistry.com	JP/AP	Geographic		1-890-25253
TOOLS	Pioneer North, LLC	US/NA			1-1653-6258
TOP	Jiangsu Bangning Science & Technology Co.,Ltd. http://www.55hl.com	CN/AP			1-1935-70970
TORAY	Toray Industries, Inc. http://www.toray.co.jp	JP/AP			1-945-91406
TOSHIBA	TOSHIBA Corporation http://www.toshiba.co.jp/	JP/AP			1-1102-7288
TOTAL	Total SA http://www.total.com	FR/EUR			1-1162-21667
TOUR	Charleston Road Registry Inc.	US/NA			1-1417-1788
TOURS	Sugar Station, LLC	US/NA			1-1648-61876
TOWN	Koko Moon, LLC	US/NA			1-1655-79604
TOYOTA	TOYOTA MOTOR CORPORATION http://www.toyota.co.jp	JP/AP			1-1717-25317
TOYS	Pioneer Orchard, LLC	US/NA			1-1650-66027
TRADE	Elite Registry Limited	GI/EUR			1-1245-40343
TRADERSHOTELS	Shangri?La International Hotel Management Limited http://www.shangri-la.com	HK/AP			1-940-16578
TRADING	Little Manor, LLC	US/NA			1-1654-94203
	IG Group Holdings PLC http://www.iggroup.com	GB/EUR			1-2047-17293

String	Applicant	Loc/Reg	Properties	IDN	Attributes	Appl. ID
TRAINING	Wild Willow, LLC	US/NA				1-1652-41660
TRANSFORMERS	Hasbro International, Inc. http://www.hasbro.com	US/NA				1-1324-55250
TRANSLATIONS	TRANSLATIONS	FR/EUR				1-850-14889
TRANSUNION	Trans Union LLC http://www.transunion.com	US/NA				1-1990-42992
TRAVELCHANNEL	Lifestyle Domain Holdings, Inc.	US/NA				1-1326-13526
TRAVELERS	Travelers TLD, LLC	US/NA				1-1841-77153
TRAVELERSINSURANCE	Travelers TLD, LLC	US/NA				1-1895-33687
TRAVELGUARD	American International Group, Inc. http://www.aig.com	US/NA				1-1700-81849
TRUST	Deutsche Post AG http://www.dp-dhl.com/de.html	DE/EUR				1-1075-15763
TRV	Travelers TLD, LLC	US/NA				1-1893-86497
TUBE	Charleston Road Registry Inc.	US/NA				1-1142-5476
	Boss Castle, LLC	US/NA				1-1656-46642
	Latin American Telecom LLC	US/NA				1-926-88379
TUI	TUI AG http://www.tui-group.com	DE/EUR				1-874-4984
TUNES	Amazon EU S.à r.l. http://www.amazon.com/	LU/EUR				1-1317-30761
TUSHU	Amazon EU S.à r.l. http://www.amazon.com/	LU/EUR				1-1318-59070
TVS	T V SUNDRAM IYENGAR & SONS LIMITED http://tvsiyengar.com	IN/AP				1-1862-71358
UBANK	National Australia Bank Limited http://www.nab.com.au	AU/AP				1-1724-54856
UBS	UBS AG http://www.ubs.com	CH/EUR				1-1942-41146
UCONNECT	Chrysler Group LLC. http://www.chryslergroupllc.com	US/NA				1-2061-81662
ULTRABOOK	Intel Corporation	US/NA				1-1695-52902
UMMAH	Ummah Digital Limited	GM/AF				1-2104-81541
UNICOM	China United Network Communications Corporation Limited http://www.chinaunicom.com	CN/AP				1-996-99850
UNICORN	Unicorn a.s. http://unicorn.eu	CZ/EUR				1-1771-82835
UNIVERSITY	Little Station, LLC	US/NA				1-1651-77163
UNO	Dot Latin LLC	US/NA				1-881-92958
UOL	UBN INTERNET LTDA. http://www.uol.com.br	BR/LAC				1-1151-36619
UPS	UPS Market Driver, Inc.	US/NA				1-1874-94992
VACATIONS	Atomic Tigers, LLC	US/NA				1-1647-84596
VANA	Lifestyle Domain Holdings, Inc.	US/NA				1-1326-7776
VANGUARD	The Vanguard Group, Inc. http://www.vanguard.com	US/NA				1-1698-41502
VANISH	Reckitt Benckiser N.V. http://www.rb.com	NL/EUR				1-1887-87120
VEGAS	Dot Vegas, Inc. http://www.dotvegas.com	US/NA	Geographic			1-846-66759
VENTURES	Binky Lake, LLC	US/NA				1-1649-44756
VERISIGN	VeriSign, Inc. http://www.verisigninc.com	US/NA				1-1145-77950
vermögensberater	Deutsche Vermögensberatung Aktiengesellschaft DVAG http://www.dvag.com	DE/EUR		IDN	A-label: xn--vermgensberater-ctb Script Code: Latn English Meaning: financial adviser	1-904-60726
vermögensberatung	Deutsche Vermögensberatung Aktiengesellschaft DVAG http://www.dvag.com	DE/EUR		IDN	A-label: xn--vermgensberatung-pwb Script Code: Latn English Meaning: financial advice	1-904-3145

String	Applicant	Loc/Reg	Properties	IDN Attributes	Appl. ID
VERSICHERUNG	dotversicherung-registry GmbH http://www.dotversicherung.de	DE/EUR	Community		1-891-92750
VET	Wild Dale, LLC	US/NA			1-1642-14231
VIAJES	Black Madison, LLC	US/NA			1-1629-12298
VIDEO	Top Level Domain Holdings Limited http://www.tldh.org	VG/EUR			1-1110-29042
	Amazon EU S.à r.l. http://www.amazon.com/	LU/EUR			1-1317-52344
	Lone Tigers, LLC	US/NA			1-1480-90854
	Uniregistry, Corp. http://www.uniregistry.com	KY/EUR			1-855-53391
VIG	VIENNA INSURANCE GROUP AG Wiener Versicherung Gruppe http://www.vig.com	AT/EUR			1-918-87536
VIKING	Viking River Cruises (Bermuda) Ltd. http://www.vikingrivercruises.com	US/NA			1-1691-8656
VILLAS	New Sky, LLC	US/NA			1-1537-30547
VIN	Holly Shadow, LLC	US/NA			1-1538-23177
VIP	I-REGISTRY Ltd., Niederlassung Deutschland http://www.i-registry.com	DE/EUR			1-1003-40726
	Top Level Domain Holdings Limited http://www.tldh.org	VG/EUR			1-1037-88001
	Charleston Road Registry Inc.	US/NA			1-1140-53549
	John Corner, LLC	US/NA			1-1532-71538
	Vipspace Enterprises LLC http://www.vipspaces.com	DE/EUR			1-851-9629
	VIP Registry Pte. Ltd. http://www.viptld.com	MY/AP			1-878-22942
VIRGIN	Virgin Enterprises Limited	CH/EUR			1-1768-35626
VISA	Visa International Service Association http://www.visa.com	US/NA			1-1338-34737
VISION	Koko Station, LLC	US/NA			1-1533-53706
VISTA	Vistaprint Limited http://www.vistaprint.com	BM/EUR			1-1033-33479
VISTAPRINT	Vistaprint Limited http://www.vistaprint.com	BM/EUR			1-1033-53103
VIVA	Saudi Telecom Company http://www.stc.com.sa	SA/AP			1-1933-773
VIVO	Telefonica Brasil S.A. http://www.telefonica.com.br	BR/LAC			1-1849-63904
VLAANDEREN	DNS.be vzw http://www.dns.be	BE/EUR	Geographic		1-1369-30849
VODKA	Top Level Domain Holdings Limited http://www.tldh.org	VG/EUR			1-1037-7152
VOLKSWAGEN	Volkswagen Group of America Inc. http://www.volkswagengroupamerica.com	US/NA			1-1262-79766
VOLVO	Volvo Holding Sverige Aktiebolag http://www.volvogroup.com	SE/EUR			1-1797-56873
VONS	Safeway Inc.	US/NA			1-1189-79924
VOTE	Monolith Registry LLC http://www.MonolithRegistry.org	US/NA			1-1013-44231
	Double Falls, LLC	US/NA			1-1530-99208
VOTING	Valuetainment Corp. http://www.valuetainment.com	CH/EUR			1-1280-72896
VOTO	Monolith Registry LLC http://www.MonolithRegistry.org	US/NA			1-1013-52757
VOYAGE	Ruby House, LLC	US/NA			1-1529-46197
VUELOS	Despegar Online SRL http://www.despegar.com	UY/LAC			1-1249-83471
WALES	Nominet UK http://www.nominet.org.uk	GB/EUR	Geographic		1-1105-18383
WALMART	Wal-Mart Stores, Inc.	US/NA			1-1244-56727
WALTER	Sandvik AB http://www.sandvik.com/	SE/EUR			1-2076-35685
WANG	Zodiac Leo Limited	HK/AP			1-857-40930

Copyright 2012 Internet Corporation for Assigned Names and Numbers

String	Applicant	Loc/Reg	Properties IDN Attributes	Appl. ID
WANGGOU	Amazon EU S.à r.l. http://www.amazon.com/	LU/EUR		1-1318-32718
WARMAN	Weir Group IP Limited http://www.weir.co.uk/	GB/EUR		1-1822-29200
WATCH	Sand Shadow, LLC	US/NA		1-1528-66412
WATCHES	Richemont DNS Inc. http://www.richemont.com	CH/EUR		1-1253-13044
WEATHER	The Weather Channel LLC http://weather.com	US/NA		1-1977-49078
WEATHERCHANNEL	The Weather Channel, LLC http://www.weather.com	US/NA		1-2117-66735
WEB	Web.com Group, Inc. http://www.web.com	US/NA		1-1009-97005
	Afilias Domains No. 3 Limited, http://www.AfiliasDomains3.info	IE/EUR		1-1013-6638
	Schlund Technologies GmbH http://www.schlundtech.com	DE/EUR		1-1013-77165
	NU DOT CO LLC	US/NA		1-1296-36138
	Ruby Glen, LLC	US/NA		1-1527-54849
	Charleston Road Registry Inc.	US/NA		1-1681-58699
	DotWeb Inc. http://www.radixregistry.com	AE/AP		1-956-26846
WEBCAM	dot Webcam Limited	GI/EUR		1-1236-11213
WEBER	Saint-Gobain Weber SA http://www.e-weber.com	FR/EUR		1-1812-10343
WEBJET	Webjet Limited http://www.webjet.com.au/	AU/AP		1-1045-73977
WEBS	Vistaprint Limited http://www.vistaprint.com	BM/EUR	Community	1-1033-22687
	Vistaprint Limited http://www.vistaprint.com	BM/EUR		1-1033-73917
WEBSITE	Top Level Domain Holdings Limited http://www.tldh.org	VG/EUR		1-1037-47594
	DotWebsite Inc. http://www.radixregistry.com	AE/AP		1-1050-30871
	Fern Edge, LLC	US/NA		1-1524-44846
WED	Atgron, Inc.	US/NA		1-1276-92005
WEDDING	Top Level Domain Holdings Limited http://www.tldh.org	VG/EUR		1-1037-16321
	Wild Madison, LLC	US/NA		1-1519-43980
	Wedding TLD LLC	US/NA		1-856-13669
WEIBO	Tencent Holdings Limited http://tencent.com	CN/AP		1-1313-41040
	Sina Corporation http://www.sina.com.cn	CN/AP		1-950-50638
WEIR	Weir Group IP Limited http://www.weir.co.uk/	GB/EUR		1-1822-6919
WHOSWHO	21st Century Communications Limited (AND/OR) ????????? http://domains.whoswho.com	HK/AP		1-1829-71938
WIEN	punkt.wien GmbH http://www.punktwien.at	AT/EUR	Community Geographic	1-1030-79531
WIKI	Top Level Design, LLC	US/NA		1-1086-78534
WILLIAMHILL	William Hill Organization Limited http://www.williamhill.com	GB/EUR		1-1755-98806
WILMAR	Wilmar International Limited http://www.wilmar-international.com	SG/AP		1-972-95481
WIN	First Registry Limited	GI/EUR		1-1226-82695
WINDOWS	Microsoft Corporation http://www.microsoft.com	US/NA		1-1129-52051
WINE	dot Wine Limited	GI/EUR		1-1223-37711
	June Station, LLC	US/NA		1-1515-14214
	Afilias Limited	IE/EUR		1-868-66341
WINNERS	The TJX Companies, Inc. http://www.tjx.com	US/NA		1-1764-23072
WME	William Morris Endeavor Entertainment, LLC http://www.wmeentertainment.com	US/NA		1-930-41059

String	Applicant	Loc/Reg	Properties	IDN Attributes	Appl. ID
WOLTERSKLUWER	Wolters Kluwer N.V. http://www.wolterskluwer.com	NL/EUR			1-1005-36512
WOODSIDE	Woodside Petroleum Limited http://www.woodside.com.au	AU/AP			1-1948-75990
WORK	Top Level Domain Holdings Limited http://www.tldh.org	VG/EUR			1-1037-87207
WORKS	Little Dynamite, LLC	US/NA			1-1518-50195
WORLD	DotWorld Inc. http://www.radixregistry.com	AE/AP			1-1071-58353
	Bitter Fields, LLC	US/NA			1-1504-13424
WOW	Charleston Road Registry Inc.	US/NA			1-1142-53389
	United TLD Holdco Ltd. http://unitedtld.com	KY/EUR			1-1255-61847
	Amazon EU S.à r.l. http://www.amazon.com/	LU/EUR			1-1318-51358
WTC	World Trade Centers Association, Inc. http://www.wtca.org	US/NA			1-1275-26828
WTF	Hidden Way, LLC	US/NA			1-1508-57100
XBOX	Microsoft Corporation http://www.microsoft.com	US/NA			1-1129-57994
XEROX	Xerox DNHC LLC http://www.xerox.com/	US/NA			1-1046-44533
XFINITY	Comcast IP Holdings I, LLC	US/NA			1-1170-40267
XIHUAN	QIHOO 360 TECHNOLOGY CO. LTD. http://www.360.cn	CN/AP			1-974-79364
XIN	Elegant Leader Limited	CN/AP			1-1152-14481
XPERIA	Sony Mobile Communications AB http://www.sonymobile.com	SE/EUR			1-1956-11092
XYZ	XYZ.COM LLC	US/NA			1-1982-70171
YACHTS	DERYachts, LLC	US/NA			1-909-89547
YAHOO	Yahoo! Domain Services Inc.	US/NA			1-1168-48888
YAMAXUN	Amazon EU S.à r.l. http://www.amazon.com/	LU/EUR			1-1318-28317
YANDEX	YANDEX, LLC http://www.yandex.ru	RU/EUR			1-977-13382
YELLOWPAGES	Telstra Corporation Limited http://www.telstra.com.au	AU/AP			1-1676-43685
YODOBASHI	YODOBASHI CAMERA CO.,LTD. http://www.yodobashi.co.jp	JP/AP			1-1809-93761
YOGA	Top Level Domain Holdings Limited http://www.tldh.org	VG/EUR			1-1037-89079
	Victor Falls, LLC	US/NA			1-1502-54392
	Uniregistry, Corp. http://www.uniregistry.com	KY/EUR			1-845-11060
YOKOHAMA	GMO Registry, Inc. http://gmoregistry.com/	JP/AP	Geographic		1-1194-80642
YOU	Amazon EU S.à r.l. http://www.amazon.com/	LU/EUR			1-1318-84751
	Charleston Road Registry Inc.	US/NA			1-1682-29217
YOUTUBE	Charleston Road Registry Inc.	US/NA			1-1417-80062
YUN	Amazon EU S.à r.l. http://www.amazon.com/	LU/EUR			1-1318-12524
	QIHOO 360 TECHNOLOGY CO. LTD. http://www.360.cn	CN/AP			1-974-89210
ZAPPOS	Amazon EU S.à r.l. http://www.amazon.com/	LU/EUR			1-1315-80866
ZARA	Industria de Diseño Textil, S.A. (INDITEX, S.A.) http://www.inditex.com	ES/EUR			1-985-40230
ZERO	Amazon EU S.à r.l. http://www.amazon.com/	LU/EUR			1-1318-14004
ZIP	Charleston Road Registry Inc.	US/NA			1-1678-17174
ZIPPO	Zadco Company	US/NA			1-1295-79595

Copyright 2012 Internet Corporation for Assigned Names and Numbers.

ZONE	Outer Falls, LLC	US/NA			1-1503-89379
ZUERICH	Kanton Zürich (Canton of Zurich) http://www.zh.ch	CH/EUR	Geographic		1-968-87792
ZULU	Top Level Domain Holdings Limited http://www.tldh.org	VG/EUR	Geographic		1-994-74713
คอม	VeriSign Sàrl http://www.verisigninc.com/en_CH/index.xhtml? loc=en_CH#/site_owners	CH/EUR	IDN	**A-label:** xn--42c2d9a **Script Code:** Thai **English Meaning:** Transliteration of com	1-1254-3015

Learning from gTLD History

See Figures A.1, A.2, A.3, and A.4.

What Happened with .tv?

A major pushback to the future release of the new gTLDs is the results companies saw with the last major domain release, .tv. Although the .tv release was overall portrayed as a failure, there were many aspects of the release that damaged the domain's popularity. Furthermore, with today's dependence on technology and push towards viewing media online, many see the relaunch of the .tv extension as inevitable.

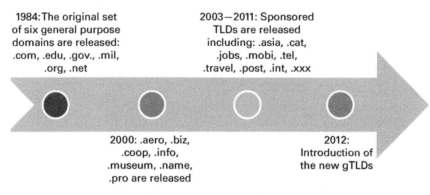

Figure A.1   The Timeline of Top-Level Domains

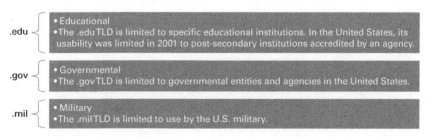

Figure A.2   Top-Level Domains

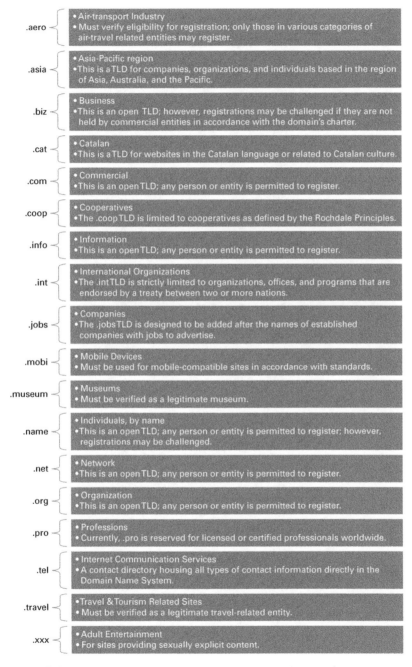

.aero	• Air-transport Industry • Must verify eligibility for registration; only those in various categories of air-travel related entities may register.
.asia	• Asia-Pacific region • This is a TLD for companies, organizations, and individuals based in the region of Asia, Australia, and the Pacific.
.biz	• Business • This is an open TLD; however, registrations may be challenged if they are not held by commercial entities in accordance with the domain's charter.
.cat	• Catalan • This is a TLD for websites in the Catalan language or related to Catalan culture.
.com	• Commercial • This is an open TLD; any person or entity is permitted to register.
.coop	• Cooperatives • The .coop TLD is limited to cooperatives as defined by the Rochdale Principles.
.info	• Information • This is an open TLD; any person or entity is permitted to register.
.int	• International Organizations • The .int TLD is strictly limited to organizations, offices, and programs that are endorsed by a treaty between two or more nations.
.jobs	• Companies • The .jobs TLD is designed to be added after the names of established companies with jobs to advertise.
.mobi	• Mobile Devices • Must be used for mobile-compatible sites in accordance with standards.
.museum	• Museums • Must be verified as a legitimate museum.
.name	• Individuals, by name • This is an open TLD; any person or entity is permitted to register; however, registrations may be challenged.
.net	• Network • This is an open TLD; any person or entity is permitted to register.
.org	• Organization • This is an open TLD; any person or entity is permitted to register.
.pro	• Professions • Currently, .pro is reserved for licensed or certified professionals worldwide.
.tel	• Internet Communication Services • A contact directory housing all types of contact information directly in the Domain Name System.
.travel	• Travel & Tourism Related Sites • Must be verified as a legitimate travel-related entity.
.xxx	• Adult Entertainment • For sites providing sexually explicit content.

Figure A.3 U.S. Top-Level Domains

APPENDIX A

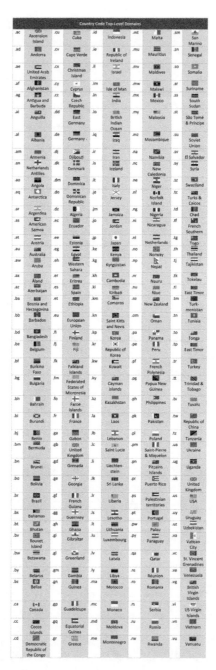

Figure A.4 Generic Top-Level Domains

History

.tv was originally released as a ccTLD, assigned to the small island of Tuvalu in the mid 1980s. This original assignment was one of the major issues with the extension. As the Internet grew and television started to became a more prominent component of the Internet, the demand for a .tv extension developed. In 1998, Jason Chapnik, a Canadian entrepreneur who was president of Information.ca, approached the Tuvalu government with an idea on how to profit from their popular country code. However, Chapnik was not the only one interested in .tv. Anton Van Couvering, former President of NetNames, had been consulting Tuvalu on how to profit from their country code. Van Couvering stepped down as a consultant in order to become a bidder for .tv through his company NetNames.

After months of negotiation in the fall of 1998, Tuvalu decided to go with Chapnik, but later agreed to license its ccTLD to IdeaLab, a California incubator. Tuvalu licensed the domain for $1 million per quarter adjustable for inflation, with a $50 million cap over 10 years. Additionally, the Tuvalu nation got a 20 percent interest in the company.

In August 2000, IdeaLab announced the three most expensive sales in .tv history. Free.tv, China.tv, and Net.tv were sold for $100,000 for the first year and an additional percentage for each year following. ChinaGo.com is the registrant of China.tv and Net.tv, and has maintained their registration to the present day. Free.tv is registered to a Pennsylvania man who has also kept the registration up to date. On January 7, 2002, IdeaLab sold its .tv international unit for $45 million to VeriSign. VeriSign took over and started doing business at .tv http://www.tv/ where premium registrations could only take place through VeriSign with a minimum two-year contract. Nonpremium registrations were $50 at.tv but other registrars such as Go Daddy, Idotz .net, Moniker, and a whole host of others offered one-year registrations for as little as $29.99 to as high as $59.99. With the release of the domain stretching over four years and no official rollout, there was little to no information on the extension for the public until nearly 2006.

After a price drop and a new marketing program, the extension responded in 2007, posting more sales than the previous three years combined.

Price

The .tv extension is one of the most expensive to purchase at $28 per domain. In addition, the renewal fees for a .tv domain are about three times the price of .com names.

The Future of .tv

Even with its negative connotation, .tv has actually become the fastest growing TLD in Internet history. Registrants of .tv include Bloomberg, Reuters, Motorola, IBM, EarthLink, eBay, MLB, HBO, Cox Communications, *The Economist*, Columbia TriStar, CNBC, and Telemundo. In addition, major search engines like Google give a .tv domain exactly the same measure as they do a .com.

Recently there has been a trend of major websites and publishers securing .tv domains to launch their online video shows. Examples include Twit.tv, TechCrunch.tv, and FordModels.tv. The other side of the trend is the popularization of Internet-based television platforms, like Google TV and Apple TV. The results of this current online craze could be the adoption of the .tv domain as the standard for websites that are compatible with Internet television (i.e., websites that have video content available and that are compatible with the Internet television platforms). This means whenever consumers are browsing on their televisions, they would first try the .tv version of the domain they are looking for.

With annual fees continuing to drop and the demand for television on the Internet rising, many see the .tv extension gaining popularity.

What's Different Now?

With the lack of public knowledge and the inconsistency of the extension .tv websites have generally received it as illegitimate or cheap. But a key aspect of the new gTLDs is that they will help promote security and legitimacy into already trusted brands. In this expansion, it's not just a handful of extensions occurring, it's large scale, and the biggest tech companies in the world will likely lead the way. When they educate the public how to navigate a new Internet, the shift will accelerate. .com may not be dead, but it will certainly be diluted in a dot-anything world. The proliferation of large businesses, particularly technology-driven businesses driving consumer behavior, will be the big differentiator. The economies of scale are significantly different this time. When Google, Bing, Yahoo!, Amazon, and others push consumers and advertise to them to access them in a new way, consumer behavior will follow.

> "One of the reasons previous top-level domains failed is because the registrations in those domains primarily came from brand owners just trying to protect their brands. .travel, .mobi, .biz were never communicated in a meaningful way to Internet users. They never had value because people didn't see them everywhere. Companies like Orbitz had no need to communicate Orbitz.travel, because they had Orbitz.com and could just redirect it. What's different now is that with so many .brand gTLDs getting involved, they will market their new location as uniquely their own and consumers may adopt this new way of getting around the Internet."
>
> Josh Bourne, Managing Partner, FairWinds Partners

What Will Happen Next?

Throughout this book, we chronicled our interviews with the global leaders in the next generation of the Internet and shared research and trends to help business navigate what to do next. While there are many uncertainties, we know for sure, things are about to change. And, while many have touted we don't need anything more than a .com world, history suggests that change comes even when people don't think they want or need it. If you simply don't believe anything will change, then hang on to your .com—it might be a bumpy ride.

Appendix B

Our Thought Leaders

We give great thanks and appreciation to our thought leaders—those who have been out in the forefront of this debate and advocating for policy to protect brand owners and consumers alike while embracing the opportunities that may develop in an expanded Internet. It was our honor and privilege to interview them and we are grateful for their time, insights, and dedication to a safe and secure Internet that benefits the planet's citizens. We feature each of them in this final section of the book.

Josh Bourne

Managing Partner, FairWinds Partners

Josh Bourne is Managing Partner and co-founder of FairWinds Partners, a consultancy that works with leading brands to improve the frequency and quality of their interactions with Internet users through the optimization of digital identifiers such as domain names and social media usernames. He is also co-founder and co-owner of DigitalDNA and Kalorama, both digital asset transactional advisory firms.

Mr. Bourne serves as President of the Coalition Against Domain Name Abuse (CADNA), a not-for-profit corporation dedicated to building awareness about and advocating action to stop illegal and unethical infringement of brands/trademarks online. He is a frequent speaker at industry events, providing perspective on the domain name system, digital marketing, and brand protection strategies.

A graduate of the University of Richmond, he received a BA in business administration with a concentration in finance and a minor in leadership studies. Josh lives with his wife, Blair, and their two sons and daughter in suburban Washington, DC.

Sarah B. Deutsch

Vice President and Associate General Counsel, Verizon Communication

Sarah Deutsch is Vice President and Associate General Counsel for Verizon Communications. Her practice covers a wide range of legal issues in the areas of global intellectual property issues, Internet policy, liability, and Internet jurisdiction. She manages Verizon's intellectual property group and is responsible for copyright, trademarks, and patent licensing matters. She has represented Verizon on a host of domestic and international Internet issues ranging from Internet governance, domain name issues, and ICANN to digital copyright issues, cybercrime, and international copyright issues.

Ms. Deutsch was one of five negotiators for the U.S. telecommunications industry who negotiated service provider provisions that resulted in the passage of the Digital Millennium Copyright Act. She was also actively involved with Congress in the passage of the Anti-Cybersquatting Act and the process that led to the creation of the UDRP.

Claudio Di Gangi

Manager, External Relations, Internet and the Judiciary, International Trademark Association

Claudio Di Gangi is Manager, External Relations, Internet and the Judiciary, for the International Trademark Association (INTA). He is responsible for working with INTA committees to manage both judicial and Internet-related policy development and advocacy issues for the Association. Mr. Di Gangi was elected as three-term Vice President of the Intellectual Property Constituency of the Internet Corporation for Assigned Names and Numbers (ICANN) from 2008 to 2010. Claudio holds degrees from Towson University (BS, political science) and St. John's University School of Law (Juris Doctor).

Cynthia L. Gibson

Executive Vice President, Legal Affairs, Scripps Networks Interactive Inc.

Cynthia Gibson is an accomplished attorney and has more than 20 years experience as a proven practitioner and leader. She has been recognized among the Best Lawyers in America and was named among the Top 50 Women Attorneys in Ohio, and Top 25 Women Attorneys in Cincinnati.

Ms. Gibson is also actively involved in the community. She serves as Vice-Chair of the Women's Leadership Council of United Way Worldwide, leading its taskforce on Women and Worldwide as well as its Council Development Committee. Locally, Gibson serves as Chair of the Women of Tocqueville for the United Way of Greater Knoxville. She also serves as a member of the board of the American Red Cross, Knoxville Area Chapter.

Gibson received a bachelor of arts degree with honors in history from Wake Forest University, and her juris doctorate degree from the University of Virginia School of Law.

J. Scott Evans

Senior Legal Director, Head of Global Brand, Domains & Copyright, Yahoo!

 J. Scott Evans received his undergraduate degree from Baylor University and his Juris Doctor cum laude in 1992 from the Louis D. Brandeis School of Law at the University of Louisville. He first served as corporate counsel for Fruit of the Loom, where he was responsible for managing the international intellectual property portfolios for Fruit of the Loom and its associate companies: the B.V.D. Licensing Corporation, Gitano, Pro Player, and Salem Sportswear, Inc. In November 1996, Mr. Evans joined Adams Evans P.A. where he continued to concentrate his practice in the areas of trademark, copyright, unfair competition, and Internet law. In November 2007, he joined the legal team at Yahoo! Inc., where he serves as a Senior Legal Director—Head of Global Brand, Domains & Copyright.

Mr. Evans served on the five-member drafting committee that assisted the staff at the Internet Corporation for Assigned Names and Number (ICANN) and with the drafting of the Uniform Dispute Resolution Policy (UDRP) and the Rules of Procedure for the UDRP. He also served as member of the Implementation Recommendation Team charged with proposing possible solutions for brand protection in new gTLDs. Evans is an active member of the International Trademark Association, where he serves as secretary, is a member of the board of directors and he serves on the executive committee. He also currently serves as a member of the U.S. Legislation Sub-Committee at INTA. Additionally, he is the immediate past-president of the Intellectual Property Constituency (IPC), the body that participates on behalf of trademark and copyright owners in the ICANN policy process. Evans has twice been voted one of the 50 Most Influential People in IP by *Managing Intellectual Property* magazine. J. Scott Evans frequently lectures on trademark and Internet policy issues, as well as domain name dispute resolution.

Nancy H. Lutz

Partner, Kelley Drye & Warren, LLP

Nancy Lutz is a partner in the Washington, DC office of Kelley Drye & Warren LLP. She protects clients' trademarks, copyrights, and domain names, including the new gTLDs, on a worldwide basis by developing legal strategies to meet their business needs. Ms. Lutz prosecutes and defends contested matters, including Uniform Domain Name Dispute Resolution Policy actions (UDRPs), before administrative bodies; advises on pre-litigation issues; manages foreign litigation; and drafts agreements relating to the foregoing. She looks forward to continuing to assist clients with their gTLD needs as the landscape evolves.

Lutz has practiced law since 1995 and has been selected as one of the best lawyers in America in trademark and copyright law. She enjoys lecturing on strategic considerations in clearing, registering, and enforcing trademarks globally and on other IP related topics. Lutz has been active with the International Trademark Association, most recently serving as Chair of the Lefkowitz Moot Court Competition. Outside of the office, she is very involved in charitable activities with an emphasis on providing hospitality to the homeless.

Steven W. Miller

Vice President and General Counsel, Intellectual Property, Procter & Gamble

Steven W. Miller is Vice President and General Counsel—Intellectual Property for the Procter & Gamble Company, joining Procter & Gamble in August 1984. In this position, he oversees about 150 patent and trademark attorneys worldwide, and advises Procter & Gamble's senior management on intellectual property issues. Mr. Miller has authored numerous P&G patents and patent applications and has been involved in a number of license agreements, acquisitions, interferences, arbitrations, and litigation, both in the United States and abroad.

Mr. Miller is currently a member of the Patent Public Advisory Committee, being appointed by Secretary of Commerce Gary Locke, in 2009; on the executive committee and vice president for the Association of Corporate Patent Counsel (ACPC); on the board of directors and past president of the Intellectual Property Owners Association Education Foundation (IPOEF); on the board of directors and past president of the Intellectual Property Owners Association (IPO); on the board of directors for the National Inventors Hall of Fame; on the steering committee for the Coalition for 21st Century Patent Reform; on the Dean's National Council for the Ohio State University Moritz College of Law; on the advisory council for Intellectual Property at the Franklin Pierce Law Center; and is a member of the American Intellectual Property Law Association (AIPLA), American Bar Association—Intellectual Property Committee, and Cincy IP.

Miller is a frequent speaker at events for the Intellectual Property Owners Association, Association of Corporate Patent Counsel, Cincy IP, and other bar associations and groups, about various IP topics including licensing and open innovation. He worked on the patent reform legislation culminating in the Leahy-Smith America Invents Act, the first major patent reform since 1952. He received a JD with honors and a BS in mechanical engineering, cum laude, from the Ohio State University. He is licensed to practice in Ohio; U.S. Patent and Trademark Office; United States District Court for the Southern District of Ohio; United States Court of Appeals for the Sixth and Federal Circuits; and the United States Supreme Court.

Jeffrey J. Neuman

Vice President, Business Affairs, Enterprise Services, NeuStar, Inc.

Mr. Neuman has over ten years of Internet, technology, and telecommunication law and policy experience with domain expertise in e-commerce, e-business, service and technology licensing, M&A, joint ventures, strategic alliances, and reseller arrangements. He is responsible for all legal services and policy for Neustar's Enterprise Services, including domain name and mobile registries, as well its media lines of business. In addition to leading the legal team for these organizations, he is responsible for the oversight of intellectual property law and policy matters, information technology licensing, as well as legal issues (including litigation) related to employment and insurance matters for the company. Mr. Neuman is the vice chair of ICANN's Generic Names Supporting Organization representing the gTLD registries and is a frequent speaker on issues involving intellectual property, domain names, online dispute resolution, and the introduction of new generic top-level domain names. He previously served as Chairman of the gTLD Registries Constituency of ICANN and participated in numerous task forces and working groups within ICANN's GNSO. Before joining NeuStar, he served as Information Technology Associate at Greenberg Traurig, LLP/Akin, Gump, Strauss, Hauer & Feld, LLP, and as an associate at the law firm of Arter & Hadden, LLP. Mr. Neuman holds a JD from the George Washington University Law School.

Russell Pangborn

Associate General Counsel for Trademarks, Microsoft Corporation

Russell Pangborn is the associate general counsel for trademarks at Microsoft Corporation. He leads a team of experienced trademark professionals in strategic counseling for Microsoft's global businesses on all aspects of trademarks including clearance, counseling, prosecution, maintenance, enforcement, licensing, litigation, and policy.

Mr. Pangborn previously held positions at Microsoft as the group manager for the Copyright & Trade Secret practice and as a senior attorney in the trademark group. Before Microsoft, he was a senior trademark attorney at Intel Corporation where he also handled all aspects of trademarks, including the enforcement of several brands of global reach. Prior to Intel, he worked in private practice with the boutique IP firm of Fulwider Patton Lee & Utecht, LLP in Southern California.

Pangborn was on the board of directors for the International Trademark Association (INTA) from 2009 to 2011 and a member of

INTA's Executive Committee in 2010 to 2011. He is also on ICANN's Intellectual Property Constituency and participated on the Implementation Recommendation Team as one of 18 legal professionals selected to propose trademark protection mechanisms to be implemented in connection with ICANN's expansion of new generic top-level domains. He is a frequent speaker at various IP association and CLE events.

Mr. Pangborn has been recognized as a leading IP attorney. In 2007, he was a finalist for the Association of Corporate Counsel's IP Attorney of the Year award, and in 2008 was featured as a top IP attorney in the IP Law & Business magazine's Top 50 under 45. The team he leads has received numerous IP industry awards, including recognition by the World Trademark Review as the 2009 Internet Team of the Year and the 2010 and 2011 Technology & Software Team of the Year.

Pangborn received his undergraduate degree from Stanford University and his JD from U.C. Hastings College of the Law. He lives in Redmond, Washington, with his wife and three children.

Krista Papac

Chief Strategy Officer, ARI Registry Services

Krista Papac has 13-plus years of strategic management and business development experience. She is responsible for strategic direction and planning for policy, information, initiatives, and industry relations for ARI Registry Services. Papac has been an active participant in the domain name industry since 2001.

Ms. Papac brings specialist knowledge of the international domain name industry to her role as chief strategy officer for ARI Registry Services. With extensive business development experience and strategic involvement in internet and technology-related industries, she provides unique insight into the upcoming opportunities presented by the advent of ICANN's new TLD program.

Papac has more than 13 years' experience identifying strategic opportunities and managing growth for a broad range of North American businesses with international focus, from startups to Fortune 1000 companies.

Her consistent successes have earned her a stellar reputation and industry recognition which, combined with her passion for tactical problem-solving, ideally suits her current role. She works closely with all facets of the business to ensure education, policy, and industry relations support ARI Registry Services mission to achieve an industry-leading position as a global provider of domain name registry services.

Ms. Papac has been involved with the International Trademark Association (INTA) since 2001, and has been an active ICANN participant, including membership on a number of ICANN policy-making groups since 2001. She is affiliated with a wide range of industry associations and contributes valuable knowledge across many forums and working groups on behalf of ARI Registry Services.

Ms. Papac holds a bachelor of science, business and information systems degree from the University of Phoenix and a masters in business administration from the University of Southern California. She is based at ARI Registry Services United States head office in California but continues to visit Australia regularly, both virtually and in person.

Katherine A. Ruwe

Senior Counsel, Global Litigation and Dispute Resolution, Procter & Gamble

Katherine A. Ruwe is currently Senior Counsel—Global Litigation and Dispute Resolution for the Procter & Gamble Company, having joined Procter & Gamble in January, 2007. Prior to Ms. Ruwe's position in Global Litigation, she was Senior Counsel in the Brand Equity group at Procter & Gamble advising global retail hair care brands on various intellectual property issues including trademarks and copyright.

Ruwe is currently a member of Cincy IP, the American Intellectual Property Law Association (AIPLA), and is a former member of the International Trademark Association (INTA) serving on several committees including the North American Anti-Counterfeiting Committee, the North American Famous and Well-Known Marks Committee, and the Emerging Issues Committee.

Ms. Ruwe received a JD from the University of Cincinnati and a BA in English, magna cum laude, from the University of Dayton. She is licensed to practice in Ohio; the United States District Court for the Southern District of Ohio; and the United States Court of Appeals for the Sixth Circuit.

Adam Scoville

Trademark and Brand Protection Counsel, RE/MAX, LLC

 Adam Scoville is in charge of trademarks, advertising substantiation, and other intellectual property issues at RE/MAX, LLC, which franchises real estate brokerage operations with nearly 90,000 sales associates, in over 6,000 franchised offices, in over 80 countries. Mr. Scoville oversees brand clearance, trademark prosecution, and infringement investigation and enforcement for RE/MAX in the United States, online, and around the world. In addition to his work at RE/MAX, he also serves on the board of directors of the International Trademark Association (where he is active as Chair of INTA's Internet Committee), and as the President of the Board of Directors for the Montessori School of Washington Park.

Ellen Shankman

Principal, Ellen B. Shankman and Associates

 Ellen B. Shankman, Esq., has more than 20 years of experience practicing trademark, Internet, licensing, and copyright law. Formerly a partner and the head of the trademark department with one of the largest intellectual property firms in Israel, she established Ellen B. Shankman and Associates as a boutique intellectual property firm specializing in global branding strategy, trademark and domain name counseling, clearance, protection, and enforcement, including the development and management of international trademark and domain name portfolios for technology and other companies. The firm proactively counsels company legal, marketing, and business development departments, with creative cost-effective strategies

to achieve marketing goals. Her clients include a wide range of companies from representation of Fortune 10 companies to small start-ups.

- Recent member of the Board of Directors of INTA.
- Represents the Israel ISOC, the administrative body responsible for Domain Name allocation under the .IL ccTLD.
- Former Chair of INTA Internet Committee and currently chair of ccTLD Subcommittee.
- Member of the ICANN Implementation Recommendation Team ("IRT").
- Former member of the Policy Council of the Generic Domain Name Supporting Organization of ICANN representing the Intellectual Property Constituency.
- Former member of the Nominating Committee of ICANN.
- She is the recipient of the 2002 INTA's first ever Volunteer Service Award for the Advancement of the Association for her work in the Internet area.
- Contributed sections on Israel trademark and Internet law, as well as the chapters on ccTLDs for number of publications.

Yasmin R. Tavakoli

Associate, Kelley Drye & Warren, LLP

Yasmin Tavakoli is an associate in the Washington, DC office of Kelley Drye & Warren LLP. Prior to joining Kelley Drye, Ms. Tavakoli earned her LLM in International Intellectual Property law from the Magister Lvcentinvs program located at the seat of the Office for Harmonization in the Internal Market (OHIM) in Alicante, Spain. Her practice focuses on international trademark portfolio management, IP licensing, opposition and cancellation proceedings, and all forms of IP litigation. Ms. Tavakoli experience with gTLDs and domain name issues includes determining brand protection strategies online, Uniform Domain Name Dispute Resolution Policy (UDRP) proceedings, counseling clients with respect to gTLD registry contracting arrangements, and assisting clients with new gTLD applications.

Fabricio Vayra

Trademark Attorney, Time Warner Inc.

Fabricio Vayra is the chief trademark attorney for Time Warner Inc. In this role, Mr. Vayra advises on all trademark issues and reviews and takes action in online infringement matters, often acting as the lead and coordinating attorney for matters that touch various Time Warner divisions (HBO, Time Inc., Turner and Warner Bros.). He also handles various Internet governance-related policy issues for the Time Warner companies, liaising with constituency groups and the Time Warner Global Policy group in Washington, DC.

Nick Wood

Managing Director, Com Laude

Nick Wood is the managing director of accredited registrar Com Laude, which is dedicated to assisting IP owners to protect their marks in the domain name system. He is also the CEO of Valideus, a consultancy assisting leading corporations to evaluate and, if appropriate, to apply for a new gTLD.

Mr. Wood was a member of the IRT (Implementation Recommendation Team) formed by the ICANN Board to recommend rights protection measures in the new gTLD process and chaired ICANN's London Consultative Day on the new gTLDs in 2009. He is a council member of MARQUES, the European Association of Trademark Owners, and sits on committees for other professional associations including INTA. Wood is an occasional lecturer at the Intellectual Property and Technology Law Centre of Queen Mary University, London, and is the co-editor of Sweet and Maxwell's *Domain Names: Global Practice & Procedure.* He sits on the Editorial Board of *Managing Intellectual Property* magazine and edited *The Perfect Sunrise* booklet.

Works Cited

Advertising Age. "The Ad Age Pop Thermometer." January 1, 2012.

Aki, Helen, Zachary Arnold, Genevieve Bennett, Chris Knight, Ashley Lin, Taj Walton, and Adam Zemel. *Case Studies in American Innovation.* Breakthrough Institute, 2009.

Allemann, Andrew. "An Easy Way to Register Domains for $2 Each." *Domain Name Wire.* March 1, 2012. http://domainnamewire.com/2012/02/29/2-dollar-domains/.

Allemann, Andrew. "Fantasy Island Returns Home to Columbia Pictures." *Domain Name Wire.* February 29, 2012. http://domainnamewire.com/2012/02/29/fantasy-island-returns-home-to-columbia-pictures/.

Allemann, Andrew. "February's Top 5 Stories on Domain Name Wire." *Domain Name Wire.* March 1, 2012. http://domainnamewire.com/2012/03/01/februarys-top-5-stories-on-domain-name-wire/.

Allemann, Andrew. "Monte Cahn and Michael Berkens Get Trademarks for "Right of the Dot." *Domain Name Wire.* February 29, 2012. http://domainnamewire.com/2012/02/29/monte-cahn-and-michael-berkens-get-trademarks-for-right-of-the-dot/.

Allemann, Andrew. "Suddenly, People Happier with ICANN." *Domain Name Wire.* March 1, 2012. http://domainnamewire.com/2012/03/01/suddenly-people-happier-with-icann/.

Allemann, Andrew. ".XXX Is Going to Make a Whole Lot of Money—Domain Name Wire." *Domain Name Wire*. October 6, 2011. http://domainnamewire.com/2011/10/06/xxx-is-going-to-make-a-whole-lot-of-money/.

Andrews, Michael D., and Brian M. Daniel. 2011. "Trademark Valuations: Basic Techniques for Building Value." *INTA Bulletin* 66 (October 15): 6–7.

Atchley, David, D. James Bidzos, and John Calys. "VeriSign Management Discusses Q4 2011 Results—Earnings Call Transcript." *Seeking Alpha*. January 26, 2012. http://seekingalpha.com/article/322517-verisign-management-discusses-q4-2011-results-earnings-call-transcript.

Barnes, Brooks. "Disney and YouTube Make a Video Deal." *New York Times*. November 6, 2011. www.nytimes.com/2011/11/07/business/media/disney-and-youtube-make-a-video-deal.html.

Bellis, Mary. "History of Post Office Technology." *About.com*. February 2, 2012. http://inventors.about.com/od/xyzstartinventions/a/zipcode.htm.

Bellis, Mary. "Putting Microsoft on The Map." *About.com*. March 15, 2012. http://inventors.about.com/od/computersoftware/a/Putting-Microsoft-On-The-Map.htm.

Blodget, Henry. "New York Times Nuts Not to Charge Subscription Fee (NYT)." *Business Insider*. February 6, 2009, http://articles.businessinsider.com/2009-02-06/tech/30051816_1_wall-street-journal-wall-street-journal-s-ad-prices.

Brand Channel. "Deloitte, Canon and Motorola Nab Dotbrand Web Addresses." *BeyondDotCom*. October 21, 2011. www.beyonddotcom.info/brands/deloitte-canon-and-motorola-nab-dotbrand-web-addresses.html.

Cabell, Diane. "UDRP Opinion Guide." *Berkman Center for Internet & Society*. August 10, 2003. http://cyber.law.harvard.edu/udrp/opinion/.

CADNA. "The Real Cost of Cybersquatting." *Learn About the Issues*. February 2012. www.cadna.org/en/issues/cadna-analysis/real-cost-of-cybersquatting.

Canon, Inc. "Canon to Begin Acquisition of the ".canon" Top-Level Domain Name." *Canon Global: News*. March 16, 2010. www.canon.com/news/2010/mar16e.html.

Carlson, Nicholas. "Facebook Connect Is A Huge Success—By The Numbers." *Business Insider*. July 1, 2009. http://articles.businessinsider.com/2009-07-01/tech/30086042_1_ceo-mark-zuckerberg-sites-user.

Cassidy, John. *Dot.con: The Greatest Story Ever Sold*. New York: HarperCollins, 2003.

Association of National Advertisers. "Coalition for Responsible Internet Domain Oversight (CRIDO)." *ANA*. December 1, 2011. www.ana.net/content/show/id/crido.

Cohen, Aaron M., Rick Docksai, Patrick Tucker, and Cynthia Wagner. "The Best Predictions of 2011." *The Futurist* (January/February 2012): 28–39.

ComScore. "ComScore Releases April 2011 U.S. Online Video Rankings—ComScore, Inc." *ComScore, Inc.* May 18, 2011. www.comscore.com/Press_Events/Press_Releases/2011/5/comScore_Releases_April_2011_U.S._Online_Video_Rankings.

Creamer, Matthew. "Hats Off to These 10 Forward-Thinking Clients." *Advertising Age.* January 8, 2012.

Delo, Cotton. "Your Guide to Who Measures What in the Online Space; Panels, Tags, Clickstream and Census-level Data—Which Service Is Right for You Depends on What You're Tracking." *Advertising Age.* September 19, 2011.

Deutsch, Sarah B., and David E. Weslow. 2011. "UDRP Hijacking Revisted: A Domain Name Register's Actions Raise Concerns." *INTA Bulletin* 66 (October): 1—2.

Efrati, Amir. "The Mounting Minuses at Google+." *Wall Street Journal.* Feb. 28, 2012. http://online.wsj.com/article/SB1000142405297020465360457724934140374239-0.html.

Electronic Frontier Foundation. "Anti-Counterfeiting Trade Agreement." *Electronic Frontier Foundation.* March 14, 2012. https://www.eff.org/issues/acta.

Elliott, Gary. "ICANN's Promises Aren't Simply Speculation, They're Outright Fantasy." *Advertising Age.* September 5, 2011.

Franklin, Curt. "How Internet Search Engines Work." *HowStuffWorks.* March 15, 2012. http://computer.howstuffworks.com/internet/basics/search-engine.htm.

Garfield, Bob, and Doug Levy. "Ignore the Human Element of Marketing at Your Own Peril." *Advertising Age.* January 2, 2012.

Garner, Rob. "Search Implications of New GTLDs." Lecture for SES, Chicago, November 18, 2011. www.slideshare.net/robgarner1/the-seo-impact-of-new-icann-top-level-domains-tlds-ses-chicago-rob-garner-seschi.

Ghedine, Jackie, Jim Whelan, Karen Egolf, Richard Skews, Nancy Coltun Webster, Barbara Knoll, Nancy Dietz, Gregory Cohane, and Katie Nelson. "Guide to Social Media & Marketing." *Advertising Age.* September 19, 2011.

HybridDomainer. "The History of the Dot TV Extension." *Hybrid Domainer.* February 7, 2011. www.hybriddomainer.com/2011/02/the-history-of-the-dot-tv-extension.html.

ICANN. "New Generic Top-Level Domains." *ICANN.* January 11, 2012. http://newgtlds.icann.org/en/.

ICANN. "Resources." *ICANN,* January 2012. www.icann.org/en/resources.

ICANN. "New STLD RFP Application.travel." *ICANN.* March 19, 2004. http://archive.icann.org/en/tlds/stld-apps-19mar04/travel.htm.

INTA. "New ICANN Chairman Meets with INTA Leaders." *INTA Bulletin* 66 (November 1, 2011).

Jansen, Jim. "Online Product Research." *Pew Internet.* September 29, 2010. http://pewinternet.org/reports/2010/online-product-research.aspx.

Jansen, Jim. "Pew Research Center's Internet & American Life Project." *Online Product Research.* September 29, 2010. http://pewinternet.org/Reports/2010/Online-Product-Research.aspx.

Jasra, Manoj. "49% of Businesses Are Investing in Social Media—Are You?" *Web Analytics World.* October 25, 2010. www.webanalyticsworld.net/2010/10/49-of-businesses-investing-in-social.html.

Kaplan, Philip J. *F'd Companies: Spectacular* Dot.com *Flameouts.* New York: Simon & Schuster, 2002.

Katz, Michael L., Gregory L. Rosston, and Theresa Sullivan. "An Economic Framework for the Analysis of The Expansion of Generic Top-Level Domain Names." *Scribd.* June 2010. www.scribd.com/doc/33189192/Economic-Analysis-of-New-Gtlds-16jun10-En.

Keller, Kevin. *Best Practice Cases in Branding: Lessons from the World's Strongest Brands, Third Edition.* Upper Saddle River, NJ: Prentice Hall, 2007.

Kim, Ryan. "Pandora Files for IPO to Keep the Music Playing." *GigaOM.* February 11, 2011. http://gigaom.com/2011/02/11/pandora-files-for-ipo-to-keep-the-music-playing/.

Little, Trevor. "International—One Month into the gTLD Window, Application Patterns Are Starting to Emerge." *World Trademark Review.* February 20, 2012. www.worldtrademarkreview.com/daily/detail.aspx?g=72c68dda-d0bf-4394-ac75-29395fe6da4d.

Lockhart, Timothy J., Kristina Rosette, and Lisa Iverson. "Avoiding Unwanted "Adult-eration" of Trademarks as .xxx Domain Names." *INTA Bulletin* 66 (September 1, 2011): 1, 4–5.

Lowenstein, Roger. *Origins of the Crash: The Great Bubble and Its Undoing.* New York: Penguin, 2004.

McAfee, Andrew. 2011. "What Every CEO Needs to Know About the Cloud." *Harvard Business Review,* November, 89-11.

McCarthy, Kieren. "Why ICANN's Domain Dispute Rules Are Flawed: Part I,—History and Problems with the Policy." *The Register.* July 11, 2001. www.theregister.co.uk/2001/07/11/why_icanns_domain_dispute_rules/.

McDermott, Eileen. "Interview: ICANN Must Clarify GTLD Protections." *Managing Intellectual Property.* February 17, 2012. www.managingip.com/Article/2981110/Interview-Icann-must-clarify-gTLD-protections.html.

Murphy, Kevin. "Europe Dislikes US-only IANA Rule." *DomainIncite.* November 14, 2011. http://domainincite.com/europe-dislikes-us-only-iana-rule/.

Murphy, Kevin. "UNICEF Looking for a.brand TLD Partner." *DomainIncite*. July 23, 2010. http://domainincite.com/unicef-looking-for-a-brand-tld-partner/.

Naseem, Javed. "The New Name-Economy Of The New World." *MediaPost Publications*. July 21, 2008. www.mediapost.com/publications/article/86768/the-new-name-economy-of-the-new-world.html.

Neff, Jeff. "How Well-Defined Is Your Brand's Ideal?" *Advertising Age*. January 16, 2012.

NetNames. "The Trademark Clearinghouse: Protecting Trademark Rights in the New GTLDs." *NetNames*. November 22, 2011. www.gtld.com/news/2011/trademark-clearinghouse-protecting-trademark-rights-new-gtlds.

New gTLD. "The Benefits of Operating a.Niche TLD." *NewgTLDsite*. January 21, 2010. www.newgtldsite.com/niche-gtlds/.

.Nxt. "All Applicants for New gTLDs." October 21, 2011, .*Nxt*. http://dot-nxt .com/applicants/all.

.Nxt. "Senate Commerce Sub-Committee Hearing on New gTLD Program." .*Nxt*. December 8, 2011. http://news.dot-nxt.com/2011/12/08/senate-gtlds-hearings-transcript.

O'Dell, Jolie. "Facebook's Ad Revenue Hit $1.86B for 2010." *Mashable*. January 17, 2011. http://mashable.com/2011/01/17/facebooks-ad-revenue-hit-1-86b-for-2010/.

OpenSRS. "Domain Service Pricing." *OpenSRS*. March 21, 2011. www.opensrs .com/site/services/domains/pricing.

Ovans, Andrea. 2011. "The Charts That Changed the World." *Harvard Business Review* (December): 34–35, 89-12.

Overstock.com. "Overstock.com Announces Purchase of O.CO Domain Name." *PR Newswire*. July 20, 2010. www.prnewswire.com/news-releases/overstockcom-announces-purchase-of-oco-domain-name-98809579.html.

Pariser, Eli. 2011. "The Troubling Future of Internet Search." *The Futurist* 45, no. 5 (September–October) 6–10.

Patel, Kunur. "Tech-Consulting Giants Slide Closer to Creative-Shop Turf." *Advertising Age*. January 16, 2012.

Perry Welty, Rachel. "Retail Isn't Broken. Stores Are." *Harvard Business Review*. December 2011: 78–82, 89-12.

Pierce, Scott D. "Big Three Networks Are All Losing Their Audience While Cable Is Gaining." *Deseret News*. October 24,1990. www.deseretnews.com/article/128752/BIG-THREE-NETWORKS-ARE-ALL-LOSING-THEIR-AUDIENCE-WHILE-CABLE-IS-GAINING.html.

PRWeb. "Hitachi to Partner with GMO Registry to Apply for and Operate ".hitachi" Domain." *Allvoices*. March 3, 2011. www.allvoices.com/news/

8357335-hitachi-to-partner-with-gmo-registry-to-apply-for-and-operate-hitachi-domain.

Public Relations Tactics. "Looking Back on What Was Trending in 2011." *PRSA Public Relations Tactics*. January 3, 2012. www.prsa.org/intelligence/tactics/articles/view/9575/1041/looking_back_on_what_was_trending_in_2011 —at this site: www.prsa.

Raad, Alexa. "Should Your Company Jump on the Dot-Brand Bandwagon?" *Advertising Age*. May 2, 2011. http://adage.com/article/cmo-strategy/facebook-apps-make-top-level-domains-irrelevant/227294/.

Rao, Leena. "LinkedIn Posts $243M In 2010 Revenue, $15.4 Million In Net Income." *TechCrunch*. March 11, 2011. http://techcrunch.com/2011/03/11/linkedin-posts-243m-in-2010-revenue-15-4-million-in-net-income/.

Reisinger, Don. "Study: More TV Viewers in U.S. 'Cutting the Cord.'" *CNET News*. April 6, 2011. http://news.cnet.com/8301-13506_3-20051202-17.html.

Roussos, Constantine. "Making Money in the Domain Name Business: Secrets, Advice and Tips to Domaining Profit." *SEO.tv*. September 4, 2010. http://seo.tv/domains/making-money-domain-name-business-secrets-advice-tips-domaining-.html.

Rueter, Thad. "Online Shoppers Spending More, but Are Less Patient about Site Problems." *Industry Statistics*. October 1, 2010. www.internetretailer.com/2010/10/01/online-shoppers-are-spending-more.

Safian, Robert. "Generation Flux." *Fast Company* 162 (February 2012): 60.

Saw, M. Astella. "The Liberalisation of the Internet." *Gandibar.net*. August 15, 2011. www.gandibar.net/public/Gandi_Liberalisation_Report.pdf.

Schumacher, Tim. "The New gTLDs Won't Change the Price Structure of the Secondary Domain Market but Danger Looms on Another Front." Newdomains.org. September 21, 2011. http://newdomains.org/news/new_gtlds_wont_change_the_price_structure_of_the_secondary_domain_market.

SEOmoz. "How Search Engines Work—The Beginners Guide to SEO." *SEOmoz*. February 25, 2012. www.seomoz.org/beginners-guide-to-seo/how-search-engines-operate.

Shearman, Sarah. "LinkedIn Ad Revenue Revealed to Be $51m in IPO Filing." *Brand Republic*. January 28, 2011. www.brandrepublic.com/news/1052059/linkedin-ad-revenue-revealed-51m-ipo-filing/.

Smith, Adam. "Brave New World—How the Trademark Community Is Preparing for New gTLDs." *World Trademark Review* 28 (December 2011). www.worldtrademarkreview.com/issues/Articles.aspx?g=1662732b-6003-484f-b562-2e048520a0bc.

Steinberg, Brian. "From Apple to Xerox: 12 Spots that Changed the Game; Love 'em or Hate 'em, These Ads Pushed the Envelope or Captured the Zeitgiest." *Advertising Age.* January 9, 2012.

Stelzner, Michael. "How Marketers Are Using Social Media to Grow Their Businesses." *Social Media Examiner.* April 2011. www.socialmediaexaminer .com/SocialMediaMarketingReport2011.pdf.

Tang, Wendy. "IReport Turns 5!" *CNN.* August 8, 2011. http://newsstream .blogs.cnn.com/2011/08/08/ireport-turns-5/.

Teicher, David. "10 Startups to Watch; Gazehawk." *Advertising Age.* September 19, 2011.

.tvFAQ. "Dot TV—.tvFAQ." *Allthings.tv.* September 24, 2010. www.allthings.tv/ web/index.php/article/tv_faq/.

U.S. Chamber of Commerce. "Facts About IP|Global Intellectual Property Center." *Global Intellectual Property Center.* 2010. www.thecacp.com/facts.

Ushistory.org. "Early American Railroads." *U.S. History Online Textbook.* 2012. www.ushistory.org/us/25b.asp.

Usselman, Steven W. *Unbundling IBM, Antitrust and the Incentives to Innovation in American Computing Business.* Stanford, CA: Stanford University Press, 2009.

Verisign. "Verisign Reports 10% Year-Over-Year Revenue Growth in 2010." *Verisign.* January 27, 2011. https://investor.verisign.com/releasedetail.cfm? ReleaseID=546077.

Wasserman, Todd. "How Tech and Social Media Companies Cashed Out in 2011." *Mashable Business.* December 26, 2011. http://mashable.com/2011/ 12/26/social-media-ipos-acquisitions-2011/.

About the Authors

Jennifer C. Wolfe, Esq., APR, SSBB

Recently named one of the top 300 global intellectual property strategists by *IAM* magazine for the second year in a row, Wolfe is the founder and CEO of Wolfe Domain, a global gTLD strategy advisory firm and co-managing partner of Wolfe-SBMC, a prominent woman-owned intellectual property law firm with offices in Cincinnati, New York City, and Spokane, Washington. She is a successful entrepreneur and was elected as the first female president of the Greater Cincinnati Venture Capital Association. She has helped found technology start-ups and serves on the boards of emerging growth companies. Clients served include: Microsoft, Nestle, Procter & Gamble, Scripps Networks Interactive, Duke Energy, First Group America, and many emerging technology companies. She is a certified Six Sigma Black Belt in process improvement, nationally accredited in public relations, and has been a regular contributor to national legal and technology publications. She was recently elected to serve on the Generic Name Supporting Organization Council of ICANN.

Anne H. Chasser

Chasser was named one of the 50 most influential people in the intellectual property world by *Managing Intellectual Property* magazine and served as commissioner of trademarks for the U.S. Patent & Trademark Office and president of the International Trademark Association. She has achieved top-level executive experience in both government and higher education administration as Associate Vice President for Intellectual Property at the University of Cincinnati and Director of Trademarks and Licensing at the Ohio State University. She has been trained in negotiation and Havard and is widely recognized as a visionary thought leader in IP. She was recently inducted into the College Licensing Hall of Fame and is a member of the Trademark Public Advisory Committee for the United States Patent and Trademark Office. She also serves as an advisor to Wolfe Domain, a leading global gTLD strategy advisory firm. This is the authors' second book.

Their first book, *Brand Rewired*, was highly recognized as a forward thinking innovative approach to brand development and protection by spanning silos within organizations.

For more information go to www.domainnamesrewired.com

Index

Printed and bound by CPI Group (UK) Ltd, Croydon, CR0 4YY

16/04/2025

14658451-0004